THE ENCYCLOPEDIA OF AFL COACHES

EVERY AFL/VFL COACH SINCE 1904

JIM MAIN

Publishing

Published by
Bas Publishing
ABN 30 106 181 542
PO Box 2052
Seaford Vic 3198
Tel/Fax: (03) 5988 3597
Web: www.baspublishing.com.au
Email: mail@baspublishing.com.au

The National Library of Australia Cataloguing-in-Publication entry:

Author:	Main, Jim, 1943-
Title:	The encyclopedia of AFL coaches : every AFL/VFL coach ever / Jim Main.
ISBN:	9781921496271 (hbk.)
Notes:	Includes index.
Subjects:	Australian football coaches--Australia--Biography.
	Australian football--Encyclopedias.
Dewey Number:	796.3360922

Front cover AFL Approval Code: ARTREQ-0094
Front cover photographs of James Hird and Alistair Clarkson supplied by Getty Images Sport
Layout and design: Ben Graham

INTRODUCTION

More than a quarter of a century ago, football historian Russell Holmesby and I started the monumental task of researching *The Encyclopedia of AFL Footballers*. The first edition of this book, published in 1992, was an instant sensation and created enormous interest. So much so that it has been revised time and time again and a tenth edition is being planned. The research for this companion publication also involved considerable research. Of course, many of those who are featured in *The Encyclopedia of AFL Footballers*, also are featured in this book, some of them as captain-coaches. In the earliest years of the VFL competition, club captains were virtual coaches, but specialised coaches were appointed in the earliest decade of the twentieth century. Carlton's Jack Worrall set the trend from 1902, even though he was not officially named as the Blues' coach until after Collingwood's Bill Strickland was appointed the Magpies' first coach in 1904. Fitzroy, on the other hand, waited until 1911 until appointing its first coach, Geoff Moriarty. There now are 18 senior club coaches, all with aspirations of premiership glory. However, many are called and few are chosen for the title of "premiership coach". Most coaches have laboured season after season without the ultimate team success, yet Geelong's Charlie Clymo landed a premiership in his only season as coach, in 1931.

Meanwhile, too many people were involved in the research and writing of this book to mention them all individually. However, special thanks to Holmesby, who provided invaluable assistance, and Richmond historian Bill Meaklim, whose knowledge of the Tigers is legendary. Also, thanks to Ben Graham for his computer expertise and design and publishing brilliance.

JIM MAIN

ABOUT THE AUTHOR

JIM MAIN is one of Australia's most experienced sports writers. He has been writing on football for more than 40 years and is the co-author (with Russell Holmesby) of *The Encyclopedia of AFL Footballers*. He is a life member of the Australian Football Media Association and, in 2003, was inducted into the Melbourne Cricket Ground Media Hall of Fame. Main, who has written more than a dozen books on football, has had his byline appear from all corners of the world, from London to Panama City and from Tokyo to Los Angeles. He was chief football writer for *The Australian* for more than a decade and has been writing his Mainline column for *Inside Football* for more than 25 years. Main also is on the selection panel for the Australian Football Hall of Fame.

ADAMS, Bill 'Bull'

PLAYING CAREER: Fitzroy 1924-26, 51 games, 17 goals. Melbourne 1931-32, 16 games, 12 goals.

COACHING CAREER: South Melbourne 1945-48, 70 games - 39 wins, 30 losses, 1 draw, 2 finals. Winning percentage - 56.

A West Australian, Adams started his senior playing career with South Fremantle, but moved to Victoria to play with Fitzroy in 1924. A strong, bullocking (hence his nickname of "Bull") player, he was a fearless follower who captained the Maroons in 1926. Adams made a name for himself as coach of consecutive Melbourne seconds premiership sides from 1932-35 and then with VFA clubs Preston and Northcote before being appointed South coach in 1945 to replace former Carlton player Joe Kelly. Adams had immediate success, taking the Swans to the infamous 1945 "Bloodbath" Grand Final against Carlton. The Swans went down by 28 points and slid down the ladder to finish seventh the following year and eighth in 1947. South then had a dismal start to the 1948 season and, after 11 rounds, Adams was asked to stand down as coach.

South officials asked Adams to attend a meeting on June 29 to explain criticism of the team Adams had made on radio. Adams was alleged to have said the team had played "like bottle-fed babies" in the previous week's match. Adams tried to explain his remarks to the South committee but then, in his own words, "tendered my verbal resignation on the spot". He added: "I bear the club no animosity, but regret such an unsatisfactory termination with a club at which I have been very happy."

He was replaced by 1938 Carlton premiership player Jack Hale, who had been coaching the Swan reserves. Adams was regarded as a disciplinarian, but not necessarily a good judge of talent. He probably is best remembered for rejecting a country youngster who was desperate to play for the Swans. Teenager Bob Davis twice tried to convince Adams to trial him with his beloved Swans, but the South coach was not interested and Davis went on to become one of Geelong's greatest players and later coached the Cats to the 1963 premiership.

ADAMSON, Ronald "Jimmy"

PLAYING CAREER: North Melbourne 1929-41, 180 games, 13 goals.

COACHING CAREER: North Melbourne 1940, 6 games – 0 wins, 6 losses, 0 draws, 0 finals. Winning percentage – 0.

A fine back pocket specialist who joined North Melbourne from Penshurst, Adamson had a superb 1939 season but was in the twilight of his career when 1933 South Melbourne premiership player Len Thomas was appointed North captain-coach for the 1940 season. However, Thomas enlisted in the army on June 3 and later was killed in action. The North committee on June 5 held an emergency meeting and named Adamson the replacement captain and joint coach with teammate Wally Carter. Adamson, a fireman, missed the following Saturday's match against Melbourne because of a bruised heel. North won just two games following Thomas' departure, but Carter was credited as being in charge in both wins (over Carlton and Hawthorn). Adamson won the 1940 North best and fairest, but former Richmond centreman Bob McAskill took over as North coach in 1941.

Adamson, who was a regular Victorian representative and was named in the Sporting Globe's team of the year in 1939, also served the Shinboners as a committeeman. He also captained North in 1937.

ALBISTON, Alec

PLAYING CAREER: Hawthorn 1936-49, 170 games, 383 goals. North Melbourne 1950, 7 games, 6 goals.

COACHING CAREER: Hawthorn 1947-49, 57 games, 12 wins, 45 losses, 0 draws, 0 finals. Winning percentage – 21.

A small but brilliant rover, Albiston joined Hawthorn from local club Kew and became an outstanding player in poor sides. He won the club best and fairest in 1941 and 1946 and was one of 12 applicants for the Hawthorn coaching position following the resignation of captain-coach Keith Shea at the end of the 1946 season. Hawthorn made it clear it wanted a playing coach and at one stage settled on Footscray ruckman Arthur Olliver, who had been Bulldog captain-coach since 1943. However, the Bulldogs refused to release their champion and although Essendon's Jack Cassin also was considered a good chance to get the Hawthorn job, Albiston finally got the nod.

The Herald reported: "Albiston's appointment followed a decision by the committee in favour of a playing coach instead of a non-playing coach. If a non-playing coach had been decided on, the job would have gone to Jack Hale, former Carlton rover, who coached Carlton Seconds last year." The newspaper also reported: "The new coach (Albiston) greatly impressed the committee at an interview by his ability to address players and his knowledge of football tactics. He has had coaching experience with junior teams while playing with Hawthorn."

Hawthorn had finished on the bottom in 1946 and Albiston could lift the Mayblooms only one position the following season. Hawthorn finished eleventh again in 1948 and when the Mayblooms collected another wooden-spoon in 1949, Albiston was dumped as both coach and captain. Former Richmond star Bob McCaskill was appointed non-playing coach for 1950, with Albiston losing the captaincy to Peter O'Donohue. Believing he had been promised an extension of his captaincy, Albiston walked out on Hawthorn and crossed to North Melbourne. His walkout sparked enormous controversy and good friend Col Austen, who had lost the 1949 Brownlow Medal to South Melbourne's Ron Clegg (but later was awarded a retrospective

medal), also walked out. Austen crossed to Richmond, where he played 51 games to 1952. Brothers Harold (Collingwood and Hawthorn) and Ken Albiston (Richmond and Melbourne) and nephew David Albiston (Hawthorn) also played in the VFL.

ALEXANDER, Ron

PLAYING CAREER: Fitzroy 1976-81, 133 games, 30 goals.

COACHING CAREER: West Coast 1987, 22 games – 11 wins, 11 losses, 0 draws, 0 finals. Winning percentage – 50.

A big-hearted ruckman, Alexander joined Fitzroy from East Perth in 1976 and made

Ron Alexander.

9

a name for himself as one of the most dedicated players in the VFL. He captained the Lions from 1979-80, but returned to Western Australia at the end of the 1981 season. Alexander, who completed a Physical Education course while living in Melbourne, was appointed captain-coach of WAFL club East Fremantle and guided the Sharks to the 1985 premiership. His record of taking East Fremantle to consecutive Grand Final appearances from 1984-86, prompted the newly-formed West Coast to appoint him its inaugural coach in 1987. The Eagles finished a creditable eighth in that debut season, but the club surprisingly dumped Alexander for local hero John Todd for the 1988 season. Alexander later became director-general of the WA Department of Sport and Recreation.

ALLAN, Ben

PLAYING CAREER: Hawthorn 1990-94, 98 games, 72 goals; Fremantle 1995-97, 47 games, 34 goals.

COACHING CAREER: Fremantle 2001, 13 games – 2 wins, 11 defeats, 0 draws, 0 finals. Winning percentage – 15.

A quick and reliable midfielder, Allan won Hawthorn's best and fairest in the premiership season of 1991. He became Fremantle's first captain when the Dockers joined the AFL in 1995, but was forced into retirement because of persistent injury problems. Allan was appointed Fremantle coach when Damian Drum was sacked halfway through the 2001 season. His first game in charge was against St Kilda at Subiaco in round 12. The Dockers were gallant in going down by 10 points and Allan had to wait until round 18 for his first win as Fremantle coach; the Dockers defeated Allan's old side Hawthorn by 16 points at Colonial Stadium. His other win as Docker coach was in the final round when Fremantle defeated Adelaide by 37 points at Subiaco. They were Fremantle's only wins for the season and although there were suggestions Allan should continue in 2002, he had made it clear he always regarded himself as a stand-in coach, willing to help the club in a crisis. Chris Connolly took over as coach in 2002.

ALVES, Stan

PLAYING CAREER: Melbourne 1965-76, 226 games, 160 goals; North Melbourne 1977-79, 40 games, 14 goals.

COACHING CAREER: St Kilda 1994-98, 115 games, 55 wins, 59 losses, 1 draw, 5 finals. Winning percentage – 48.

One of the best wingers of his era, Alves proved the value of perseverance as he originally was rejected by Melbourne before having a glittering career with the Demons. He was club captain from 1973-76, but moved to North in 1977 after

Stan Alves (left) looks relaxed in the St Kilda coaching box.

being offered to Carlton and achieved a lifetime ambition in playing in the Roos' 1977 premiership team. Alves on retirement provided expert commentary on ABC radio and his insight made it obvious he would turn to coaching. He spent four seasons as a specialist coach with St Kilda before being appointed senior coach to replace former Carlton star Ken Sheldon for the 1994 season.

Alves introduced a new regime of discipline with St Kilda and, in his fourth season, took the Saints to the 1997 Grand Final. The Saints went into the match, against Adelaide, with key ruckman Peter

Everitt sidelined by injury but the Saints looked the likely winners in leading by 13 points at half-time. However, the Crows produced a blistering second half which included eight goals in the final quarter, including five from Darren Jarman. Alves was criticised for not moving full-back Jamie Shanahan from Jarman and the eventual 31-point defeat was the beginning of the end for Alves at St Kilda coach. Although Alves guided the Saints to another finals series in 1998, he was dumped after a semi-final defeat by Melbourne.

Alves, in his book *Sacked Coach,* wrote

that the Saints had "gone from chocolates to boiled lollies" in just six weeks and that supporters "wanted blood and plenty of it". St Kilda president Andrew Plympton called Alves to a meeting a few weeks after the Demon defeat and was told to resign or be sacked. Alves later told the club he would not bow to pressure and wrote in his book that he "was given 10 minutes to empty the (his) locker". He said the official explanation for his sacking was that he had "lost the players".

It was the end of Alves' coaching career yet, in his five years at Moorabbin, proved he was an innovative mentor and prepared to think outside the square. He encouraged new levels of leadership, implemented new training techniques and urged his players to adopt corporate-type self-improvement techniques. Alves, at the time of his sacking, was St Kilda's second most successful coach – behind only 1966 flag mentor Allan Jeans. His 115-game tenure also was second only to Jeans (332) and since surpassed only by Grant Thomas (123) and Ross Lyon (121).

ANGUS, George

> **PLAYING CAREER:** Collingwood 1902-1911, 157 games, 64 goals.
>
> **COACHING CAREER:** Collingwood 1909-11, 60 games, 41 wins, 17 losses, 2 draws, 6 finals, 1 premiership. Winning percentage – 68.

Angus had the unusual record of serving as Collingwood's unofficial playing coach over the 1909 season even though he was not club captain. The Magpies' captain that season was Bob Nash, whose son Laurie became a champion South Melbourne centre half-forward. However, Angus was Collingwood captain in 1910-11 and continued as unofficial club coach over these seasons. Angus, who had played in the 1902-03 premiership sides, guided the Magpies to the 1910 flag and played on a half-forward flank in the 14-point Grand Final defeat of Carlton. Angus was injured during the big match and, without reserves in that era, was a "lame duck" on the forward line.

However, the 1910 Collingwood annual report had this to say of him: "Angus both before and after he was lamed set his men a noble example of pluck and earnestness." Angus left Collingwood at the end of the 1911 season when he was appointed captain-coach of VFA club Williamstown. He was replaced as Magpie captain by the legendary Jock McHale, who also was officially appointed coach. Angus' son Les played nine games with the Magpies in 1928 and grandson Geoff Angus played 73 games with Hawthorn from 1967-73, including the Hawks' 1971 premiership side.

ARKLAY, Tom

PLAYING CAREER: Geelong, 1933-41 and 1944, 137 games, 45 goals.

COACHING CAREER: Geelong, 1944, 18 games, 1 win, 17 losses, 0 draws, 0 finals. Winning percentage – 6.

A Geelong stalwart, Arklay had a sparkling playing career with the Cats and played on a half-back flank in the 1937 premiership side. He retired when Geelong went into recession at the end of the 1941 season, but was on the committee when Geelong applied for readmission from the 1944 season. The Cats had to wait until early March for the VFL to approve its participation in the 1944 season and, when given the nod, appointed Arklay as non-playing coach in an honorary capacity.

Arklay's task was a daunting one as Geelong virtually had to start all over again, but at least was able to recall a number of its pre-war players from other clubs. Among those who returned to the Cats were Lindsay White, who had been playing with South Melbourne, and George Gniel, who had won Carlton's best and fairest in 1943. Arklay's first task as coach was to advise all potential players that training for the new season would start on March 10.

Arklay's first game in charge was against Footscray at the Western Oval, with the Bulldogs defeating the Cats by 58 points. In fact, Geelong did not score in the first quarter and Arklay would have been aware of the enormity of his task. Geelong the following week played its first "home" game at Kardinia Park since 1941 after mainly playing in the VFL at the Corio Oval from 1897. The Geelong team was piped onto the ground, but South defeated the Cats by 19 points.

Geelong's lack of manpower forced the 30-year-old Arklay into making a comeback and he played in seven games in 1944. The Cats won just one game under Arklay, by 25 points against Hawthorn at Kardinia Park in round 14. Arklay resigned as coach in January,

1945, notifying Geelong that he would run a sheep property at Casterton. He was replaced by another former Geelong player in Jack Williams.

ARTHUR, Graham

PLAYING CAREER: Hawthorn, 1955-68, 232 games, 201 goals.

COACHING CAREER: Hawthorn, 1964-65, 36 games, 17 wins, 19 losses, 0 draws, 0 finals. Winning percentage – 47.

A brilliant half-forward, Arthur was captain of Hawthorn's first premiership side, in 1961, and was a logical successor to coach John Kennedy when the Hawk mentor was appointed headmaster at Stawell Technical School before the start of the 1964 season. Arthur therefore was appointed captain-coach, but if the players believed they would get some relief from the punishing Kennedy training routines, they were wrong as Arthur was just as tough a task-master.

Hawthorn won 13 games and missed the finals by just two match points in 1964 and although Arthur averaged

almost 20 possessions a game, the Hawk committee believed he would serve the club better as non-playing coach in 1965. Arthur therefore retired as a player and Hawthorn appointed John Peck captain. This arrangement lasted just two games and, in the lead-up to Hawthorn's round three match against Collingwood at Victoria Park, Hawthorn announced that Arthur would make a comeback and captain the Hawks against the Magpies.

Although Arthur had lost none of his class,

Graham Arthur in a posed training shot.

he was unable to lift the Hawks and even missed four games through suspension following an incident against Essendon at the Glenferrie Oval in round 13. Hawthorn won just four games to collect the wooden spoon that season and it seemed certain John Kennedy would return from Stawell to resume as Hawthorn coach. However, Kennedy agreed to another year in the country and the Hawks appointed former player Peter O'Donoghue as non-playing coach. Arthur remained as club captain to his retirement in 1968.

AUSTIN, Rod

PLAYING CAREER: Carlton, 1972-85, 220 games, 20 goals.

COACHING CAREER: Fitzroy – 1989-90, 44 games, 19 wins, 25 losses, 0 draws, 0 finals. Winning percentage – 43.

The media touted former Carlton utility Rod Austin as the obvious replacement for David Parkin as Fitzroy coach when Parkin resigned at the end of the 1988 season. Austin had played under Parkin at Carlton and won himself a handsome reputation as coach of Victorian State of Origin teams. Fitzroy had finished twelfth (in a 14-team competition) in 1988, but Austin lifted the Lions to sixth position in his first season in charge. Fitzroy won 12 of its 22 games and missed the finals by one game and percentage.

However, the Lions slipped back to twelfth position in 1990, through no fault of Austin. Fitzroy even then was experiencing enormous financial difficulties and had extremely limited resources. Austin therefore resigned at the end of the season and later joined the AFL in an administrative capacity. Former Essendon defender Robert Shaw replaced Austin as coach from 1991.

AYRES, Gary

PLAYING CAREER: Hawthorn – 1978-93, 269 games, 70 goals.

COACHING CAREER: Geelong – 1995-99, 116 games, 65 wins, 50 losses, 1 draw, 6 finals. Winning percentage – 56. Adelaide – 2000-04, 107 games, 55 wins, 52 losses, 0 draws, 6 finals. Winning percentage – 51.

Hawthorn premiership coach Allan Jeans once described reliable Hawk defender Gary Ayres as the best player he had seen in "heavy traffic". Nothing seemed to ruffle Ayres and this also was characteristic of his coaching. Ayres, who played in eight Grand Finals for five premierships, was obvious coaching material and was given the Geelong job in 1995 following the retirement of Malcolm Blight, who later coached Adelaide to two premierships.

Ayres quickly won himself a reputation as a tough task-master, with Geelong playing tough, accountable football. The former Hawk guided his team to the 1995 Grand Final, only for the Cats to go down by 61 points to Carlton in the Grand Final. Although Geelong made the finals again over the following two seasons, the Cats eventually slid down the ladder and Ayres was replaced by Mark Thompson at the end of the 1999 season.

A career coach, Ayres was appointed Adelaide coach in 2000 and, after a slow start, became the first coach to take the Crows to three consecutive finals series, from 2001-03, with a highest position of fourth. Then, when the Crows slid down the ladder during the 2004 season, the Adelaide board told Ayres his contract would not be renewed. Ayres stepped down from his position on June 21 and was replaced by Neil Craig. Ayres to that stage was Adelaide's longest-serving coach, with 107 games. He also had become only the 28th man to coach 200 or more VFL/AFL games. Ayres later was appointed coach of VFL (formerly VFA) club Port Melbourne.

Gary Ayres coached both Geelong and Adelaide.

BAGGOTT, Jack

PLAYING CAREER: Richmond 1927-35, 128 games, 140 goals. Essendon 1936-27, 19 games, 0 goals.

COACHING CAREER: Essendon 1936-39, 60 games – 22 wins, 38 losses, 0 draws, 0 finals. Winning percentage – 37. South Melbourne – 1940, 18 games, 7 wins, 11 losses, 0 draws, 0 finals. Winning percentage – 39.

The South African-born Jack Baggott was a star key position player with Richmond after joining the Tigers from Dimboola and played in the 1932 and 1934 premiership sides. However, he left Richmond before the start of the 1936 season to accept the position as captain-coach of Essendon. The Dons had finished the 1935 season in eighth position under coach Charlie May and believed Baggott's playing and premiership experience would boost a young Essendon side. However, the Bombers remained stagnant and, after finishing eighth, tenth and then seventh under his guidance, he felt he did not have the confidence of the Essendon committee and resigned. He was replaced

J. BAGGOTT
Richmond

by the unusual combination of former player Harry Hunter and star rover Dick Reynolds as co-coaches. Baggott was out of a coaching job for less than 12 months as South Melbourne appointed him its

1940 coach as it wanted 1939 captain-coach Herbie Matthews to concentrate on his playing career. It was a controversial decision as Baggott was not considered a top-line coach and his tenure at the Lake Oval lasted just one season. The Swans, after finishing tenth in 1940, replaced Baggott with former Footscray coach Joe Kelly. Baggott continued his coaching career with VFA club Brunswick.

BAILEY, Dean

PLAYING CAREER: Essendon, 1986-89 and 1991-92, 53 games, 19 goals.

COACHING CAREER: Melbourne, 2008-11, 83 games, 22 wins, 59 losses, 2 draws, 0 finals. Winning percentage – 26.5.

Bailey played 60 games with SANFL club Glenelg after leaving Essendon and started his coaching career with Queensland club Mt Gravatt. He was appointed an assistant coach with Essendon in 2000 and later filled an identical position with Port Adelaide. Bailey was appointed Melbourne coach for the start of the 2008 season, but inherited a poor playing list and the Demons collected the wooden-spoon in each of his first two seasons. The Demons improved to twelfth in 2010, but appeared to mark time the following season. When Geelong humiliated Melbourne by 186 points at Skilled Stadium, in round 19, 2011, there

was immediate speculation Bailey would be sacked. The axe fell the following day, but Bailey exited with dignity. His sacking followed a board meeting at the home of club vice-president Don McLardy, but Bailey insisted he had not seen his demise coming. However, he caused a storm of controversy in suggesting that he had done "what was best for the Melbourne Football Club" in his first two seasons, raising suggestions that the Demons might have tanked for draft selections.

BALDOCK, Darrel

PLAYING CAREER: St Kilda, 1962-68, 119 games, 237 goals.

COACHING CAREER: St Kilda 1987-89, 62 games, 18 wins, 44 losses, 0 draws, 0 finals. Winning percentage – 29.

Exalted among the St Kilda faithful, Baldock was captain of the Saints' first premiership side, in 1966. One of the most brilliant centre half-forwards in football history, he had freakish ability and, at the end of his VFL playing career, returned to his native Tasmania. Baldock became a member of the island state's parliament and he shocked the football world when he decided to accept the St Kilda coaching position in 1985. However, he eventually decided that he could not juggle his parliamentary duties with coaching at VFL level and former player Graeme Gellie continued to coach the

Darrel Baldock directs traffic at training.

have coached two years ago was to fly in (from Tasmania). The club accepted that but they were really clutching at straws, and I just didn't want to do it. The second time I still didn't want the job, but I suppose the club members were able to convince me that St Kilda was moving to a new era." St Kilda had finished on the bottom of the ladder in Gellie's third and final season of 1986 and although Baldock lifted the Saints' intensity, he suffered a stroke late in the season and had to temporarily hand over the coaching duties to 1966 premiership teammate Allan Davis. Although Baldock was advised to take a year off, he was back in harness for the 1988 season and remained St Kilda coach until the end of the following season. The Saints finished bottom and then twelfth in those two seasons. St Kilda fans realised that despite Baldock's lack of success as a coach, this was mainly due to a poor playing list and his ill health at a critical time in the club's history.

Saints without Baldock taking charge for even one match. Baldock said at the time: "It wasn't a publicity stunt. I suppose there had been a lot of wishful thinking and I wasn't in the position to continue."

All that changed two years later when he not only accepted the coaching position, but threw heart and soul into his new role. Baldock said at the time that St Kilda's skill levels were appalling and he realised that he had to start with the basics. He also said: "The only way I could

BALME, Neil

PLAYING CAREER: Richmond, 1969-79, 159 games, 229 goals.

COACHING CAREER: Melbourne, 1993-97, 98 games, 41 wins, 57 losses, 0 draws, 3 finals. Winning percentage – 42.

A ferocious ruckman/forward in his playing days with Richmond after being

Neil Balme at work during his playing days with Richmond.

recruited from WA club Subiaco, Balme moved to South Australian club Norwood at the end of his VFL career and was so successful in that position that Melbourne lured him back to Victoria to coach the Demons from 1993 to replace John Northey. Balme took over a poor list, but lifted the Demons to fourth position in only his second season.

A great teacher rather than a disciplinarian, Balme had the Demons playing with great flair and defeated Carlton by 27 points in a 1994 qualifying final and then Footscray by 79 points in the first semi-final, with Garry Lyon kicking 10 goals. However, eventual premier West Coast thrashed Melbourne by 65 points in a preliminary final at the WACA in what turned out to be the Demons' last final under Balme's coaching. Melbourne

slid down the ladder from there, but it was still a surprise when Balme was sacked late in the 1997 season, with Greg Hutchison taking over as caretaker coach for the rest of the season. He was bitterly disappointed with his dismissal, but later shrugged: "You get over it." Balme later became Geelong's General Manager, Football Operations, and played a big part in assembling the Cats' 2007, 2009 and 2011 premiership sides.

BARASSI, Ron Jnr

PLAYING CAREER: Melbourne, 1953-64, 204 games, 195 goals. Carlton, 1965-69, 50 games, 35 goals.

COACHING CAREER: Carlton, 1965-71, 146 games, 98 wins, 47 losses, 1 draw, 9 finals, 2 premierships. Winning percentage – 67. North Melbourne, 1973-80, 198 games, 130 wins, 65 losses, 3 draws, 24 finals, 2 premierships. Winning percentage – 65. Melbourne – 1964 and 1981-85, 111 games, 34 wins, 77 losses, 0 draws, 0 finals. Winning percentage – 30. Sydney Swans, 1993-95, 59 games, 13 wins, 46 losses, 0 draws, 0 finals. Winning percentage – 22.

Ron Barassi was born to coach. Not only did his father, Ronald James Barassi, play 58 games with Melbourne from 1936-40 before being killed at Tobruk in World War II, but young Ron lived with legendary Demon coach Norm Smith in the Melbourne suburb of Pascoe Vale while he attended Preston Technical School. Barassi was one of the first to join a VFL club under the father-son rule and, almost from his debut in 1953, seemed destined for greatness. Barassi, who played mainly as a ruck-rover, was captain of Melbourne's 1964 premiership side at 28 years of age, but his career turned dramatically the following summer when Carlton president George Harris pursued him to be captain-coach of the Blues.

Harris was elected Carlton president as leader of a reform group in December, 1964, and although it was not announced at the time, the group always intended snaring Barassi's signature. Carlton

secretary Harry Bell months earlier had filed a report indicating that Barassi wanted to coach at VFL level. It was music to Carlton's ears and, following an informal luncheon in which Barassi indicated that he was interested in moving to Carlton, the Blues stepped up their campaign. However, Barassi eventually telephoned Harris to say he was not interested in the job after all. Undeterred, Harris rang Barassi at seven the following morning and spoke to the Demon captain for three hours. Harris refused to hang up until Barassi gave him a commitment and eventually won him over.

Carlton announced Barassi's appointment

Ron Barassi rides high after guiding North Melbourne to premiership success.

at a press conference at Princes Park on December 22, 1964, but no one knew how much money was involved. Harris many years later indicated that there had been a signing fee, but refused to elaborate. Barassi immediately cracked the whip at Princes Park and his new regime of discipline had an immediate effect when Carlton defeated Hawthorn by 37 points at the Glenferrie Oval in his first game in charge. Barassi, who ruled his players with an iron first, guided the Blues to the 1968 and 1970 flags as a non-playing coach. The 1968 flag was Carlton's first for 21 years and, in 1970, the Blues came from 44 points down at half-time to win by 10 points.

Barassi retired as Carlton coach at the end of the 1971 season, but spent just one season out of harness before being lured to Arden Street as North Melbourne coach. The ambitious Kangaroos were determined to take full advantage of the VFL's short-lived 10-year rule but realised that, apart from signing players, they also needed a quality coach. It now is part of football's folklore that Barassi signed a dinner napkin to signal his intention to join the Roos as senior coach. Part of the agreement was that North would pay Barassi a signing fee to help him with his office furniture business. North recruited stars of the calibre of Essendon's Barry Davis, Geelong's Doug Wade and South Melbourne's John Rantall and, with Barassi in charge, won its first premiership

in 1975. The Roos also triumphed in 1977 after originally playing a Grand Final draw with Collingwood. Barassi, in the week leading up to the replay, asked the players' wives and girlfriends if he could have their men for one more week so they could land the ultimate reward. He trained his side very lightly in the lead-up to the match and his tactics paid off with North's second flag.

Barassi was severely injured in a motor accident while at North and at one stage oversaw training on crutches and again "retired" at the end of the 1980 season. Again, however, he was lured back to coaching, this time by his old club Melbourne. Barassi, who said when he joined Carlton in 1965 that he could never coach the Demons while Smith was there, agreed to take over the coaching from Carl Ditterich in 1981. For the first time in his coaching career, Barassi did not have the playing talent for success and Melbourne finished no higher than eighth (1982 and 1983) in his five seasons in charge.

Barassi's last coaching hurrah was as unexpected as it was dramatic. Barassi, who had always said he one day would like to coach in Sydney, was given this opportunity in 1993 after the Sydney Swans sacked Gary Buckenara early in the season. While former Swan centreman Brett Scott briefly took over, Barassi sat at the back of a grandstand at Princes Park while he took notes during a Swans-

North game. With the full co-operation of the AFL, Barassi took over as coach of the struggling Swans and, after several humiliating defeats, worked minor miracles. However, Barassi later said that he was not aware that the Swans were in such desperate trouble and, in fact, he described their situation when he joined them as "disgraceful", in terms of both amenities and morale. The Swans' highest position under Barassi might have been a humble twelfth in his final season of 1995, but he paved the way for future success and gave the club the credibility it craved and, after two and a half seasons, he agreed to step down in favour of a younger coach. It was no coincidence that Rodney Eade guided the Swans to a Grand Final the season after Barassi's departure and it is why the great man will always be revered by Swan fans.

BARKER, Syd Snr

PLAYING CAREER: Richmond, 1908, 2 games, 1 goal. Essendon, 1921-24, 57 games, 23 goals. North Melbourne, 1927, 9 games, 1 goal.

COACHING CAREER: Essendon, 1922-24, 43 games, 31 wins, 11 losses, 1 draw, 7 finals, 2 premierships. Winning percentage – 72. North Melbourne, 1927, 18 games, 3 wins, 15 losses, 0 draws, 0 finals. Winning percentage – 17.

A dispute over where Essendon should play its home games early in the 1920s led to the club snaring the services of two key VFA players, Syd Barker and Vin Irwin. North had unsuccessfully tried to amalgamate with Essendon for the 1921 season and subsequently saw itself ejected from the VFA. Barker, a follower who had captained North, soon made an impact in the VFL and, after playing just 13 games with Essendon in 1921, was appointed club captain for the 1922 season, and eventually took over the coaching role following the departure of former St Kilda star Sam Gravenall late in

S. BARKER
NTH. MELBOURNE

the season. Essendon that season shifted from the East Melbourne Cricket Ground to Windy Hill, so Barker therefore had the honour of being Essendon's leader in its first match at Windy Hill, in a victory over Carlton.

Essendon finished third in Barker's first season as captain and coach after finishing on the bottom the previous season. The Dons went on to win the 1923 flag and made it consecutive premierships in 1924. The 1924 premiership was won under a round-robin finals system and Essendon, after winning its first two finals matches, went down to Richmond. Barker blasted his players and when VFA premier Footscray defeated Essendon in a charity match the following week, the black and red was split wide open, with some players accusing other of "taking a dive".

Barker retired and was replaced as captain-coach by Frank Maher. However, he was appointed captain-coach of North Melbourne for the 1927 season. He was almost 40 years of age, but had been a North stalwart in its VFA days and North fans welcomed the return of one of their great favourites. However, Barker played just nine games in his comeback season, with the Roos finishing above only Hawthorn. He remained as non-playing coach for the 1928 season, but North again finished above only Hawthorn and he was replaced by his 1928 captain, former Collingwood star Charlie Tyson.

Barker, who was born in Abbotsford, had played two games with Richmond in 1908. A fireman throughout his VFL career, he died on March 24, 1930, at just 42 years of age. Argus football writer "Old Boy" wrote this tribute to Barker: "He was not a brilliant player but was remarkably sound and solid. He invariably made the best of use of the ball. He was a good leader, a sound judge of human nature and always got the best out of his men. Speeches to his teams before entering the field were masterpieces of brevity and sound common sense." The North best and fairest award is named in honour of Syd Barker. Son Syd Junior played 41 games with North from 1930-33.

BARTLETT, Kevin

PLAYING CAREER: Richmond, 1965-83, 403 games, 778 goals.

COACHING CAREER: Richmond, 1988-91, 88 games, 27 wins, 61 losses, 0 draws, 0 finals. Winning percentage – 31.

A champion rover, Barlett joined Richmond as a skinny teenager and worked his way through the ranks and, after retiring in 1983 on 403 games with the Tigers, became a highly-respected media commentator. However, he always seemed destined to coach Richmond and, when Richmond parted company with Tony Jewell (for the second time) at the end of the 1987 season, Bartlett put his hand up to take over. Richmond had collected the wooden-spoon in 1987, with just five wins, and no one expected miracles from Bartlett. In fact, the Football Record for the opening round in 1988 reflected the magnitude of his task. It reported: "It seems that Bartlett will need all his old football talents and durability in his new role as the men he is coaching stand on the 14th rung and look skyward. But, as they say in football, all teams are on equal footing with the commencement of each season. Kevin Bartlett did not play in a wooden spoon team at Richmond. Instead, he saw much of the football action at the other end of the scale. He is now planning a return visit."

Bartlett had a taste of what was to come when Melbourne defeated Richmond by 46 points in his first match as coach. However, he lifted Richmond to 10th position by the end of the season, with eight wins and above (in order) North Melbourne, Fitzroy, the Brisbane Bears and St Kilda. Unfortunately for Bartlett, he coached Richmond when its playing stocks were near an all-time low and that 10th position was the best the Tigers could manage in his four years in charge and the Tigers even collected another wooden spoon in 1989. Bartlett returned to the media when he was replaced as coach by former St Kilda and Hawthorn premiership coach Allan Jeans in 1992.

Bartlett later became a popular radio identity with SEN.

BEAMES, Percy

PLAYING CAREER: Melbourne, 1931-44, 213 games, 323 goals.

COACHING CAREER: Melbourne – 1942-44, 48 games, 19 wins, 29 losses, 0 draws, 0 finals. Winning percentage – 40.

One of Melbourne's greatest players, Beames was nominated as best on ground in each of the three Demon premiership sides from 1939-41 and was the obvious choice as captain-coach when Frank "Checker" Hughes announced his retirement for "business reasons" on February 20, 1942. Beames might have been taking over a side that had won the three previous Grand Finals, but he faced an enormously difficult task as several key players (including Ron Barassi Senior, Harold Ball and Syd Anderson) had been killed in World War II. Besides, all clubs found it difficult to field full-strength teams because of the number players in the services. Melbourne finished eighth in Beames' first season as captain-coach and then seventh the following year when he announced his retirement as a player. He was coach again in 1944 but the Demons again missed the finals in finishing eighth. Beames, who also was a champion cricketer who once made 226 not out for Victoria, stepped down when Hughes returned as coach for 1945 and became one of Australia's most respected sports journalists, covering cricket and football for The Age. Beames died on March 28, 2004, at 92 years of age.

BECKWITH, John

PLAYING CAREER: Melbourne, 1951-60, 176 games, 19 goals.

COACHING CAREER: Melbourne, 1968-70, 65 games, 19 wins, 46 losses, 0 draws, 0 finals. Winning percentage – 29.

Beckwith was Melbourne captain during part of Melbourne's golden era under the coaching of Norm Smith. A fine back pocket who was recruited from Black Rock, he led the club from 1957-1959, with Melbourne winning the 1957 and 1959 flags under

John Beckwith.

his captaincy. Beckwith, keen to coach at senior level, moved to country club Colac at the end of 1960 and won himself an enviable reputation there (winning two Hampden Football League flags) before returning to Melbourne after five years to become Smith's assistant coach. Beckwith was on a hiding to nothing when he took over as senior coach from the start of the 1968 season as Melbourne parted company with Smith in acrimonious circumstances and he had to step into a coaching legend's boots. While Smith was an autocratic disciplinarian, Beckwith adopted an entirely different approach. He believed the Demon players under Smith had become too worried about making mistakes and therefore urged them to play with more flair. Unfortunately, Beckwith did not have enough talent for success and the Demons' best year in his three seasons as coach was in his first, of 1968, when they finished eighth. Beckwith resigned at the end of the 1970 season to concentrate on his nursing home business, with former teammate Ian Ridley taking over from 1971.

BELCHER, Allan

PLAYING CAREER: Collingwood, 1904, 4 games, 1 goal. Essendon, 1906-19, 176 games, 40 goals.

COACHING CAREER: Essendon, 1910, 19 games, 12 wins, 7 losses, 0 draws, 1 final. Winning percentage – 63.

While brother Vic elected to play with South Melbourne, Allan started his VFL career with Collingwood before joining Essendon in 1906. One of the most powerful ruckmen of his era, he also had great leadership qualities and was appointed captain-coach of the Same Old for the 1910 season, replacing non-playing coach Dave Smith and captain Bill Griffith. It was Belcher's only season in the joint roles, although he was club captain from 1912-15 and, indeed was Essendon's 1912 premiership captain under the coaching of John Worrall. Ironically, Essendon defeated Vic's South Melbourne in the Grand Final in a rare case of brothers opposing each other in a premiership decider.

Essendon finished fourth in Belcher's only season as captain-coach, going down to Collingwood by 58 points in a semi-final. Although he briefly retained the captaincy for the following season under Worrall's coaching, Belcher's playing career was severely hampered by injuries, while ill-health dogged him following his retirement in 1919. His health deteriorated over the following two years and he died of a brain tumour on Monday, July 2, 1921. Just 36 years of age, he left behind a wife, Margaret, and two children, Allan and Linda. A notice which referred to Belcher having been a "late captain of the Essendon League Football Club" in The Argus the following Monday read: "Though lost in sight, in memory dear. The final bell has rung."

BELCHER, Vic

PLAYING CAREER: South Melbourne, 1907-20, 226 games, 62 goals.

COACHING CAREER: South Melbourne, 1914-15 and 1917, 53 games, 31 wins, 21 losses, 1 draw, 4 finals. Winning percentage – 58. Fitzroy, 1922-24 and 1926-27, 93 games, 49 wins, 42 losses, 2 draws, 9 finals, 1 premiership. Winning percentage – 53.

Vic Belcher coached Fitzroy to the 1922 flag.

northern suburb of Brunswick, this was an unusual request, but the youngster obliged and, when he had the chance to join a VFL club, he chose South Melbourne while brother Allan played for Collingwood and then Essendon.

Belcher was a powerful ruckman who generally was considered best on ground in the 1909 Grand Final defeat of Carlton and was elected South captain in 1913 even though the club had a playing coach in Harvey Kelly. The following year, when the South players again elected Belcher as captain, the club committee also named him coach. Belcher led the Southerners to the 1914 Grand Final, but they went down to Carlton by six points. Belcher remained captain-coach in 1915, but with South in recess during World War I in 1916, he did not resume duties until 1917. However, he was replaced as coach by Herb Howson in 1918, with Henry "Sonny" Elms as assistant coach and Jim Caldwell taking over the captaincy. Belcher hid his disappointment well and played a huge part in South's five-point defeat of Collingwood in the Grand Final.

Belcher retired as a player at the end of the 1920 season and, later that year, won a bravery medal after rescuing a boy from

Belcher, until the 2012 season, was the only man to have played in two South/Sydney VFL/AFL premiership sides, in 1909 and 1918. Yet Belcher became a South player only because of a childhood connection. As a boy, he liked hitching a ride on the local baker's cart. However, the baker insisted that young Belcher could only ride with him if he barracked for his club, South Melbourne. As the Belchers lived in the drowning in the Maribyrnong River on Melbourne Cup day. Belcher was appointed non-playing Fitzroy coach in 1922 and guided the Maroons to the flag in his first season in charge. He coached Fitzroy for another two seasons before being replaced by Chris Lethbridge in 1925 and returning for two more seasons, Belcher also coached Brunswick to a VFA flag as well as coaching Tasmanian club City (Launceston) for one season. On return to Victoria, he briefly took up boundary umpiring but had one last hurrah as a coach as Fitzroy enticed him back to Brunswick Street in 1944 as an assistant to captain-coach Fred Hughson. Belcher therefore played a hand in the Maroons' Grand Final defeat of Richmond that year. Belcher died on January 6, 1977, at 88 years of age. He was a life member of both the South Melbourne and Fitzroy Football Clubs.

BENTLEY, Perc

PLAYING CAREER: Richmond, 1925-40, 263 games, 275 goals.

COACHING CAREER: Richmond, 1934-40, 133 games, 86 wins, 46 losses, 1 draw, 8 finals, 1 premiership. Winning percentage – 65. Carlton, 1941-55, 281 games, 167 wins, 110 losses, 4 draws, 11 finals, 2 premierships. Winning percentage – 59.

Although Bentley spent his entire playing career with Richmond, he is a revered Carlton identity as he not only coached the Blues to the 1945 and 1947 premierships, but gave Carlton more than two decades of service as coach and then as chairman of selectors, vice-president and delegate to the VFL. A tough, relentless ruckman recruited from local club Burnley, Bentley gave Richmond wonderful service and was captain of the Tigers' 1932 and 1934 premiership sides. He was Tiger captain-coach from 1934-40, but Carlton then sought his services as captain-coach in the lead-up to the 1941 season when it heard that Richmond was not happy with his tactics in losing the 1940 Grand Final against Melbourne. Although Richmond bucked at the prospect of Bentley playing against the Tigers, it finally cleared him to Carlton on the condition that he be only the Blues' non-playing coach. Bentley was always Carlton's first choice to replace 1938 premiership coach Brighton Diggins, who had enlisted in the army early in 1941.

Bentley masterminded Carlton's defeat of South Melbourne in the 1945 "Bloodbath" Grand Final, with his insistence that the Blues play tough, aggressive football reaping the ultimate reward, even if the tactics upset the purists. Bentley, who had a massive presence at Princes Park even after he stood down at the end of the 1955 season, once said this of coaching: "It requires the same patience and knowledge as school teaching. Just as some brilliant students do not succeed as teachers, many great footballers flop badly when they take on coaching." A creative football thinker, Bentley was the

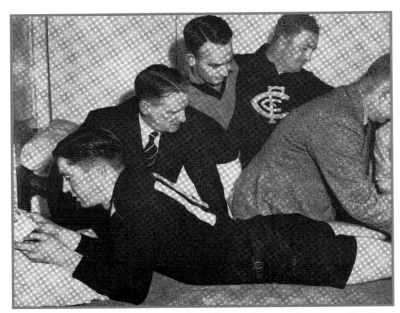

Perc Bentley (in CFC jumper) with (L-R), Bert Deacon, Carlton secretary Harry Bell and club captain Ern Henfry in 1947.

first to use the system of resting a ruckman in a forward pocket. He encouraged the full-forward to act as a decoy, allowing the resting ruckman to drop into the goal square. Bentley died in 1982 at 75 years of age.

BICKLEY, Mark

PLAYING CAREER: Adelaide, 1991-2003, 272 games, 77 goals.

COACHING CAREER: Adelaide, 2011, 6 games, 3 wins, 3 losses, 0 draws, 0 finals. Winning percentage – 50.

A tough and reliable midfielder, Bickley captained the Crows' 1997-98 premiership

sides. Originally from South Adelaide, he was appointed an Adelaide assistant coach in 2009 and was promoted to the senior position when Neil Craig stepped down after St Kilda thrashed the Crows by 103 points in round 18, 2011. He was rated a good chance to take the role in his own right from 2012, but a disastrous final round 95-point hiding at the hands of West Coast saw the Crows appoint Brenton Sanderson senior coach.

BIRT, John

PLAYING CAREER: Essendon, 1957-67, 194 games, 303 goals.

COACHING CAREER: Essendon – 1971, 22 games, 4 wins, 17 defeats, 1 draw, 0 finals. Winning percentage – 18.

A brilliant rover recruited from Ballarat College, Birt not only played in Essendon's 1962 and 1965 premiership flag sides, but won the club best and fairest in 1961, 1965 and 1967. He left the Bombers at the end of the 1968 season to coach SA club West Torrens, but returned to Essendon in controversial circumstances in 1971 when he was appointed coach in place of former teammate Jack Clarke. Essendon shocked the football world when it dumped Clarke at the end of the 1970 season, with the club announcing it would advertise all coaching positions. Clarke, who had been in charge for three seasons, just before his sacking complained that he never felt he was in charge of selection, but the Bombers' slide to eleventh in 1970 was the real catalyst for his removal. The Essendon committee turned to Birt, but the former club champion lasted just one season, with Essendon again finishing eleventh. Essendon replaced Birt with former Collingwood captain Des Tuddenham, who was appointed playing coach. Birt moved to Hawthorn as reserves coach

and later held administrative positions with Collingwood and Fitzroy.

BISSET, Jack

PLAYING CAREER: Richmond, 1928 and 1931, 38 games, 9 goals. South Melbourne, 1932-36, 90 games, 9 goals.

COACHING CAREER: South Melbourne, 1933-36, 80 games, 63 wins, 17 losses, 0 draws, 10 finals, 1 premiership. Winning percentage – 79.

An itinerant ruckman, Bisset was in the right spot at the right time when he landed the job as South Melbourne coach in 1933. The position in 1932 had been held by West Australian Johnny Leonard, who played

John Birt.

a major role in South's "Foreign Legion" recruitment policy. However, Leonard had to return to the west in his employment with a football manufacturer and South therefore turned to Bisset, who had joined the red and white from Richmond in 1932. Bisset, born in the tiny Victorian hamlet of Labertouche, played for a succession of country clubs before making an impression in the VFA with Port Melbourne and then in Stawell. He caught Richmond's eye and he joined the Tigers in 1928, but eventually lost his place in the side to a very young Jack Dyer and moved to South.

Leonard recommended to South that Bisset be named his replacement as captain-coach and the Swans finished second on the ladder in 1933 before going on to defeat Richmond by 42 points in the Grand Final. Bisset, who had one of the greatest sides of any era, was desperately unlucky not to win more flags with the Swans as they were runners-up each season from 1934-36. In 1935, champion South full-forward Bob Pratt was knocked down by a truck two nights before the Grand Final and, to make matters worse, Bisset had his skull fractured early in the Grand Final against Collingwood. The legendary Roy Cazaly replaced him as coach in 1937 and the Swans slumped from runner-up in 1936 to ninth in Cazaly's first season as coach. Bisset remains the only coach to guide South/Sydney to four consecutive Grand Finals and, in 2003, was named coach of the Swans' Team of the Century. Bisset, who also was a keen racehorse owner, enlisted in the army during World War II and son Raymond played for Melbourne reserves. Daughter Dawn maintained the Bisset connection with football when she married 1953 Collingwood premiership winger Des Healey. Bisset died of a stroke in 1965 at 64 years of age.

BLAKEY, John

PLAYING CAREER: Fitzroy 1985-92, 135 games, 38 goals. North Melbourne 1993-2002, 224 games, 72 goals.

COACHING CAREER: Brisbane Lions, 2005, 1 game, 0 wins, 1 loss, 0 draws, 0 finals. Winning percentage – 0.

A wonderfully committed and reliable defender/utility, Blakey played in the Kangaroos' 1996 and 1999 premiership sides and on his retirement in 2002 joined the Brisbane Lions as an assistant coach. He was called on to coach the Lions in a match against the Western Bulldogs at Telstra Dome in round 18, 2005, when senior coach Leigh Matthews was unavailable following the death of his mother. Blakey knew earlier in the week he was likely to be coach for that match and all pre-match plans already had been mapped out. The Bulldogs defeated the Lions by 28 points in Blakey's only match as a senior coach. He joined the Sydney Swans as an assistant coach at the end of the 2006 season.

BLIGHT, Malcolm

PLAYING CAREER: North Melbourne, 1974-82, 178 games, 444 goals.

COACHING CAREER: North Melbourne, 1981, 16 games, 6 wins, 10 losses, 0 draws, 0 finals. Winning percentage – 38. Geelong, 1989-94, 145 games, 89 wins, 56 losses, 0 draws, 15 finals. Winning percentage – 61. Adelaide – 1997-99, 74 games, 41 wins, 33 losses, 0 draws, 8 finals, 2 premierships. Winning percentage – 55. St Kilda, 2001, 15 games, 3 wins, 12 losses, 0 draws, 0 finals. Winning percentage – 20.

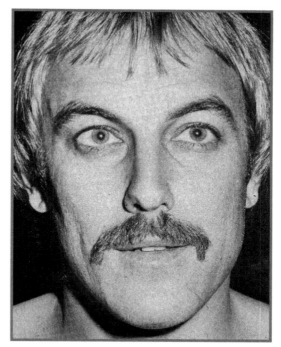

Malcolm Blight.

Blight had a glittering playing career in both South Australia and Victoria, winning Magarey and Brownlow Medals. After playing in North Melbourne's 1975 and 1977 premiership sides, his playing experience and football nouse made him the natural successor when legendary coach Ron Barassi stepped down at the end of the 1980 season. North appointed Blight captain-coach, even though it seemed the days of a playing coach had passed. Blight therefore became the last captain-coach and, after just 16 games, he was replaced by former teammate Barry Cable. Blight's demise at Arden Street followed six consecutive defeats, but even North officials acknowledged their coach had been handed a poisoned chalice.

Blight returned to his old South Australian club Woodville as captain-coach in 1983 and was so impressive that Geelong lured him back to Victoria as coach to replace John Devine in 1989. Blight lifted the Cats from ninth position to runner-up (to Hawthorn) in his first season and took the Cats to two other Grand Final losses (in 1992 and 1994) in his six-year tenure at Kardinia Park. Blight insisted on fast, open, high-scoring football and was desperately unlucky not to have guided the Cats to at least one flag as they went down to the Hawks by just six points in a brutally physical 1989 Grand Final. The Geelong coach was criticised for his placement of skipper Mark Bairstow on a wing against West Coast champion Peter Matera in the 1992 Grand Final. Matera won the Norm Smith Medal as best on ground in the Eagles' 28-point triumph. Blight also courted controversy through his sometimes unorthodox treatment of players and coaching techniques. During one quarter-time break he made Cat defender Austin McCrabb stand 10 metres away from the rest of the playing group as punishment for a botched kick-in.

Blight resigned as Geelong coach at the end of the 1994 season and, after spending a couple of seasons in the media, was appointed Adelaide coach for the start of the 1997 season. He immediately sparked controversy by sacking several veterans, including Andrew Jarman and Chris McDermott, but had the last laugh as the Crows won both the 1997-98 flags. The 1997 premiership won Blight credit as a master tactician as his move of Darren Jarman to full-forward turned the Grand Final against St Kilda. Jarman kicked six goals in the Crows' come-from-behind 31-point victory. Blight resigned after the Crows finished 13th in 1999 and again turned to the media, winning enormous respect for his insight and tactical awareness. The football world then was shocked when St Kilda lured Blight out of retirement in 2001. However, there was an even greater shock later in the season when the Saints sacked Blight after the round 15 loss to, ironically, Adelaide. He was replaced by director of football Grant Thomas, with St Kilda president Rod Butterss questioning Blight's commitment

Francis Bourke.

to the Saints. Blight reacted by saying: "I couldn't give a rat's tossbag whether he thought I could coach or whether anyone thinks I can coach. I'm happy with what I did." Blight returned to the media as a commentator with the Ten network and, in 2010, joined the Gold Coast board.

BOURKE, Francis

PLAYING CAREER: Richmond, 1967-1981, 300 games, 71 goals.

COACHING CAREER: Richmond, 1982-83, 46 games, 26 wins, 20 losses, 0 draws, 2 finals. Winning percentage – 57.

One of Richmond's favourite sons, Bourke was renowned for his courage and commitment. He was seen even early in his Tiger career as a future coach and Richmond saw the opportunity to bring this to fruition following a disappointing 1981 Tiger season. The Tigers, after winning the premiership under Tony Jewell's coaching in 1980, slipped to seventh the following season and the Richmond hierarchy ruthlessly chopped Jewell off at the knees. Bourke went straight from a playing career to senior coach from one season to the next and started his off-field role brilliantly. He guided Richmond to the 1982 minor premiership but, after a 23-point victory over bitter rival Carlton in the second semi-final, went down to the Blues by 18 points in the Grand Final. Bourke insisted that he would not take injured players into the Grand Final and subjected defender Mick Malthouse to ruthless physical tests on the Thursday night before the big game. Malthouse's injured shoulder did not stand up to Bourke's scrutiny and he was ruled out. Richmond slipped to tenth the following season amid rumours of player discontent. It was claimed that some of the senior Tiger players believed training was too rigorous and there also were suggestions that several players would seek clearances to rival clubs. Bourke resigned at the end of the season and was replaced by former Tiger ruckman Mike Patterson.

BREW, Ray

PLAYING CAREER: Carlton, 1923-26 and 1928-31, 118 games, 31 goals.

COACHING CAREER: Carlton, 1926 and 1928, 37 games, 22 wins, 15 losses, 0 draws, 1 final. Winning percentage – 59.

When Ray Brew was appointed Carlton captain-coach for the 1926 season, he

Ray Brew, as depicted in the magazine Table Talk.

became the youngest captain-coach in VFL history, a record he stills holds. He was just 22 years and 122 days when he led Carlton to victory over Hawthorn at the Glenferrie Oval in his first game in charge. However, Carlton knew it had a born leader in Brew, who had joined the Blues from St Kevin's and Newman Colleges. Brew made his debut with Carlton in 1923 while studying law at the University of Melbourne and at one stage he not only played with the Blues, but was the club's honorary solicitor.

Originally tied to Essendon, Brew was cleared to Carlton without a fuss as the Dons had no idea of his enormous potential. His debut in the third round of the 1923 season was one of the sensations of the season as he was a late inclusion and took the field without a number. Carlton fans therefore had to guess the identity of their new rover. Brew represented Victoria the following season but, after being captain-coach in 1926, he missed the following season because of appendix surgery. He therefore was replaced by Horrie Clover before returning to his old position in 1928. Although the Blues finished fourth, they decided they needed a non-playing coach and appointed former Collingwood and Richmond star Dan Minogue, with Brew club captain in 1929-30 and appointed to retain the position for 1931. However, he injured a knee in a pre-season practice match and, after missing the opening match of the season, broke down against Geelong in round four and was forced into premature retirement. Ferociously competitive, Brew was one of the toughest players of his era and demanded that his players follow the same take-no-prisoners approach. He was dogged by illness for much of his playing career and he retired at just 28 years of age.

BRITTAIN, Wayne

PLAYING CAREER: Did not play at VFL/AFL level.

COACHING CAREER: Carlton, 2001-02, 46 games, 18 wins, 28 losses, 0 draws, 2 finals. Winning percentage – 39.

Although Brittain had no senior coaching experience when he was appointed to the Carlton job to replace David Parkin in 2001, he was always expected to get the job. Parkin had taken a step sideways the previous season, with Brittain taking on more and more responsibility as an assistant coach. Brittain was a rarity among coaches as he had no VFL/AFL playing experience. His first VFL experience was as skills and rehabilitation coach with the Brisbane Bears in 1994. A former player with Queensland club Windsor Zillmere, he had coached that club for seven years and also had coached in Cairns. He was appointed assistant coach at Carlton in 1996 and won himself a reputation as a wily strategist. Brittain, who had been linked with Brisbane and St Kilda in coaching speculation, guided Carlton to the finals (sixth) in his first season, but the Blues collected the wooden-spoon position for the first time in its history the following season. Carlton reacted by replacing him with former North Melbourne premiership coach Denis Pagan. Brittain's coaching career, unfortunately, coincided with Carlton's bleakest years.

BROSNAN, Jeremiah 'Gerald'

PLAYING CAREER: Fitzroy, 1900-09, 131 games, 160 goals.

COACHING CAREER: University, 1910-12 and 1914, 72 games, 12 wins, 60 losses, 0 draws, 0 finals. Winning percentage – 17. Melbourne, 1920, 16 games, 5 wins, 11 losses, 0 draws. Winning percentage – 31.

G. BROSNAN FITZROY

A star forward, Brosnan joined Fitzroy from Ballarat after earlier trying to break into VFL ranks with Geelong and Essendon. He was Fitzroy captain from 1903-05 and therefore was unofficial coach of the Maroons in their 1904-05 premiership triumphs. However, he stood down from the captaincy in 1906 in favour of rover Ern Jenkins. The Fitzroy Annual Report of 1905 reported that Brosnan was "retiring from active service", although this was misleading as the Fitzroy crowd favourite

continued as a player to 1909. He was appointed coach of the University club in 1910 and spent three seasons with the Students, with a highest finish of sixth, in 1910. Brosnan was on a hiding to nothing as University coach as players drifted in and out of the team, depending on studies, examinations and other factors. However, he was enormously popular with his players and, after he stepped down at the end of the 1912 season, he took a close interest in their professional careers. Brosnan became a football writer with The Winner newspaper and took a particular interest in the exploits of sports identities, especially footballers, fighting in World War I. He was heart-broken over the deaths in action of many of the players he coached, including University's George Elliott and Jack Doubleday. Brosnan coached Melbourne in 1920, taking the Fuchsias to eighth position. Indeed, Brosnan broke a 19-game Melbourne losing streak when his side defeated South Melbourne in the opening round of the 1920 season.

BROWN, Vic

PLAYING CAREER: Did not play at VFL/AFL level.

COACHING CAREER: University, 1913, 18 games, 0 wins, 18 losses, 0 draws, 0 finals. Winning percentage – 18.

A small advertisement in the Argus of February 22, 1913, called for applications regarding the vacant coaching position of the University club. Applicants had to send details to the honorary club secretary, Gerald Brosnan, by 4pm on February 28. Ironically, Brosnan had been University coach over the previous three seasons and now was involved in seeking his own replacement as coach. The successful applicant was Victor Upton Brown, who still holds a place in VFL/AFL history as the only man to umpire and coach at the highest level. Brown, who had been a teacher at Wesley College from 1902-

10, had umpired six VFL matches in 1909. Unfortunately, University did not win any of its 18 games under his coaching and Brosnan stepped into the breach again for the 1914 season, University's last in the VFL. Because the Students did not have a coach in their first two seasons, of 1908-09, Brosnan and Brown therefore were the only men to coach the club in the VFL. Brown holds a unique place in VFL/AFL history as both a coach and as an umpire.

BUCKENARA, Gary

PLAYING CAREER: Hawthorn, 1982-90, 154 games, 293 goals.

COACHING CAREER: Sydney Swans, 1992-93, 25 games, 3 wins, 21 losses, 1 draw, 0 finals. Winning percentage – 12.

After the Sydney Swans failed to lure Essendon coach Kevin Sheedy to the harbour city at the end of the 1991 season, they turned their attention to Hawthorn's Gary Buckenara, who might have been a rookie AFL coach, but appeared to have all the relevant qualifications for a senior position. Originally from WA club Subiaco, he had played in four Hawthorn premiership sides. Buckenara started his coaching career in fine style, with the Swans thrashing Essendon by 61 points in a Foster's Cup match at Lavington. After a bye in the opening round of the home and away season, they pipped eventual premier West Coast by three points at the SCG in round two. However, the Swans finished the season on the bottom with just three wins and a draw. Their last win of the season was against the Brisbane Bears, by 74 points, at the SCG in round eight and defeat after demoralising defeat followed. Then, when the run of outs continued in 1993, the Swans sacked Buckenara following an 86-point rout by Essendon at the SCG in round four. Ironically, Buckenara declared straight after that defeat: "Today was rock bottom. We're scratching our heads for answers and we're not going to find them in the text-books or video-tapes." The Swans had lost their previous 19 matches and Buckenara was temporarily replaced by former Swan centreman Brett Scott and then the legendary Ron Barassi.

BUCKLEY, Nathan

PLAYING CAREER: Brisbane Bears, 1993, 20 games, 21 goals. Collingwood, 1994-2007, 260 games, 263 goals.

COACHING CAREER: Collingwood, 2012, 25 games, 17 wins, 8 losses, 0 draws, 3 finals. Winning percentage – 68.

One of the greatest footballers of the modern era, the seven-time All-Australian and Brownlow Medallist was always going to coach Collingwood. After retiring in 2007, he spent two years as an assistant coach with the AFL-AIS Academy before becoming heir apparent to senior Magpie coach Mick Malthouse. Buckley was part of an unusual arrangement in which Malthouse was to become director of coaching from 2012. However, the 2010 premiership coach elected not to take up this appointment and Buckley assumed control. Although the Magpies ran into horrific injury problems early in 2012, it was obvious Buckley was determined to make his own mark as Collingwood coach and he tinkered with the Malthouse playing style. This brought a raft of criticism when Collingwood struggled in early 2012, but the Magpies went on to a preliminary final defeat by Sydney.

BUNTON, Haydn

PLAYING CAREER: Fitzroy, 1931-37 and 1942, 119 games, 207 goals.

COACHING CAREER: Fitzroy, 1936, 18 games, 2 wins, 16 losses, 0 draws, 0 finals. Winning percentage – 11.

One of football's greatest players, Bunton joined Fitzroy from Albury, but had to delay his playing career because of a VFL investigation into an alleged signing fee – illegal at that time. Bunton won the Brownlow Medal in his debut season of 1931 and won again in 1932 and 1935. He crossed to WA club Subiaco in 1938 and won three Sandover Medals before briefly returning to Fitzroy in 1942 during war service. After former Collingwood

Haydn Bunton.

player Percy Rowe stood down as Fitzroy coach at the end of the 1935 season, the Maroons made the obvious decision of appointing Bunton captain-coach. The Fitzroy Annual Report of 1935 had this to say of Bunton: "If there were 36 Buntons in each match, umpires could almost be done without." Scrupulously fair, the only doubt about Bunton as a coach was whether he was ruthless enough to lift Fitzroy from its seventh position of 1935.

Bunton had the worst possible start to his coaching career when Carlton defeated Fitzroy by 76 points in an opening round match at the Brunswick Street Oval. Fitzroy's season went from bad to worse and the Maroons finished on the bottom of the ladder with just two wins (over Geelong in round five and Melbourne in round 13). However, Bunton was desperately unlucky as star winger and vice-captain Charlie Cameron was injured early in the season and forced to retire. Fitzroy reacted by relieving Bunton of his coaching duties, with former Maroons captain Gordon Rattray taking over but with Bunton retaining the captaincy. Fitzroy's Annual Report for 1936 thundered: "The almost unbroken succession of defeats; the failure of the team, except for sporadic flashes of brilliance, to function as a team; these circumstances are, unfortunately, too well known to require detailed recapitulation."

CABLE, Barry

PLAYING CAREER: North Melbourne, 1970 and 1974-77, 115 games, 133 goals.

COACHING CAREER: North Melbourne, 1981-84, 76 games, 40 wins, 36 losses, 0 draws, 4 finals. Winning percentage – 53.

A brilliant West Australian rover who had two stints with North Melbourne and played in the Roos' 1975 and 1977 premiership sides, he won three Sandover Medals with Perth. He returned to WA at the end of 1977 but, late in 1981, received an SOS from North. Champion forward Malcolm Blight had been appointed coach in 1981 (with Wayne Schimmelbusch as captain) after the great Ron Barassi had stepped down as coach but, after just six wins over the first 16 rounds, North realised it was asking too much of the South Australian. Blight stood down and Cable took over as coach, guiding the Roos to four wins over the final six rounds. Cable lifted the Roos to fourth in 1982, but after finishing on top of the ladder the following year, North crashed out in "straight set" losses to Hawthorn and Essendon. North finished eleventh in

Barry Cable lifted the Roos.

1984 and Cable was replaced as coach by Hawthorn legend John Kennedy .

CAHILL, John

PLAYING CAREER: Did not play at VFL/ AFL level.

COACHING CAREER: Collingwood, 1983-84, 47 games, 27 wins, 20 losses, 0 draws, 3 finals. Winning percentage –

57. Port Adelaide, 1997-98, 44 games, 19 wins, 23 losses, 2 draws, 0 finals. Winning percentage – 43.

When John Cahill was appointed Port Adelaide's inaugural coach in 1997, he said he wanted the AFL newcomer to win eight games in its debut season. The Power did better than that, winning 10 games and drawing another (with the Brisbane Lions) to finish ninth and out of the finals only on percentage. Cahill at that time was the oldest coach in the AFL and able to call on a wealth of experience. One of the Port Adelaide Magpies' most celebrated players, he also made a name for himself as coach of the South Australian club. In what was considered a shock move at the time, he was appointed Collingwood coach in 1983 and, in his second season, guided the club to third position. However, he eventually returned to South Australia and was handed the Port Magpies' coaching position again in 1988. He stepped down during the 1996 season

John Cahill.

to help prepare the Power for its debut the following season. Cahill coached the Power for two seasons before being replaced by another Port favourite son in Mark Williams.

CALDWELL, Jim

PLAYING CAREER: South Melbourne, 1909-19, 155 games, 34 goals.

COACHING CAREER: Carlton, 1925, 11 games, 4 wins, 7 losses, 0 draws, 0 finals. Winning percentage – 36. South Melbourne, 1929, 4 games, 1 win, 3 losses, 0 finals. Winning percentage – 25.

A brilliant winger during his playing career with South Melbourne, James McIlwrick Caldwell was desperately unlucky not to be a dual premiership player as he missed South's 1909 flag triumph through suspension. He was captain of South's 1918 premiership side and, after leaving South at the end of the following season, was captain-coach of Williamstown and then country club Rutherglen. He then was a shock choice as Carlton's non-playing coach in 1925. Carlton had appointed Blues' stalwart Paddy O'Brien as playing coach but, when the players refused to elect him as club captain, Carlton faced an agonising dilemma. The club was split down the middle and the only solution was to appoint an alternative coach, with Caldwell getting the job and O'Brien cleared to Footscray. Carlton won just five games to finish ninth under Caldwell in 1925 and the former South star was appointed coach for the following season. Although the Argus in March, 1926, reported that the Blues were looking forward to the new season under Caldwell, Carlton replaced him with Ray Brew as captain-coach.

Caldwell returned to South as coach in 1929, replacing former Collingwood star Charlie Pannam, but lasted just four games before standing down in favour of another former player in Fred Fleiter. Caldwell's only win in these four games was against St Kilda (by 26 points at the Lake Oval) in round two. Caldwell's football thinking was too unorthodox for South officials and, for example, he experimented with star full-forward Ted Johnson on a half-back flank. Caldwell died on August 20, 1929, just months after he was replaced as South coach. The Argus reported the day after his death: "Footballers will regret to learn of the death of James Caldwell, who recently retired from the position of coach to the South Melbourne Football Club. He came to South Melbourne as a junior from Williamstown and was regarded as a first-class player ... He had been in the Melbourne Hospital since July 31 and died yesterday morning. He leaves a wife and two daughters."

CAMERON, *Charlie*

PLAYING CAREER: North Melbourne, 1926-34, 122 games, 19 goals. Fitzroy, 1934-36, 23 games, 52 goals.

COACHING CAREER: North Melbourne, 1932, 4 games, 1 win, 3 losses, 0 draws, 0 finals. Winning percentage – 25. Fitzroy, 1948, 19 games, 9 wins, 10 defeats, 0 draws, 0 finals. Winning percentage – 47.

A small, but brilliant winger who was a regular Victorian representative, Cameron was in charge at North Melbourne for four games in 1932 when regular captain-coach Dick Taylor was unavailable. He moved to Fitzroy in 1934 and, after being appointed captain the following season when 35 years of age, had a heart attack. Despite the odds, Cameron eventually returned to senior action and, after playing four games in his final season of 1936, became playing coach of the

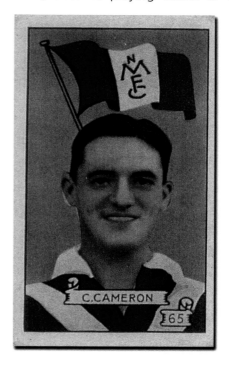

C.CAMERON

reserves. He also coached Tasmanian club Cananore, VFA club Yarraville and Ballarat East. Cameron was non-playing coach of Fitzroy in 1948, but stepped down after one season (the Maroons finished seventh after a promising start to the season), citing business reasons.

CAMPBELL, Garnet

PLAYING CAREER: Essendon, 1923-33, 157 games, 51 goals.

COACHING CAREER: Essendon, 1931-33, 54 games, 22 wins, 32 losses, 0 draws, 0 finals. Winning percentage – 41.

A highly-skilled centreman or winger, Campbell was named Essendon captain-coach in 1931 to replace Charlie Hardy and held the position for three years. Although the Dons finished sixth in both 1931 and 1932, they collected the wooden spoon in 1933, with just two wins, and Campbell was replaced by Charlie May as coach and Keith Forbes as captain. Campbell later coached VFA club Sandringham.

CAMPBELL, Graham

PLAYING CAREER: Fitzroy, 1956-64, 151 games, 154 goals.

COACHING CAREER: Fitzroy 1972, 1974 and 1978, 26 games, 8 wins, 18 losses, 0 draws, 0 finals. Winning percentage – 31.

A wonderfully loyal Fitzroy identity, Campbell played in the Lions' 1955 Under 19s premiership side and, after graduating to the seniors, proved himself a reliable rover/forward. He left Fitzroy at the end of the 1964 season to be captain-coach of suburban club Reservoir and returned to Fitzroy in 1971 as reserves coach, taking charge for one match in 1972. Campbell also was appointed Fitzroy coach for the final three rounds of 1974 following the resignation of Graham Donaldson and also guided the Lion reserves to the 1974 premiership. He then was appointed coach of West Perth and took the WAFL club from last to premier in his first season in charge. However, Fitzroy eventually lured him back to Victoria and he coached the Lions to the 1978 night premiership. Campbell could have continued as Fitzroy coach, but his family wanted to return to West Australia. He therefore coached West Perth to his "retirement" in 1981. Then, after a year in the media, he moved to South Australia to coach Glenelg and later became a television commentator in Adelaide.

CARTER, Wally

PLAYING CAREER: North Melbourne, 1929-40, 137 games, 32 goals.

COACHING CAREER: North Melbourne, 1940, 1948-53 and 1958-62, 214 games, 96 wins, 117 losses, 1 draw, 7 finals. Winning percentage – 45.

Carter will always be remembered for being coach of North Melbourne's first Grand Final side, in 1950. A brilliant player after being recruited locally, he had had a brief stint as coach in 1940 following the resignation of Len Thomas, who had enlisted in the army. Carter, after a stint as reserves coach, was appointed to the senior position in his own right in 1948 to succeed Bob McCaskill and lifted the Shinboners from tenth to eighth and, in 1949, to third (going down by 17 points to Essendon in the preliminary final). The following season, in the lead-up to the round six match against Essendon at Arden Street, the Argus ran a photograph of Carter "talking tactics" with his players. When North defeated the reigning premier by 15 points, the football public realised that the Shinboners were genuine premiership challengers. It was Essendon's only defeat of the season and it therefore was no surprise when the Bombers defeated North by 38 points in the Grand Final. North failed to make the finals under Carter over the next three seasons and, in 1954, he was appointed coach of VFA club Williamstown. He guided the Seagulls to consecutive flags over the 1954-55 seasons but North then tried to lure him back to Arden Street. However, the Seagulls insisted he was tied to them by contract and refused to release him. Carter said he would love to return to North, but admitted this was "in the hands of the gods". Williamstown won a third consecutive flag and Carter returned to North as coach in 1958. He immediately lifted the club to the preliminary final, with the Roos going down to eventual premier Collingwood by 20 points. Carter remained in charge to 1962, but then was replaced by Alan Killigrew.

CASHMAN, Jack

PLAYING CAREER: Fitzroy, 1926-31 and 1934, 76 games, 102 goals. Carlton, 1934-35, 17 games, 32 goals.

COACHING CAREER: Fitzroy, 1934, 2 games, 1 win, 1 loss, 0 draws, 0 finals. Winning percentage – 50.

A top follower/forward recruited from Fitzroy Juniors, Cashman abandoned his VFL career at the end of the 1931 season to accept a coaching position with Tasmanian club Cananore. From there, he was appointed captain-coach of West Perth and coached it to the 1932 premiership. Fitzroy therefore lured him back as captain-coach for the 1934 season as the replacement for former Essendon star Frank Maher. However, Cashman's VFL coaching career lasted just two games. The Maroons defeated North Melbourne by 11 points at Brunswick Street in the opening round but, after the following week's 24-point defeat by Footscray at the Western Oval, Cashman resigned. He told the Fitzroy committee that "because of the unfavourable attitude of a section of the club's members and supporters" he felt he could not continue as coach or player. It was reported at the time that the Fitzroy committee "accepted Cashman's resignation with regret". He was cleared to Carlton where he played 17 games (for 32 goals) before leaving Princes Park after just five games in 1935 to play in the VFA and was a member of Yarraville's premiership side that season.

CASSIDY, Jim

PLAYING CAREER: Did not play at VFL/AFL level.

COACHING CAREER: Footscray, 1926, 7 games, 1 win, 6 losses, 0 draws, 0 finals. Winning percentage – 14.

Cassidy played with Footscray in its VFA era and also was captain-coach of another VFA club, Yarraville. He made his Footscray debut as a 16-year-old in 1898 and went on to have a 50-year association with the club, serving in many capacities, including several terms as head trainer. Cassidy coached the Tricolours from 1912-14 and, at one stage, had the unusual title of trainer-coach. He was appointed coach to replace Con McCarthy in 1926 and therefore was Footscray's second VFL coach, even though he was forced to resign because of ill-health after just seven games. His only win as a VFL coach was against Hawthorn at the Glenferrie Oval in round five, 1926. Regarded as a shrewd tactician, Cassidy was an influential figure at the Western Oval and, in 1940, was awarded life membership of the VFL Trainers' Association.

CAZALY, Roy

PLAYING CAREER: St Kilda, 1911-20, 99 games, 39 goals. South Melbourne, 1921-24 and 1926-27, 99 games, 128 goals.

COACHING CAREER: South Melbourne, 1922 and 1937-38, 46 games, 10 wins, 35 losses, 1 draw, 0 finals. Winning percentage – 22. Hawthorn, 1942-43, 30 games, 10 wins, 20 losses, 0 draws, 0 finals. Winning percentage – 33.

One of football's most iconic identities, Cazaly not only was a St Kilda and South Melbourne champion, but coached numerous clubs in an extraordinarily long career in both Victoria and Tasmania. A fitness fanatic, Cazaly adhered to a strict diet (he refused to eat fried food) and soaked his feet in ice after every game he played. It was obvious during his VFL playing career that he yearned to coach and, in fact, was captain-coach of country club Minyip in 1925 before returning to the Lake Oval the following year. Then, when he retired from VFL football in 1927, he accepted the position of captain-coach of Tasmanian club Launceston City. He spent three years with City before being appointed coach of VFA club Preston for the 1932 season. Cazaly insisted that many of the Preston players were unwilling to work hard enough for success and sacked 13 of them in favour of youth.

However, Cazaly returned to Tasmania the following season as captain-coach of North Hobart, winning the flag that season and taking the club to a losing Grand Final in 1933. Then, in 1934, Cazaly was appointed captain-coach of another Tasmanian club, New Town, leading it to its first flag the following year. Finally, in 1937, he was handed his big chance to coach at VFL level. Ironically, he was negotiating the coaching position with Fitzroy when South asked him to take over from Jack Bisset. Cazaly jumped at the opportunity to coach his old side and the Hobart Mercury noted in its February 17, 1931, edition: "Cazaly will leave Hobart with the knowledge that he has made numerous friends, not only in the sphere of sport, but in other circles."

Although South had reached the 1936 Grand Final (going down to Collingwood) in Bisset's final season, it was the end of an era. Several key players had either retired or moved on and the Swans fell to ninth in Cazaly's first year as coach. They finished on the bottom the following year and the club replaced Cazaly with Herbie Matthews as captain-coach. Cazaly, at 47 years of age, was appointed captain-coach of VFA club Camberwell in 1940 and, in 1942, was handed the non-playing reins with Hawthorn. Although Hawthorn finished eleventh in Cazaly's first season in charge, the brown and gold jumped to fifth in 1943, missing the finals on percentage to fourth-placed Carlton. Cazaly had made a huge impact at the Glenferrie Oval, especially as he changed the club's nickname from the Mayblooms to the Hawks. He dropped this bombshell on the players before the match against Essendon on May 15, 1943. He told them: "I expect all players to live up to the name." Cazaly moved back to Tasmania the following season to open a massage business and again coach New Town. He died in Hobart in 1963, aged 70.

CHADWICK, Bert

PLAYING CAREER: Melbourne, 1920-27, 142 games, 45 goals. Hawthorn, 1929, 17 games, 0 goals.

COACHING CAREER: Melbourne, 1925-27, 58 games, 42 wins, 15 losses, 1 draw, 5 finals, 1 premiership. Winning percentage – 72. Hawthorn, 1929, 18 games, 4 wins, 14 losses, 0 draws, 0 finals. Winning percentage – 22.

Chadwick had a delayed start to his football career because of service with the Royal Flying Corp (later the RAAF) in World War I. On return from Europe he played in the VFA with Prahran and wrote to Melbourne asking for the chance to play at VFL level. Chadwick made his senior debut in 1920 and the big-hearted ruckman was appointed club captain in 1924. Former Fitzroy star Gordon Rattray stepped down as coach at the end of the 1924 season and Chadwick was appointed captain-coach. Melbourne finished third in his first year in charge and then won the 1926 premiership, defeating Collingwood by 57 points in the Grand Final. Chadwick had revitalised Melbourne by insisting on hard, vigorous football.

Melbourne, then known as the Fuchsias, had been renowned for their fast, open play, but Chadwick gave them the hard edge necessary for success. As esteemed football writer Hugh Buggy suggested in a feature in the Argus in 1950, Chadwick's Melbourne "abandoned the over-genteel methods of their predecessors and with a vigour which previously they did not seem to possess".

Chadwick retired the following season when Melbourne finished fifth, but was persuaded to take on the captain-coach position (in an honorary capacity) with VFL newcomer Hawthorn in 1929. Although the Mayblooms improved to tenth from being wooden-spooner the previous season, Chadwick stepped down to concentrate on his business career. He returned to Melbourne as a committeeman and was chairman from 1950-62. Chadwick was chairman of the Melbourne Cricket Club from 1965-79 and also served as chairman of Victoria's Gas and Fuel Corporation. He was knighted in 1974 and died on October 27, 1983, at 86 years of age.

CLARK, *Norman*

PLAYING CAREER: Carlton, 1905-12, 125 games, 3 goals.

COACHING CAREER: Carlton, 1912, 1914-18 and 1920-22, 150 games, 102 wins, 42 losses, 6 draws, 7 finals, 2 premierships. Winning percentage – 68. Richmond 1919, 19 games, 12 wins, 7 losses, 0 draws, 3 finals. Winning percentage – 63. St Kilda, 1925-26, 35 games, 14 wins, 21 losses, 0 draws, 0 finals. Winning percentage – 40. North Melbourne, 1931, 10 games, 0 wins, 10 losses, 0 draws, 0 finals. Winning percentage – 0.

A wonderfully talented sportsman, Clark not only was a brilliant footballer, but also won the 1899 Stawell Gift. Carlton recruited him from South Adelaide and he was involved in the Blues' first five premiership sides, as a player in the three triumphs from 1906-8 and as coach in 1914-15. Clark, known as "Hackenschmidt" because the powerfully built defender reminded Carlton fans of a

Norman Clark (centre)
with Carlton teammates.

favourite American wrestler of that name, was a highly controversial character who wore his heart on his sleeve. During one match as coach he walked onto the playing arena and had to be restrained by police. He coached Carlton in 1912 and, when replaced by Jack Wells the following year, coached VFA club Brighton for one season before moving back to Princes Park. Clark also coached Richmond in 1919 and North Melbourne in its final VFA season of 1924 before coaching St Kilda over the 1925-26 seasons. He coached another VFA club, Prahran, in 1929, before being appointed to a second stint with North, this time in the VFL, in 1931. However, North failed to win a game under Clark's coaching and he was dumped after a 72-point defeat by Hawthorn in round 10. This was an ignominious defeat as the Mayblooms were second last on the ladder. Clark was replaced by John Pemberton, who had played three games with Richmond in 1908 after starring with the Tigers in its VFA days. Clark died in December, 1943, at 65 years of age.

CLARK, Wally

PLAYING CAREER: Fitzroy, 1955-62, 105 games, 120 goals.

COACHING CAREER: Fitzroy, 1963, 1 game, 1 win, 0 losses, 0 draws, 0 finals. Winning percentage – 100.

Hugely-popular with Fitzroy fans because of his courage and never-say-die spirit, Clark was a clever rover who was playing coach of the reserves in 1963 when he was called up to take charge of the seniors for one match. Lion captain-coach Kevin Murray was selected to represent Victoria in Adelaide, with Fitzroy scheduled to play premiership favourite Geelong at the Brunswick Street Oval in round 10. The ground was in an atrocious condition and Clark cut his reserves playing duties short to take a shower in preparation for the senior match. Fitzroy, against the odds, defeated Geelong by 36 points, giving Clark a 100 per cent record as a senior coach. It was Fitzroy's only win of the 1963 season and Clark capped his own season by winning the Gardiner Medal as the VFL reserves' best and fairest. He later coached Tasmanian club Latrobe to a premiership.

CLARKE, Ansell

PLAYING CAREER: Carlton, 1929-37, 145 games, 242 goals. St Kilda, 1938-40, 26 games, 47 goals.

COACHING CAREER: St Kilda, 1938-40, 47 games, 24 wins, 23 losses, 0 draws, 2 finals. Winning percentage – 51.

A classy rover recruited locally, Edward Augustus Ansell Clarke captained Carlton in 1937 after winning the club best and fairest the previous season. But, after playing 145 games with the Blues, he was approached by St Kilda on the eve of the

1938 season. The Saints over the previous season had been coached by Dan Minogue but, when the former Collingwood and Richmond star (he also played one game for Hawthorn) indicated he wanted to step down, the Saints were left in a quandary. They approached Richmond defender Kevin O'Neill but, when St Kilda realised the Tigers would not clear him, they turned to Clarke. Carlton at first blocked Clarke's move, but he was released just in time for the start of the new season. Carlton president Ken (later Sir Kenneth) Luke said: "In view of his wonderful services and because he had the opportunity of bettering himself, the committee felt that it could not deny him that opportunity and congratulated him on his appointment." St Kilda, which officially had started the season with Minogue as coach, finished eighth in Clarke's first season and, in 1939, the Saints finished the home and away season in fourth position. It was the first time they had made the finals since 1929 and they defeated Richmond by 30 points in the first semi-final before going down by 29 points to Collingwood in the preliminary final. St Kilda slipped to eleventh position the following year and World War II then ended Clarke's career. Clarke served in the RAAF Construction Squadron in Papua-New Guinea and the Pacific Islands during the war and, on his return from service, was a Carlton recruiting officer for many years while working as a courier. He was still playing golf well into his 80s. Former Melbourne champion Ivor Warne-Smith, writing in the Argus in 1936, described Clarke as "the best rover in the League". Warne-Smith also wrote: "He thinks about the game before he runs onto the field, and he thinks about it while he is playing. At Carlton they tell me that many wise moves on the field and many little points about ways to check opponents have been given to them by Clarke."

CLARKE, Jack

PLAYING CAREER: Essendon, 1951-67, 263 games, 180 goals.

COACHING CAREER: Essendon, 1968-70, 65 games, 33 wins, 30 losses, 2 draws, 3 finals. Winning percentage – 51.

A brilliant centreman, Clarke played in the 1965 Essendon premiership side and was captain of the 1962 flag side. He was appointed coach of Essendon the year after he had been dropped by predecessor John Coleman. Clarke said when handed the Bomber coaching job: "I don't propose to make any radical changes in training routine. But I want to try and put more fun and enjoyment back into football ... I have felt for some time that League football is taken too seriously." The players responded superbly to Clarke's new regime and the Bombers made the 1968 Grand Final only to go down to Carlton by just three points, with full-forward Geoff Blethyn missing a late shot for goal which would have given Essendon victory. Despite high expectations, Essendon finished sixth the following year and, in 1970, was rocked by an unprecedented strike by senior players Don McKenzie, Geoff Pryor, Daryl Gerlach, Barry Davis and Geoff Gosper over a pay dispute. The dispute was not settled until after the opening round match against Carlton and the Bombers did not recover, finishing the season in eleventh position. The Essendon hierarchy reacted by voting to end Clarke's tenure as coach and he was replaced by another former player in John Birt. Clarke reacted by saying that he never had full control at selection and felt he did not have the full support of the club committee.

Jack Clarke.

CLARKSON, Alastair

PLAYING CAREER: North Melbourne, 1987-95, 93 games, 61 goals. Melbourne, 1996-97, 41 games, 24 goals.

COACHING CAREER: Hawthorn, 2005- , 188 games, 107 wins, 80 losses, 1 draw, 10 finals, 1 premiership. Winning percentage – 54.

Clarkson's main claim to fame as a player was being regarded as the protagonist while playing for North Melbourne in the infamous "Battle of Britain" match against Carlton in London in 1987. A qualified teacher with two university degrees, he immersed himself in coaching at the completion of his playing career and had stints as an assistant coach with St Kilda and Port Adelaide and also coached VFL club Werribee and South Australian club Central District. He defeated a large field, including former Hawk greats Gary Ayres, Rodney Eade and Terry Wallace, to take over at Hawthorn for the start of the 2005 season and was given a brief to rebuild the team. Clarkson performed this task to perfection, lifting the Hawks from mediocrity to a surprise premiership triumph in 2008. Under Clarkson, Hawthorn played fast, play-on football with a heavy reliance on defensive zoning. He was criticised for Hawthorn's high-possession game, but insisted it was the right game-plan. Most opposition teams found it difficult to counter this style of play and, in the 2008 Grand Final defeat of Geelong, the Hawks also were prepared to concede behinds. Hawthorn fell away after that flag triumph, but Clarkson revamped his side and playing style to become a serious challenger in 2011. However, the Hawks crashed out to Collingwood by just three points in a preliminary final after having the game all but won at three-quarter time. Clarkson said no defeat had ever hurt so much and vowed the Hawks would bounce back from that heartbreak. However, the Hawks in 2012 went down to the Sydney Swans in the Grand Final.

CLEGG, Ron

PLAYING CAREER: South Melbourne, 1945-54 and 1956-60, 231 games, 156 goals.

COACHING CAREER: South Melbourne, 1958-59, 36 games, 15 wins, 21 losses, 0 draws, 0 finals. Winning percentage – 42.

"Argus" 1953 Football Portraits: 12.—Ron Clegg (Sth. Melb.)

Born November 17, 1927; joined South Melbourne 1945; previous experience with South Melbourne Boys; position in the field—centre half-back; vice-capt. 1952; played in 120 games; kicked 92 goals; Interstate Team 1951, 1950, 1949; won Brownlow Medal 1949.

Recruited from the Melbourne Boys' Club, Clegg was South's greatest player in the years following World War II and could dominate at centre half-forward or centre half-back. He shared Brownlow Medal honours with Hawthorn's Col Austen in 1949 and was appointed Swan captain in 1953. Following a brief stint with North Albury, he returned to the Lake Oval and was appointed captain-coach in 1958, replacing another Swan Brownlow Medal winner in Herbie Matthews. Clegg, known as "Smokey" because of his job as a cigarette sales representative, by then was in the twilight of his career and South finished ninth in both 1958 and 1959. He retired as coach at the end of the 1959 season and was replaced as coach by 1933 Swan premiership half-back Bill Faul. South over the entire 1950s was known more for its social activities than its football prowess and not even Clegg's brilliance could lift the Swans out of the doldrums. Clegg died in 1990 at just 62 years of age.

CLOVER, Horrie

PLAYING CAREER: Carlton, 1920-24 and 1926-31, 147 games, 397 goals.

COACHING CAREER: Carlton, 1922-23 and 1927, 45 games, 26 wins, 18 losses, 1 draw, 2 finals. Winning percentage – 58.

Although Clover grew up a Melbourne supporter, he became a Carlton legend. He served in World War I, but spent several months in hospital on his return to Australia and did not make his VFL debut until 1920 after being recruited from Maryborough. He was in just his third season when he was named Carlton captain. Then, when Norman Clark was dumped as coach that season, he became captain-coach over the rest of the season. The players voted him to continue in 1923, but this caused resentment in a Carlton era of split loyalties and intrigue. Carlton slipped from fourth to seventh and, the following year, he was replaced as coach by former star Fitzroy forward Percy Parratt. Clover took seriously ill during the season and was replaced as captain by Paddy O'Brien, but he eventually returned to action and was appointed captain-coach for the 1927 season. Carlton changed coaches with almost monotonous regularity in the 1920s and

Clover's second reign lasted just one season. The Blues finished fourth under Clover in 1927, going down to Richmond by just six points in the first semi-final, but Carlton appointed Ray Brew as captain-coach for the following season. The loyal Clover therefore was Carlton vice-captain from 1928-30. Clover later served the Blues as club president.

CLYMO, Charlie

PLAYING CAREER: St Kilda, 1907-09, 43 games, 21 goals.

COACHING CAREER: Geelong, 1931, 21 games, 17 wins, 4 losses, 0 draws, 3 finals, 1 premiership. Winning percentage – 81.

Clymo had the perfect coaching record – one season for one premiership. A talented follower/forward with St Kilda after being recruited from Golden Point, he returned to the country club as captain-coach in 1910, only to have his playing career cut short by a leg injury. He won flags with Golden Point in 1910 and 1914 and, following the resumption of the Bendigo competition at the completion of World War I, from 1919-22. Clymo also coached Ballarat Imperials to a premiership in 1929 and, after taking this club to another Grand Final the following season, Geelong took notice of his coaching credentials and installed him as coach in place of Arthur "Bull" Coghlan. A blacksmith, Clymo also was captain of the Ballarat Fire Brigade and refused to take up the Geelong appointment until the completion of the Country Fire Brigades celebrations in February, 1931. He then declared that he would be living in Geelong for six months and sought leave of absence from his employment with a brick manufacturer in Ballarat.

Clymo took on a Geelong side which had been runner-up to Collingwood in 1930 and it therefore was no surprise when the Cats topped the ladder in 1931. Defeat by Richmond in the second semi-final proved a stumbling block to Geelong's premiership ambitions, but the Cats then defeated Carlton in the preliminary final before defeating Richmond by 20 points in the Grand Final. For some unknown reason, Clymo then ended his association with Geelong. It has been suggested that Coghlan and star defender Reg Hickey had told the committee they would not play under Clymo for another season and also that Clymo simply wanted to return to Ballarat. Clymo died on October 8, 1955, just shy of his 71st birthday.

COGHLAN, Arthur

PLAYING CAREER: Geelong, 1922-25 and 1927-32, 145 games, 10 goals.

COACHING CAREER: Geelong, 1929-30 and 1933-34, 80 games, 48 wins, 31 losses, 1 draw, 7 finals. Winning percentage – 61.

A powerful, bullocking ruckman, Coghlan

should have played in Geelong's 1925 premiership side, but had to sit on the sidelines because of suspension following a vicious clash with VFL newcomer North Melbourne. Geelong fans were so incensed that 500 fans rallied in the street in protest. Coghlan was appointed captain-coach in 1929 to replace Tom Fitzmaurice and lifted Geelong from ninth to seventh, and to a Grand Final loss (to Collingwood) the following year. Inexplicably, Geelong replaced him with former St Kilda player Charlie Clymo in 1931 and even named Ted Baker as a replacement captain. Coghlan took the demotion hard, but remained loyal to Geelong and played in the 1931

A. COGHLAN
Geelong

premiership side under Clymo's coaching. It is believed Coghlan complained to the club committee about Clymo's coaching and this might have had something to do with the premiership mentor's one-year tenure. Geelong named key defender Reg Hickey as captain-coach for 1932 but, when the Cats slipped to fifth position, they turned to Coghlan once more and he had a second term as non-playing coach and took them to preliminary finals in 1933 and 1934

COLEMAN, John

PLAYING CAREER: Essendon, 1949-54, 98 games, 537 goals.

COACHING CAREER: Essendon, 1961-67, 133 games, 90 wins, 40 losses, 3 draws, 8 finals, 2 premierships. Winning percentage – 68.

When the great Dick Reynolds retired as Essendon coach at the end of the 1960 season, the Bombers had to step into the unknown. Reynolds had been in charge for more than two decades and the Bombers had not won a flag since 1950. Although Essendon advertised the senior coaching position, it had only one man in mind – former club goalkicking legend John Coleman. When Coleman declared he was available, Essendon had no hesitation in appointing him coach. However, Coleman's coaching career was delayed because of a bout of hepatitis, with Jack Clarke and Bill Hutchison stepping into the breach.

John Coleman – Bomber hero.

Coleman, whose magnificent playing career had been ended by a serious knee injury in 1954, had a shaky start to his coaching career as the Bombers finished seventh in 1961. However, the Bombers dropped only two matches during the 1962 home and away season and then defeated Carlton by 32 points in the Grand Final. Coleman, whose insistence on team unity and discipline was non-negotiable, again was an Essendon hero, little more than a decade after being a member of the 1949-50 flag sides.

Essendon slipped to fifth position the following year, but bounced back to make the 1964 finals. Essendon finished third, but crashed out to Geelong in the first semi-final. It proved a disastrous day for the Bombers as Coleman was reported after running onto the field to remonstrate with umpire Ron Brophy during a brawl. The Essendon coach later was severely reprimanded. Then, in 1965, Coleman took Essendon to another flag, defeating St Kilda by 35 points in the Grand Final. After finishing fourth in 1966, crashing to St Kilda in the first semi-final, there were suggestions the Bombers needed an overhaul. When the Bombers went down in the opening two rounds of the 1967 season, Coleman showed his ruthless streak by dropping club champions Jack Clarke and Hugh Mitchell. Essendon struggled throughout the rest of the season and finished sixth – its lowest position under Coleman's coaching since 1961. Essendon was shocked at the end of the season when Coleman resigned on medical advice because of fears for his health. Ironically, he was replaced by Clarke. Sadly, Coleman died following a heart attack at his Dromana hotel on April 5, 1973.

CONDON, Dick

PLAYING CAREER: Collingwood, 1897-1900 and 1902-06, 148 games, 101 goals. Richmond, 1908-09, 32 games, 26 goals.

R.CONDON COLʷ°.

COACHING CAREER: Collingwood, 1905-06, 37 games, 26 wins, 11 losses, 0 draws, 3 finals. Winning percentage – 70. Richmond 1908-09, 36 games, 12 wins, 24 defeats, 0 draws, 0 finals. Winning percentage – 33.

One of the finest footballers of his era, Condon also was one of the most controversial. Recruited locally, he was a star rover or centreman with dazzling skills, but had a selfish, unruly streak. He missed the entire 1901 season after abusing a boundary umpire. Regardless, he was appointed Collingwood coach in 1905, with Charlie Pannam club captain. Collingwood, under Condon, went down to Fitzroy by 13 points in the Grand Final. Condon played as a rover and, the following season, he saw the Magpies slip to third position and he was replaced as coach by Ted Rowell. Collingwood officials claimed that Condon caused dissension among the players and he left to play and coach in Tasmania. Condon then was Richmond's inaugural VFL coach in 1908, again with Pannam as club captain. Condon moved to Richmond without a clearance and the Magpies never forgave him. However, the Tigers finished above only Geelong in 1908 and then eighth the following season, with Condon again falling out with teammates and he was replaced by Alex Hall for the 1910 season. He moved to Sydney and disappeared from the football scene.

However, legendary Collingwood coach Jock McHale once said that Condon taught him everything he knew and said that the former Magpie rover and his teammates of the earliest years of the twentieth century "deserve the credit for Collingwood's success". McHale said: "They perfected our way of playing and I am just passing it on." McHale told of how Condon, on a club trip to Tasmania, told his players to use handball and short passing to open up a game and, on return to the mainland, used the tactic to perfection in a match against Geelong. McHale added: "The system has been rattling sides ever since." Condon died in Sydney on December 27, 1946, at 70 years of age.

CONNOLLY, Chris

PLAYING CAREER: Melbourne, 1982-87 and 1989, 84 games, 38 goals.

COACHING CAREER: Hawthorn, 2001, 1 game, 1 win, 0 losses, 0 draws, 0 finals. Winning percentage – 100. Fremantle, 2002-7, 129 games, 67 wins, 62 losses, 0 draws, 4 finals. Winning percentage – 52.

A talented onballer, Connolly had his playing career cut short by a severe knee injury and, on retirement at just 26 years of age, became an assistant coach with Melbourne in 1991 and in 1992 was appointed coach of the Eastern Ranges. He was appointed an assistant coach with Hawthorn in 1996 and was in charge for one game (a last-gasp victory over Carlton) when senior coach Peter Schwab was unavailable because of a heart complaint during the 2001 season. Connolly's fine record won him the senior Fremantle coaching job in 2002 and the following season he guided the Dockers to their first finals series. Then, in 2006, he guided the Dockers to their first finals win (over Melbourne in a semi-final) before they went down to the Sydney Swans in a preliminary final. Despite his fine record, he was dumped in favour of Mark Harvey

Graham Cornes.

during the 2007 season. However, Connolly still holds the record for the most games (129) by a Docker coach.

CORNES, Graham

PLAYING CAREER: North Melbourne, 1979, 5 games, 10 goals.

COACHING CAREER: Adelaide, 1991-94, 89 games, 43 wins, 45 losses, 1 draw, 3 finals. Winning percentage – 48.

A hugely talented key forward, Cornes was a star with South Australian club Glenelg who joined North Melbourne at 31 years of age and played just five games with the Roos. He became a highly-respected coach at Glenelg and masterminded several South Australian defeats of Victoria in State of Origin matches. He therefore was a natural choice when the Adelaide Crows sought a coach for its inaugural season of 1991. Cornes seemed to court controversy and, at one stage, asked his players to run over hot coals – only for defender Nigel Smart to burn his feet. Cornes spent four seasons as Adelaide coach, taking the Crows to a preliminary final (defeated by Essendon after leading by 42 points at half-time) in 1993. The second half fadeout prompted him to say: "Anyone who takes satisfaction from today's game and where we finished really doesn't deserve to pull on the guernsey." When the Crows finished eleventh in 1994 he was replaced by Robert Shaw.

S. COVENTRY
Collingwood

COVENTRY, Syd

PLAYING CAREER: Collingwood, 1922-34, 227 games, 62 goals.

COACHING CAREER: Footscray, 1935-37, 36 games, 8 wins, 26 losses, 2 draws, 0 finals. Winning percentage – 22.

One of the greatest players of his era, Coventry was a powerful ruckman who was captain of the four consecutive Collingwood premiership sides from 1927-30. He won the 1927 Brownlow Medal but, by the end of the 1934 season, was nearing 35 years of age. However, this did not deter Footscray from seeking his clearance as captain-coach for the 1935 season. Collingwood, naturally, was horrified by the prospect of their great champion playing against them, even though it was obvious his best days were well behind him. The Magpies blocked the move and relented only when the Bulldogs agreed that Coventry would be non-playing coach.

The move was a major sensation at the time and, apart from anything else, the Bulldogs had to notify current coach Alby Morrison that he was about to be replaced. Morrison knew nothing about Coventry's arrival until he was taken into a corridor at the Western Oval and saw Coventry there. Morrison graciously stepped aside as coach, but retained the captaincy that season. Coventry, who had been offered 12 pounds a week to join Footscray in 1930, five years later stamped his authority at the Western Oval. He told the players he would not tolerate second-class efforts and lifted the training tempo. However, Footscray finished above only North Melbourne in 1935, with two wins and two draws. The Bulldogs finished tenth with five wins the following year and when there was no improvement early in 1937, there were internal rumblings about Coventry's coaching.

The Footscray committee called on

Coventry to explain the team's 33-point defeat by Collingwood at Victoria Park in round four and the former Magpie great took exception to suggestions that he had over-trained his players. Coventry resigned as coach, saying that he had slept on the criticism and had decided that because the Footscray committee was dissatisfied with his coaching he had no alternative but to resign. The coaching duties fell to former Carlton winger Joe Kelly, who had guided the Bulldog reserves to the premiership the previous season. Coventry returned to Collingwood as a committeeman, was Magpie vice-president from 1939 and club president from 1950-62.

CRAIG, Neil

PLAYING CAREER: Did not play at VFL/AFL level. Played 321 games as a midfielder with SANFL clubs Norwood, Sturt and North Adelaide.

COACHING CAREER: Adelaide, 2004-11, 166 games, 92 wins, 74 losses, 0 draws, 9 finals. Winning percentage – 55.

Craig coached Norwood from 1991-95 and, as a qualified sports scientist, was appointed the Crows' fitness coach in 1997 and was Gary Ayres' assistant coach from 2001 until Ayres stepped down with nine rounds to play in 2004. Craig was appointed interim coach and held the position in his own right from 2005 to his resignation late in 2011. His departure followed a humiliating 103-point defeat by St Kilda at Etihad Stadium. Craig fell on his own sword, but won plenty of admirers with his honesty and dignity at his farewell press conference. Craig was unlucky not to have taken the Crows to a Grand Final as they finished third in 2006, going down to eventual premier West Coast by just 10 points in a preliminary final at AAMI Stadium. The Crows also finished fourth in 2005, again going down to West Coast in a preliminary final, this time by 16 points at Subiaco.

CROCKER, Darren

PLAYING CAREER: North Melbourne, 1985-98, 165 games, 119 goals.

COACHING CAREER: Kangaroos, 2009, 10 games, 3 wins, 6 losses, 1 draw, 0 finals. Winning percentage – 30.

A great Kangaroos' stalwart, Crocker was an invaluable member of the 1996 premiership side, kicking three goals, but was hampered by a knee injury late in his playing career. On retirement, he joined Richmond as an assistant coach, but moved back to Arden Street in 2005 as an assistant coach and was caretaker senior coach for 10 games after Dean Laidley resigned his position during the 2009 season. Brad Scott took over as senior coach in 2010 and Crocker reverted to being an assistant coach with the Roos.

CROWE, Jim

PLAYING CAREER: Carlton, 1929-34, 83 games, 37 goals. Collingwood, 1936-37, 21 games, 0 goals.

COACHING CAREER: Footscray, 1947, 19 games, 8 wins, 10 defeats, 1 draw, 0 finals. Winning percentage – 42.

A fine utility with both Carlton and Collingwood, Crowe played in the Blues' losing 1932 Grand Final side and then the 1936 Collingwood premiership side. He played just eight games with the Magpies in his final senior season of 1937 before joining Footscray as captain-coach of the Bulldogs reserves over the second half of the season. Crowe retained that position to the start of World War II in 1939 and then abandoned his playing career when he joined the army, eventually reaching the rank of captain. After Arthur Olliver had been Footscray captain-coach from 1943-46, Crowe was a surprise choice as non-playing coach for the 1947 season. The Argus reported that the Bulldog committee had "long discussions" on whether to appoint a playing or non-playing coach, with Crowe getting the nod ahead of a big list of applicants, including Footscray players Joe Ryan and Harry Hickey. Crowe wasted no time instructing his players that he would demand nothing less than total commitment and full dedication to training. However, the Bulldogs slipped from fourth in 1946 to ninth in Crowe's only season as coach and, in 1948, the Bulldogs returned to Olliver as captain-coach. Crowe complained during the 1947 season that his instructions to players sometimes were countermanded by some committeemen.

CUBBINS, Bill

PLAYING CAREER: St Kilda, 1915, 1919-26 and 1928-30, 149 games, 42 goals. Footscray, 1931-32 and 1934, 33 games, 0 goals.

COACHING CAREER: St Kilda, 1930, 18 games, 8 wins, 10 defeats, 0 draws,

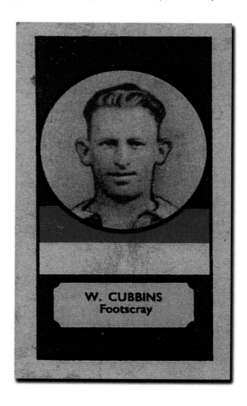

W. CUBBINS
Footscray

0 finals. Winning percentage – 44. Footscray, 1931-34, 60 games, 34 wins, 26 losses, 0 draws, 0 finals. Winning percentage – 57.

One of St Kilda's greatest full-backs, Cubbins grew up barracking for the Saints and was recruited from South St Kilda. He made his VFL debut in 1915 at just 16 years and three months before enlisting in the army to fight in World War I. A natural leader, he captained the Saints in 1922, 1925 and 1928-29, with these stints interrupted by disputes with the club committee. When George Sparrow was coach in 1929, it was said that Cubbins, as captain, devised all the tactics and it therefore was only natural that he would replace Sparrow for the 1930 season.

Footscray, in the lead-up to the 1931 season, swooped to appoint Cubbins as captain-coach and he almost immediately lifted spirits and results. In fact, the Bulldogs at one stage looked like making the finals for the first time, only to falter over the second half of the season to finish fifth, behind fourth-placed Collingwood only on percentage. Footscray slipped to seventh the following season and when the Bulldogs finished ninth the following season there were suggestions during the season that Cubbins would be replaced as coach. Cubbins had retired as a player at the end of the 1932 season, but made an unsuccessful comeback against his old side St Kilda

in round five. 1934. However, he played poorly and was jeered by his own fans, not only during the match but at training the following week. Cubbins resigned, but his players voted for him to continue as non-playing coach. The Footscray committee rejected this plea, dumped Cubbins and appointed Alby Morrison captain-coach. It was a sad end to Cubbins' career as Footscray struggled over the next few years. Cubbins, who had coached Warrnambool in 1927 before returning to St Kilda the following year, died in 1968.

CURCIO, Frank

PLAYING CAREER: Fitzroy, 1932-36, 1938-43 and 1945-48, 249 games, 17 goals.

COACHING CAREER: Fitzroy, 1956, 1 game, 0 wins, 1 loss, 0 draws, 0 finals. Winning percentage – 0.

Curcio was a lion-hearted ruckman who gave Fitzroy wonderful service and his professional career as a violinist belied his on-field strength and vigour. Curcio later served on the club committee and was one of three Fitzroy vice-presidents in 1956 when captain-coach Bill Stephen was selected to represent Victoria at the Carnival in Perth. Curcio therefore stepped in as coach for the round 10 clash with Carlton at the Brunswick Street Oval. The match proved to be a disaster for the Maroons as they failed to goal over the first half and eventually went down by 36 points.

DANIHER, Neale

PLAYING CAREER: Essendon, 1979-81, 1985 and 1989-90, 82 games, 32 goals.

COACHING CAREER: Melbourne, 1998-2007, 223 games, 108 wins, 114 losses, 1 draw, 12 finals. Winning percentage – 49.

A richly-talented key position defender whose playing career was truncated by severe knee injuries, Daniher played briefly with VFA club Werribee before returning to Windy Hill as a specialist coach in 1992. He then moved to Fremantle as an assistant to senior coach Gerard Neesham before being named Melbourne's senior coach for the start of the 1998 season. Daniher was appointed ahead of a large field of applicants, including incumbent Greg Hutchison, who had taken over as coach following the departure of Neil Balme during the previous season. Daniher worked minor miracles with the Demons, lifting them from bottom position to the finals (fourth) in his debut season. Although the Demons crashed the following season, Daniher's team bounced back to make the 2000 Grand Final against Essendon. The Bombers thrashed the Demons by 60 points, but Daniher won praise for lifting what generally was considered a mediocre Melbourne list to such heights. Daniher continued to have a roller-coaster reign with the Demons, but was criticised by some supporters for being too slow in making changes during a match. Although the Demons made the finals six times under Daniher, he was replaced by Mark Riley 13 rounds into the 2007 season, with Dean Bailey taking over the following season. Daniher, known as "the Reverend" during his 10-year tenure with Melbourne, is third (with 223 games in charge) on the Demons' list of long-serving coaches, behind club legends Norm Smith (307) and Frank "Checker" Hughes (258).

DARE, Norm

PLAYING CAREER: Fitzroy, 1968-74 and 1977, 72 games, 24 goals.

COACHING CAREER: Brisbane Bears, 1990, 22 games, 4 wins, 18 losses, 0 draws, 0 finals. Winning percentage – 18.

A handy winger with Fitzroy and, over the 1975-76 seasons, with SANFL club West Torrens, Dare spent two years as Fitzroy's assistant coach on retirement as a player. He moved to Queensland in 1980 to coach Kedron and took this club to a flag in his first season in charge. Dare moved to Southport in 1982 and won three more flags to 1988 before joining the Brisbane Bears as an assistant coach. Then, when the Bears replaced Paul Feltham after the former North player took charge following the dumping of Peter Knights, Dare was handed the senior job for 1990. The Bears finished on the bottom of the ladder and Dare voluntarily stepped aside in favour of Robert Walls. He remained as an assistant coach to 1993 before turning to football administration. However, Dare returned to coaching as an assistant coach with North Melbourne (1996-2000) and Geelong (2001-03). He then returned to Southport and guided the Sharks to the 2005 flag. Dare in 2003 was named the coach of Queensland's Team of the Century.

DAVIS, Allan

PLAYING CAREER: St Kilda, 1966-75, 173 games, 303 goals. Melbourne, 1976-77, 41 games, 36 goals. Essendon, 1978-79, 33 games, 27 goals. Collingwood, 1980, 3 games, 1 goal.

COACHING CAREER: St Kilda, 1987, 4 games, 2 wins, 2 losses, 0 draws, 0 finals. Winning percentage – 50.

A clever half-forward, Davis played in the 1966 St Kilda premiership side and later became an assistant coach to flag captain Darrel Baldock. Davis then took over when Baldock suffered a mild stroke towards the end of the 1987 season. He was in charge for four games, the Saints defeating Footscray and Collingwood, but going down to Richmond and West Coast. Baldock resumed coaching the following season.

DAVIS, Barry

PLAYING CAREER: Essendon, 1961-72, 218 games, 65 goals. North Melbourne 1973-75, 71 games, 54 goals.

COACHING CAREER: Essendon, 1978-80, 67 games, 30 wins, 36 losses, 1 draw, 1 final. Winning percentage – 45.

One of the finest half-backs of his era, Davis played in the 1962 and 1965 Essendon premiership sides and, after moving to North Melbourne under the now-defunct 10-year rule, captained the 1975 Roo premiership side. One of the Bombers' favourite sons, Davis was appointed Essendon coach in 1978, replacing former Fitzroy star Bill Stephen. The Bombers were in a trough, with finishes of tenth and ninth under Stephen over the 1976-77 seasons and Davis' appointment immediately lifted club morale. Membership numbers rocketed, but the poor run continued. Essendon finished tenth in Davis' first season in charge, but the Bombers remained patient as they knew the team was in a rebuild phase. Davis took the

Barry Davis.

Bombers to the finals in his second season in charge, but an 81-point thumping by Fitzroy in the elimination final left Essendon again worried about its future. Davis said mid-season in 1980 that he would resign if the Bombers did not make the finals and kept his word when Essendon finished a disappointing seventh; he was replaced by former Richmond defender Kevin Sheedy.

DAVIS, Bob

PLAYING CAREER: Geelong, 1948-58, 189 games, 149 goals.

COACHING CAREER: Geelong, 1960-65, 115 games, 72 wins, 38 losses, 5 draws, 8 finals, 1 premiership. Winning percentage – 63.

In his typically self-effacing manner, Davis used to describe himself as the last of the non-thinking coaches. Regardless, the former champion Geelong half-forward guided his beloved Cats to the 1963 premiership. Yet Davis was extremely reluctant to take over from mentor Reg Hickey in the lead-up to the 1960 season. He indicated that there was no way known he would apply for the position while Hickey still wanted the job. Davis, under long-serving Geelong president and tireless secretary Leo O'Brien, set about rebuilding a Geelong side which had finished tenth in Hickey's final season in charge. The Cats recruited heavily, with star East Perth ruckman Graham "Polly" Farmer the jewel in the crown. Davis once said that Farmer brought a new dimension to ruck play with his clever tap-work and sensational handball skills. The Cats, after finishing ninth in Davis' first season in charge, won the 1961 night premiership and finished sixth. They then were unlucky in going down to Carlton in the 1962 preliminary final when full-forward Doug Wade was penalised for a hold on the Blues' Peter Barry.

Then, in 1963, Davis courted controversy when he criticised Hawthorn for its rugged style of play, with Hawk coach John Kennedy threatening legal action. It therefore was ironic that the Cats met the Hawks in the Grand Final. Davis' pre-match preparations, to say the least, were unusual. He invited players' friends and relatives into the rooms pre-match and even had a piano accordionist strolling around to "relax" the players. When the Cats took the field at the MCG, they were led out by colourful children's television entertainer "Happy" Hammond in his signature check jacket and pork-pie hat. Davis was laughing and joking with his entourage over the final 15 minutes as the Cats ran away to win by 49 points. Although Geelong finished third and then fourth over the following two seasons under Davis, he was asked to apply for his position at the end of the 1965 season. Shocked, he resigned and returned to his media career. He remained a hugely influential identity at Geelong for many years and, until Mark Thompson guided the Cats to the 2007 premiership, was known as "the last living Geelong premiership coach".

Bob Davis, the Geelong flier who guided the Cats to the 1963 flag.

DEANE, Colin

PLAYING CAREER: Melbourne, 1925-30, 82 games, 53 goals. St Kilda, 1933, 3 games, 0 goals.

COACHING CAREER: St Kilda, 1933, 18 games, 6 wins, 12 losses, 0 draws, 0 finals. Winning percentage – 33.

A fine follower, Deane was a multi-talented sportsman who represented Tasmania in King's Cup rowing and also was a top-class cricketer. He represented Tasmania at the 1924 Carnival in Melbourne and then signed with Melbourne. He played in Melbourne's 1926 premiership side and then was so impressive in coaching the Melbourne reserves to the 1932 premiership (defeating Essendon in the Grand Final) that St Kilda swooped to appoint him captain-coach in 1933. Deane played just three games with the Saints before seriously injuring a thigh and was forced to resign his position as club captain. He continued as coach, but St Kilda at that time was a club divided and, after finishing ninth in Deane's only season as coach, the club replaced him with

Brownlow Medal winner Colin Watson, who had returned to the Saints from South Warrnambool to play under Deane in 1933. Deane died in Melbourne on December 9, 1952, at just 52 years of age.

DEVINE, John

PLAYING CAREER: Geelong, 1960-66, 118 games, 6 goals.

COACHING CAREER: Geelong, 1986-88, 66 games, 28 wins, 37 losses, 1 draw, 0 finals. Winning percentage – 42.

One of the toughest half-backs of his era, Devine played in the Cats' 1963 premiership side. Originally from Colac, he became a highly-successful coach with North Hobart and was lured back to Kardinia Park to replace Tom Hafey in 1986. An old-time blood and thunder coach, Devine showed Cats fans his methods in his debut in charge. With Geelong trailing Fitzroy badly at three-quarter time at Kardinia Park in the opening round of 1986, he took his players as close to the fence as possible on the members' side of the ground and implored the Cats to play with more passion. Geelong fans applauded their new coach's fiery speech, but the Cats still went down by 28 points. Devine spent three seasons in charge at Kardinia Park but was unable to lift the Cats to higher than sixth position, in his second season. He did not have

the talent for success and also inherited "problem player" Mark Jackson, whom he had to part company with in 1986.

DIBBS, Charlie

PLAYING CAREER: Collingwood, 1924-25, 216 games, 1 goal. Geelong, 1936, 7 games, 0 goals.

COACHING CAREER: Geelong, 1936, 7 games, 3 wins, 4 losses, 0 draws, 0 finals. Winning percentage – 43.

When Geelong was looking for a coach to replace former Fitzroy forward Percy Parratt at the end of the 1935 season, it announced that the club wanted a playing coach. The Cats therefore cast a wide net in their search for the right man and finally selected champion Collingwood defender Charlie Dibbs, who had played in five Collingwood premiership sides – 1927-30 and 1935. Dibbs was 31 years at the start of the 1936 season, but Geelong believed his experience would be invaluable. Although Geelong thrashed Footscray by 75 points in the opening round, North Melbourne by six points the following week and Melbourne by 70 points in round three, its form fell away dramatically from there and the Cats went down to St Kilda, Fitzroy and Richmond over consecutive weeks. Then, after lowly Hawthorn defeated Geelong by 43 points at the Glenferrie Oval, Dibbs resigned. He told the Geelong committee that he was "not in the best of health" and could not fully devote himself to his coaching duties. It proved to be a blessing in disguise for the Cats as his replacement, champion centre half-back Reg Hickey lifted Geelong to fifth position that season and the Cats went on to win the flag the following year under Hickey's stewardship. Dibbs immediately after his resignation crossed to the Ford club in the Geelong Football League and later was captain-coach of industrial club MacRobertson's in the Melbourne Saturday Morning League and then of Tasmanian club Latrobe and then the Essendon reserves.

DIGGINS, Brighton

PLAYING CAREER: South Melbourne, 1932-36, 65 games, 21 goals. Carlton, 1938-40, 31 games, 6 goals.

COACHING CAREER: South Melbourne, 1935, 2 games, 2 wins, 0 losses, 0 draws, 0 finals. Winning percentage – 100. Carlton, 1938-40, 56 games, 38 wins, 18 losses, 0 draws, 2 finals, 1 premiership. Winning percentage – 68.

Although West Australian Brighton Diggins played in South Melbourne's 1933

Premiers in 1938, captain-coach Brighton Diggins is sitting fourth from the left, second front row.

premiership side, he is best remembered as being captain-coach of Carlton's 1938 premiership side. Originally recruited from Subiaco, Diggins made a huge impression with South as a follower and was the Swans' vice-captain under captain-coach Jack Bisset. Then, when Bisset moved to VFA club Port Melbourne after the 1936 season, most observers believed Diggins would be appointed the new South coach. Although the Swans named former player Roy Cazaly as non-playing coach, Diggins believed they would honour a promise to name him captain. However, the Swans named Laurie Nash as captain and Diggins immediately resigned as vice-captain. He told South he would continue as a player, only for the Swans to drop him. Diggins walked out on the Swans and subsequently was swamped with offers from rival clubs. He eventually declared he wanted to play with Carlton but, when South refused to clear him, he decided to stand out of football over the 1937 season and returned to Western Australia. South relented in the lead-up to the 1938 season and Carlton appointed Diggins captain-coach. A natural leader who used a physical training expert to prepare his team, Diggins guided the Blues to the flag in his first season in charge. Diggins was the perfect captain-coach as he was big, strong and set a fine example in protecting his smaller players. Carlton finished fifth under Diggins in both 1939 and 1940, but he was forced to retire as a player four games into the 1940 season after breaking a hand. He resigned at the

end of 1940 to enlist in the army and, after the war, wrote on football matters for the Argus. He died in 1971 at just 60 years of age.

DITTERICH, Carl

PLAYING CAREER: St Kilda, 1963-72 and 1976-78, 203 games, 156 goals. Melbourne, 1973-75 and 1979-80, 82 games, 43 goals.

COACHING CAREER: Melbourne, 1979-80, 44 games, 11 wins, 33 losses, 0 draws, 0 finals. Winning percentage – 25.

One of football's most volatile characters, Ditterich made a name for himself as a

Carl Ditterich (left) in his Melbourne days.

ferociously-competitive ruckman with St Kilda. He missed the Saints' 1966 premiership victory because of suspension and, in 1979, was a shock appointment as Melbourne captain-coach. Melbourne believed it needed an on-field protector and Ditterich had played with the Demons from 1973-75, but had returned to St Kilda for another three seasons before taking on the Melbourne coaching job. The big, blond Demon leader started his regime by dumping 26 players and instituting a bold player input scheme. Although Ditterich led by example, the Demons finished above only St Kilda in 1979 and improved only marginally to finish ninth the following season. Melbourne then replaced him with club "Messiah" Ron Barassi in 1981.

Brian Dixon had a busy schedule.

DIXON, Brian

PLAYING CAREER: Melbourne, 1954-68, 252 games, 41 goals.

COACHING CAREER: North Melbourne, 1971-72, 44 games, 6 wins, 37 losses, 1 draw, 0 finals. Winning percentage – 14.

Dixon was an unorthodox choice as North Melbourne coach in the lead-up to the 1971 season. The Roos were in the doldrums and had collected the wooden spoon under former North winger Keith McKenzie in 1970. Dixon had had a sparkling playing career with Melbourne, winning five premiership medallions, had

coached VFA club Prahran but, at the time of his appointment with the Roos, was the sitting State Member for St Kilda and was Victoria's Minister for Youth, Sport and Recreation. A tough task master, Dixon demanded nothing less than full commitment, but did not have the player material for success. At one stage it was suggested former Footscray champion Ted Whitten would make a comeback with the Roos after retiring as a Bulldog in 1970. However, Dixon demanded that Whitten prove himself in a practice match and the man known as "Mr Football" pulled the plug on his comeback plan. North finished ninth under Dixon in 1971 but when the Roos collected the wooden spoon in 1972 he was replaced by Ron Barassi. Dixon was the Sydney Swans' CEO from late 1982 to mid-1983.

DONALD, Wally

PLAYING CAREER: Footscray, 1946-58, 205 games, 1 goal.

COACHING CAREER: Footscray, 1952 and 1953, 2 games, 1 win, 1 loss, 0 draws, 0 finals. Winning percentage – 50.

A back pocket in Footscray's 1954 premiership side, Donald had been recruited from local club Braybrook and gave the Bulldogs wonderful service over many years. As Footscray vice-captain, he had two games as club coach (one in each of the 1952-53 seasons) when captain-coach Charlie Sutton was unavailable. In one of these games, against St Kilda at Yallourn in the Propaganda Round (eight) in 1952, Donald moved himself to the forward line and kicked the only goal in his 205-game VFL career. There were suggestions that Donald would replace Sutton as Bulldog captain-coach in 1953, but the Footscray hierarchy decided to retain the status quo and Sutton led the Bulldogs to the 1954 flag. Donald later coached Mornington Peninsula club Crib Point and Footscray District club St Albans.

DONALDSON, Graham

PLAYING CAREER: Carlton, 1955-62, 106 games, 83 goals.

COACHING CAREER: Carlton, 1969, 1 game, 1 win, 0 losses, 0 draws, 0 finals.

Graham Donaldson.

Winning percentage – 100. Fitzroy, 1971-74, 84 games, 34 wins, 49 losses, 1 draw, 0 finals. Winning percentage – 39.

A big-hearted ruckman in his playing career with Carlton, Donaldson was Ron Barassi's assistant coach when the Blues won the 1968 premiership. He had coached the Blues in one game when Barassi was unavailable during the 1969 season and, after Carlton won another flag in 1970, rival clubs sought

Donaldson's services. He was offered the North Melbourne and Fitzroy positions and plumped to take on the Lions on a three-year contract from 1971. Succeeding Bill Stephen, Donaldson lifted the Lions from ninth to sixth in his first season to have Carlton making enquiries about his possible return to Princes Park following the resignation of Barassi as the Blues' coach. Donaldson said he wanted to honour his contract and remained with Fitzroy until he was replaced by Graham Campbell three games before the end of the 1974 season.

DONNELLY, Gerald

PLAYING CAREER: Melbourne, 1925, 12 games, 4 goals. North Melbourne, 1926 and 1930, 14 games, 5 goals. Essendon, 1930, 3 games, 0 goals.

COACHING CAREER: North Melbourne, 1926, 14 games, 0 wins, 13 losses, 1 draw, 0 finals. Winning percentage – 0.

An itinerant footballer, Donnelly joined Melbourne in 1925, only for North Melbourne to protest that he was tied to the Shinboners. The talented winger therefore crossed to Arden Street the following season and, bizarrely, found himself coaching the team when former St Kilda coach Wels Eicke stepped down. Donnelly had been appointed captain for the season and, after club official Stan Thomas took charge for one match, found himself as club captain-coach. North did not win a game under Donnelly's coaching, but it did draw in its clash with fellow-struggler Hawthorn at the Glenferrie Oval in round 13. North appointed Syd Barker as coach for the following season and although Donnelly was asked to captain the side, he declined and ended his VFL playing career with Essendon in 1930.

DROHAN, Eddie

PLAYING CAREER: Fitzroy, 1898-1902, 75 games, 5 goals. Collingwood, 1903-08, 96 games, 54 goals.

COACHING CAREER: Melbourne, 1910, 18 games, 4 wins, 14 losses, 0 draws, 0 finals. Winning percentage – 22. St Kilda, 1911, 18 games, 2 wins, 16 losses, 0 draws, 0 finals. Winning percentage – 11.

A member of Fitzroy's 1898-99 premiership sides, Drohan was a highly-skilled winger who was a master of the stab-pass and also played in Collingwood's 1903 flag side. He retired in 1908 and spent a season as an umpire before being appointed non-playing coach of Melbourne. The Fuchsias in 1910 won just four games under Drohan and finished above only St Kilda (one win). Remarkably, the Saints convinced him to switch clubs the following season, but again with little success. The Saints won just two games to finish above only University (one win).

Drohan was an opening batsman with Collingwood in District cricket, was a Collingwood delegate to the VFL and was an assistant coach at Hawthorn. He died on August 4, 1938, at 64 years of age.

DRUM, Damian

PLAYING CAREER: Geelong, 1982-89, 63 games, 34 goals.

COACHING CAREER: Fremantle – 1999-2001, 53 games, 13 wins, 40 losses, 0 draws, 0 finals. Winning percentage – 25.

A solid and reliable half-back, Drum had his playing career truncated by injuries and, after a stint with VFA club Werribee, coached rival club Port Melbourne. He then made a big impression as an assistant coach with the Sydney Swans and was handed the senior Fremantle job in 1999 following the departure of inaugural coach Gerard Neesham. The Dockers failed to flatter under Drum, with a season's best finish of twelfth in 2000. He was dumped during the following season and temporality replaced by former Hawthorn premiership player Ben Allan. Drum in 2002 was elected to the Victorian Legislative Council.

DUGDALE, John

PLAYING CAREER: North Melbourne, 1955-70, 248 games, 358 goals.

John Dugdale.

COACHING CAREER: North Melbourne, 1977, 1 game, 0 wins, 0 losses, 0 draws, 0 finals. Winning percentage – 0.

A hugely talented key position player for North Melbourne over his long playing career, Dugdale coached VFA club Coburg from 1973-75 before returning to Arden Street as assistant coach to Ron Barassi. Dugdale, who also served the Roos as chairman of selectors, coached North in one game when Barassi was unavailable during the 1977 premiership season. He also served the Roos as an administrator and spent more than 30 years with his beloved club.

DYER, Jack

PLAYING CAREER: Richmond, 1931-49, 312 games, 443 goals.

COACHING CAREER: Richmond, 1941-52, 226 games, 135 wins, 89 losses, 2 draws, 10 finals. 1 premiership. Winning percentage – 60.

One of football's greatest identities, Dyer started with Richmond in 1931 as a 17-year-old and went on to become a club legend. He played in the Tigers' 1934 premiership side and built himself a reputation as one of the most feared ruckmen in the competition. Known as "Captain Blood" because of his fearless swashbuckling style, it was obvious in the late '30s that Dyer eventually would coach Richmond. His time came in 1941 in controversial circumstances which split the Richmond Football Club. Richmond considered making Dyer captain-coach in place of Perc Bentley in 1940, but "Captain Blood" had to wait until the following year before the Tigers gave him the nod, with Bentley joining Carlton. The Tigers finished fourth in Dyer's first season and they then were runners-up to Essendon in 1942. However, the Tigers won the 1943 flag, defeating Essendon by just five points in the Grand Final at Princes Park. Dyer was Richmond's hero as he kicked a brilliant drop-kick goal to give the Tigers the lead in the final quarter. He finished with three goals in his greatest triumph.

Although the Dyer-led Tigers made the Grand Final the following year, they went down to Fitzroy by 15 points at the Junction Oval. Dyer had kicked nine goals in a brilliant performance against Essendon in the previous week's preliminary final, so placed himself at full-forward for the Grand Final. He kicked just one goal and was well held by Fitzroy captain-coach Fred Hughson. It was the end of a Richmond era as the Tigers did not make another Grand Final until they defeated Geelong in the 1967 Grand Final. Dyer's Tigers slid down the ladder after the 1944 Grand Final defeat and "Captain Blood" took them into only one other finals series – in 1947, when they went down to Fitzroy in the first semi-final. Dyer retired as a player at the end of the 1949 season, but was non-playing coach until the end of the 1952 season, when he was replaced by Alby Pannam. Dyer was so upset at being replaced by the much smaller Pannan, who had played just two games with Richmond after a tremendous career with Collingwood, that he was not seen at Punt Road for two years. After running hotel and milk bar businesses and at one time serving with the Victoria Police, Dyer at the end of his coaching career became a much-loved media identity, especially through his mangling of the Queen's English. He died on August 23, 2003, in his 90th year.

EADE, Rodney

PLAYING CAREER: Hawthorn, 1976-87, 229 games, 46 goals. Brisbane Bears, 1988-90, 30 games, 3 goals.

COACHING CAREER: Sydney Swans, 1996-2002, 152 games, 81 wins, 69 losses, 2 draws, 8 finals. Winning percentage – 53. Western Bulldogs, 2005-11, 162 games, 88 wins, 72 losses, 2 draws, 11 finals. Winning percentage – 54.

A classy winger, Tasmanian Eade played in four Hawthorn premiership sides, but joined the Brisbane Bears in 1988 and became the club's reserves coach. Eade then joined North Melbourne as an assistant coach in 1992 and took the reserves to the 1995 premiership, defeating the Sydney Swans in the Grand Final. The Swans were so impressed that they sought Eade's services as the replacement for retired coach Ron Barassi. The only problem was that Fitzroy also wanted Eade as its coach and the Swans had to move fast. They telephoned Eade as soon as he landed in Melbourne after an interview in Sydney and he accepted the position on the spot. Eade had a tough initiation to senior coaching as Adelaide thrashed the Swans in the opening round of 1996. However, the Swans eventually grasped Eade's requirements of running to back each other up and the red and white made its first Grand Final since going down to Carlton in 1945. North Melbourne defeated the Swans, but Eade had made a big impression as an innovative and tactically brilliant coach.

The Swans did not reach the same heights as 1996 under the rest of Eade's tenure as club coach, but he guided them to four of the next five finals series. But, when the

Rodney Eade.

Swans struggled in 2002, he went to the club committee to ask about his future. When told he would not be reappointed for the following season, he resigned and was replaced by Paul Roos with six rounds to play. Eade spent the 2003-04 seasons on the sidelines, but was touted as a possible candidate for every AFL coaching position that fell vacant. He eventually was appointed the Western Bulldogs' coach for 2005 and beyond and immediately gave his new club respectability. The Bulldogs, playing fast, systematic football under the wily Eade, made preliminary finals in 2008-09, but history repeated itself when the Bulldogs struggled in 2011. When Eade asked about his future, he again was told there would be no new contract and he resigned in the lead-up to round 22 and was temporarily replaced by former Collingwood and Sydney star Paul Williams. Eade then joined Collingwood to assist new senior coach Nathan Buckley.

EASON, Alec

PLAYING CAREER: Geelong, 1909-15 and 1919-21, 150 games, 80 goals. Richmond, 1916, 12 games, 8 goals.

COACHING CAREER: Geelong, 1920, 16 games, 5 wins, 11 defeats. 0 draws, 0 finals. Winning percentage – 32. Footscray, 1929, 18 games, 6 wins, 11 losses, 1 draw, 0 finals. Winning percentage – 33.

The best rover of his era, Eason was known as "Bunny" because he was said to be as fast as a rabbit. Geelong's 1915 best and fairest, he crossed to Richmond the following year and then missed a large chunk of football because of service in World War I. Footscray sought his services to play in the VFA when he returned to football in 1919, but he played another three seasons with Geelong before Footscray finally won his services in 1922. Meanwhile, Eason was elected Geelong captain-coach for the 1920 season but, after seven consecutive defeats to start the season, he was always likely to be a short-term Geelong coach, although the club did not have an official coach in 1921 (with Harold Craven as captain). Eason, after joining Footscray, guided the Tricolours to the 1923 and 1924 VFA premierships and, after coaching Sunshine in the Victorian Junior Football Association, was appointed Footscray's non-playing coach for the 1929 season. The Tricolours finished ninth under Eason, with six wins and a draw, but he was replaced at the end of the season when star Footscray centreman and club favourite Allan Hopkins was appointed captain-coach. Eason later served the Bulldogs for many seasons as chairman of selectors. He died on May 5, 1956, after collapsing at the Geelong railway station on his way to the round four Geelong-Richmond match at Kardinia Park; he was 66 years of age.

EASON, Bill

PLAYING CAREER: Geelong, 1902-15, 220 games, 187 goals.

COACHING CAREER: Geelong, 1912-13, 37 games, 21 wins, 16 losses, 0 draws, 1 final. Winning percentage – 57.

A more versatile player than brother "Bunny" Eason, Bill Eason could star in the centre or even in defence and when Geelong looked to replace Dave Hickinbotham as coach in 1912, it turned to club captain Eason and named him captain-coach. Hickinbotham even told the Geelong Advertiser that "nobody could coach the team but the captain". To 1912, the Geelong players elected their captain in the rooms before their opening round match. But, in 1912, they broke with tradition to elect Eason coach on the Thursday night before the opening round of the season. Eason immediately lifted Geelong into its first VFL finals series for nine years, only for the Pivotonians to go down to Carlton in the first semi-final. After Geelong finished fifth the following year during which Eason became the first Geelong player to notch 200 VFL games (in round 15 against Fitzroy), Billy Orchard was elected club captain and therefore playing coach. Eason continued as a player with Geelong until 1915.

EDWARDS, Arthur 'Titch'

PLAYING CAREER: Fitzroy, 1936-39 and 1944-45, 36 games, 22 goals.

COACHING CAREER: Fitzroy, 1961, 1 game, 1 win, 0 losses, 0 draws, 0 finals. Winning percentage – 100.

A handy rover/forward in his playing career with Fitzroy, Edwards stood in as the Lions' coach for one game – for one win – when senior coach Len Smith was coach of the Victorian team at the 1961 Brisbane Carnival. Edwards, whose career was interrupted by four years of army service in World War II, at one stage was captain-coach of the Fitzroy reserves and later coached Gippsland club Leongatha (taking it from last to premier in his first season) and Queensland club Coorparoo.

EICKE, Wels

PLAYING CAREER: St Kilda, 1909-24 and 1926, 197 games, 61 goals. North Melbourne 1925-26, 21 games, 0 goals.

COACHING CAREER: St Kilda, 1919 and 1924, 19 games, 7 wins, 12 losses, 0 draws, 0 finals. Winning percentage – 37. North Melbourne, 1925-26, 20 games, 5 wins, 15 losses, 0 draws, 0 finals. Winning percentage – 25.

Famous for making his debut with St Kilda at 15 years and 315 days, Eicke gave his club wonderful service at centre half-back and was appointed captain-coach in 1919 at just 25 years of age. Of course, he was a 10-year VFL veteran by then but, unfortunately, his tenure was marked by controversy and St Kilda fell from fourth under Jimmy Smith in 1918 to seventh in 1919. Along the way, St Kilda suffered the indignity of South Melbourne kicking 17 goals in one quarter against Eicke's men. The Saints appeared to be at war with each other and, in 1920, Eicke refused to play while another man – believed to be Billy Schmidt – was still at the club. George Sparrow and then Charlie Ricketts took over the coaching, but Eicke eventually returned to the Saints and he spent part of the 1924 season as captain-coach. The following season Eicke was appointed North Melbourne's coach

Wels Eicke.

for its inaugural VFL season of 1925. North finished tenth in its debut season, but when the Shinboners struggled the following season and failed to win a game under Eicke, he quit after playing just four games and returned to St Kilda, where he played another three games that season. He then ended his long VFL career, but coached VFA club Prahran and in the amateurs and served the Saints as a committeeman and selector. Eicke died on February 10, 1980, at 86 years of age.

ELLIOTT, Fred 'Pompey'

PLAYING CAREER: Melbourne 1899, 12 games, 4 goals. Carlton, 1900-01 and 1903-11, 197 games, 86 goals.

COACHING CAREER: Carlton, 1909-11, 47 games, 34 wins, 11 losses, 2 draws, 3 finals. Winning percentage – 72.

Elliott, a tireless follower, played in Carlton's 1906 and 1908 premiership sides and captained the Blues under the coaching of John Worrall in 1908. Elliott retained the captaincy for 1909, but when Worrall resigned following player unrest, Elliott took over coaching duties. Elliott guided the Blues to the finals, but they went down by two points to South Melbourne in the Grand Final. A reform group took control of the club the following year and, although top players George Johnson, Frank Caine, Fred Jinks and Charlie Hammond left Carlton to join VFA club North Melbourne, Elliott still managed to guide the Blues to top position before going down by 14 points to Collingwood in the Grand Final. Elliott coached the Blues to fourth position in 1911, a remarkable effort considering Carlton also was the centre of bribery allegations, but then retired and was

"PAST & PRESENT CHAMPIONS."

(29) **F. ELLIOTT.**
CARLTON FOOTBALL CLUB.

replaced as coach by Norman Clark and as captain by Jack Wells.

ELMS, Henry 'Sonny'

PLAYING CAREER: Did not play at VFL/ AFL level.

COACHING CAREER: South Melbourne, 1918-19, 33 games, 27 wins, 6 losses, 0 draws, 3 finals, 1 premiership. Winning percentage – 82.

A champion South winger in the 1880s when the club played in the VFA, Elms in 1918 was asked to be an assistant to non-playing coach Bert Howson. Although most record books indicate that Howson and Elms were appointed co-coaches in 1918, this is not accurate. South's 1918 annual report, released in February, 1919, said: "Mr H. (Herbert) Howson was appointed coach, with Elms his assistant." Regardless, the AFL recognises both as South's coaches over the 1918-19 seasons, with Howson and Elms taking the Southerners to the 1918 flag. South ended the two-year Howson-Elms partnership before the start of the 1920 season, when it appointed former player Arthur "Poddy" Hiskins non-playing coach. Elms died on September 15, 1928, and was buried at the Melbourne General Cemetery. Pall-bearers included Howson and former South and Geelong star Peter Burns. The Argus reported that "many football officials and former players" gathered at the graveside.

ERWIN, Mick

PLAYING CAREER: Collingwood, 1962-65, 29 games, 4 goals. Richmond, 1965-68, 33 games, 37 goals.

COACHING CAREER: Collingwood, 1982, 12 games, 3 wins, 9 losses, 0 draws, 0 finals. Winning percentage – 25.

A tough, relentless ruckman, Mick Erwin coached VFA club Prahran and also played in a Port Melbourne premiership side before being appointed an assistant to coach Tom Hafey at Collingwood. When Hafey sensationally was dumped after just one win from 10 games during the 1982 season, Erwin took over as senior coach. He guided the Magpies to victories over St Kilda and Footscray in his first two matches in charge and then against Geelong in the final round, with the Magpies finishing above only St Kilda and Footscray. Erwin was replaced by South Australian John Cahill the following season.

EVERETT, Allan

PLAYING CAREER: Geelong, 1934-40, 117 games, 25 goals.

COACHING CAREER: Geelong, 1940, 12 games, 7 wins, 5 losses, 0 draws, 1 final. Winning percentage – 58.

Geelong had three coaches in 1940, starting with Reg Hickey and followed by Les Laver (two games) and then Everett, who had assumed the captaincy following the retirement of Reg Hickey. It was a dramatic season for the Cats as club vice-captain Tom Quinn retired after being dropped to the reserves, therefore elevating Everett to the captaincy. Everett might have coached the Cats for just 12 games, but they made the finals in 1940, going down to Essendon in the first semi-final. Everett's other claim to fame was being the last captain of a Geelong side at the Corio Oval as the Cats moved to Kardinia Park the following season. Everett retired at the completion of the 1940 season.

FARMER, Graham "Polly"

PLAYING CAREER: Geelong, 1962-67, 101 games, 65 goals.

COACHING CAREER: Geelong, 1973-75, 66 games, 24 wins, 42 losses, 0 draws, 0 finals. Winning percentage – 36.

Farmer was a superb ruckman who changed the game with his clever tap work and brilliant long, penetrating handball. Geelong recruited him from East Perth and he played a huge part in the Cats' 1963 premiership triumph. He left the Cats after Geelong's 1967 Grand Final loss to Richmond and returned to Western Australia. He was captain-coach of two West Perth premiership sides and, in 1973, he returned to Kardinia Park as non-playing coach to succeed Bill McMaster. However, Farmer was unable to lift the Cats and they finished eleventh, sixth and eleventh in three seasons as coach. Farmer, who was nicknamed "Polly" because he was as talkative as a parrot when growing up in Western Australia, might not have succeeded in his stint as Geelong coach, but will always be remembered as a Cat legend.

Graham Farmer - a Cat legend.

FAUL, Bill

PLAYING CAREER: South Melbourne, 1932-38, 117 games, 2 goals.

COACHING CAREER: South Melbourne, 1960-61, 36 games, 12 wins, 0 draws, 24 losses, 0 finals. Winning percentage – 33.

W. FAUL.
STH. MELBOURNE.

A wonderfully reliable half-back after South Melbourne recruited him from WA club Subiaco, Faul played in the Swans' 1933 premiership side. He left the Swans in 1938 to accept the position as captain-coach of VFA club Prahran, thus starting a long coaching career. He had two stints with Prahran and also had two stints with VFA rival Northcote. Faul coached Prahran to the 1951 premiership and also coached the VFA at the 1950 Carnival before moving to another VFA club in Moorabbin. Faul's coaching reputation improved even further when Moorabbin won the 1957 flag. It therefore was no surprise when the Swans in 1960 named him senior coach to replace the retired

Ron Clegg. Faul spent two years in charge at the Lake Oval but, after finishing eighth in 1960, the Swans slumped to eleventh the following year. Faul years later lamented that he did not have the players for success. He ended his coaching career in the amateurs, with the Old Brighton Grammar, AJAX and National Bank clubs. He died of a heart attack in the car park at Waverley Park after watching a VFL match there on September 17, 1974, at 65 years of age.

FELTHAM, Paul

PLAYING CAREER: North Melbourne, 1970-76, 128 games, 78 goals. Richmond, 1978, 7 games, 8 goals.

COACHING CAREER: Brisbane Bears, 1989, 7 games, 4 wins, 3 losses, 0 draws, 0 finals. Winning percentage – 57.

A talented winger who played in North Melbourne's inaugural premiership side of 1975, Feltham was the Brisbane Bears' sports psychologist in 1989 when the club sensationally sacked coach Peter Knights. The axe fell four days after Geelong thrashed the Bears by 74 points in the first night match at Carrara, on July 15. Feltham guided the Bears to four wins in seven games, but was not reappointed and was replaced by former Fitzroy player Norm Dare for the 1990 season.

FINDLAY, Bill

PLAYING CAREER: Footscray, 1933-34, 5 games, 8 goals. North Melbourne, 1935-45, 158 games, 352 goals.

COACHING CAREER: North Melbourne, 1942-43, 21 games, 7 wins, 13 losses, 1 draw, 0 finals. Winning percentage – 32. Footscray, 1961, 1962, 1964 and 1966, 5 games, 2 wins, 3 losses, 0 draws, 0 finals. Winning percentage – 40.

One of the finest rovers of his era, Findlay also was an iron-man as he played more than 200 consecutive games with North Melbourne and VFA club Port Melbourne. He took over as North coach during the 1942 season when Bob McCaskill was called away on war service and held the position for the following season. North finished ninth in both 1942 and 1943. McCaskill returned as coach in 1944, but Findlay continued as a player until 1945. He then was appointed captain-coach of Port Melbourne and, in 1949, was named playing coach of the North reserves under senior coach Wally Carter. Findlay was appointed assistant coach at Footscray in 1961 and stood in when club captain-coach Ted Whitten was unavailable in five matches over the next few years.

FITZMAURICE, Tom

PLAYING CAREER: Essendon, 1918-20 and 1922-24, 85 games, 30 goals. Geelong, 1925-28, 49 games, 20 goals. North Melbourne, 1932-35, 54 games, 196 goals.

COACHING CAREER: Geelong, 1928, 18 games, 6 wins, 12 losses, 0 draws, 0 finals. Winning percentage – 33. North Melbourne, 1934-35, 16 games, 0 wins, 16 losses, 0 draws, 0 finals. Winning percentage – 0.

Although Fitzmaurice could not get a game with his school (CBC North Melbourne) football team because he was regarded as too big and awkward, he became a star ruckman with Essendon,

TOM FITZMAURICE

Geelong and North Melbourne. He missed the 1921 season when he was transferred to Sydney in his job with a bank, but played in the 1923-24 premiership sides. However, he walked out on the Dons over the claim that some teammates had accepted bribes to "throw" the end-of-season charity match against VFA premier Footscray. Fitzmaurice therefore joined Geelong and was appointed coach in 1928. He accepted the position only on condition that his fee would be shared by the rest of the team. Geelong slid from third to ninth in Fitzmaurice's only season in charge and he then coached country club Mortlake for a season and then VFA club Yarraville for three seasons before being enticed to join North Melbourne as captain-coach when Dick Taylor resigned during the 1934 season. North finished on the bottom and when it continued to struggle the next year, Fitzmaurice also resigned. He told the club that the continued failure of the team had caused him to lose enthusiasm. Although North asked Fitzmaurice to reconsider his decision, he told them his decision was final and he was replaced by former South Melbourne star Paddy Scanlan. Fitzmaurice later coached in Tasmania and in Canberra. Fitzmaurice, who also was a talented singer and athlete, was responsible for burning cancelled bank notes in his bank job and used to light his cigars with 10 pound ($20) notes.

FLEITER, Fred

PLAYING CAREER: South Melbourne, 1919-25, 71 games, 11 goals.

COACHING CAREER: South Melbourne, 1929, 14 games, 6 wins, 8 losses, 0 draws, 0 finals. Winning percentage – 43.

Part of the famous following group also comprising Roy Cazaly and Mark Tandy, Fleiter was a bullocking ruck-rover who found himself non-playing coach in 1929 when 1918 premiership captain Jim Caldwell stepped down because of serious illness just four rounds into the

Fred Fleiter (right) hams it up with Roy Cazaly (left) and Mark Tandy (centre).

season. Caldwell was just 40 years of age when he died later that year. Fleiter did not want the South coaching position on a permanent basis and, after South finished eighth in 1929, he stepped aside for former club champion Paddy Scanlan.

FOOTE, Les

PLAYING CAREER: North Melbourne, 1941-51, 134 games, 105 goals. St Kilda, 1954-55, 33 games, 4 goals.

COACHING CAREER: St Kilda, 1954-55, 36 games, 5 wins, 30 losses, 1 draw, 0 finals. Winning percentage – 14.

Foote, a brilliant centreman, left North Melbourne to be captain-coach of NSW country club Berrigan in 1952 after also considering an offer from North Launceston. He was just 27 years of age when he turned his back on the VFL, but was far too good a footballer to be playing in the bush. St Kilda realised this when it was looking for a coach to replace Col Williamson as coach in 1954 and was successful in signing Foote as a marquee captain-coach. He said at the time: "I have been out of the big game in Melbourne for two years. Now I am going to get fit and show the St Kilda boys everything I know about football. St Kilda has been moving forward in the last couple of years and I hope we can go one or two better this season. You must remember it takes a great effort to get to the top.

What St Kilda needs is more barrackers to yell their heads off." Although Foote won St Kilda's 1954 best and fairest, his brilliance did not rub off on his team. The Saints collected the wooden spoon and a repeat in 1955 saw Foote relinquish his position, announcing his retirement in the lead-up to the final round match against Richmond, and he was replaced by former St Kilda player Alan Killigrew.

FORBES, Keith

PLAYING CAREER: Essendon, 1928-37, 152 games, 415 goals. North Melbourne, 1938-39, 31 games, 50 goals. Fitzroy, 1940, 4 games, 10 goals.

COACHING CAREER: North Melbourne, 1938-39, 36 games, 12 wins, 24 losses 0 draws, 0 finals. Winning percentage – 33.

Recruited by Essendon from VFA club Coburg, Forbes was a goalkicking rover who was a regular Victorian representative. Runner-up in the 1930 and 1935 Brownlow Medal counts, he was named North Melbourne captain-coach to replace Paddy Scanlan in 1938. Forbes lifted North from the bottom to ninth but after the Shinboners finished ninth again the following year the club turned to South Melbourne star Len Thomas as coach for 1940. Forbes had been suspended in highly unusual circumstances while North coach against Richmond in round 16, 1939.

He was booked for disputing umpire Morgan's decisions but, in a feature in the Sporting Globe in 1955, Forbes explained that he had queried umpire Morgan about speaking to Richmond player Martin Bolger by name instead of by number. However, he admitted he added "you big so-and-so" to his comment and copped a six-match ban. Forbes, unavailable for the first four rounds of 1940, joined Fitzroy and also enlisted in the army. He played just four games for the Maroons, kicking five goals in his final match (against Melbourne) before serving in the army. He was farming in Gippsland in 1946 when he agreed to be captain-coach of local side Welshpool and then coached Yarram, playing his last game at 44 years of age.

FRANCIS, Jim

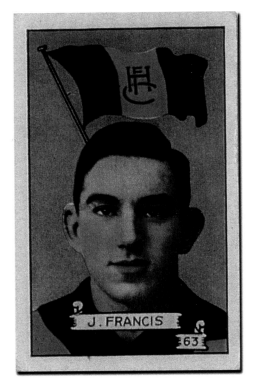

PLAYING CAREER: Hawthorn, 1929-33, 61 games, 26 goals. Carlton, 1934-43, 162 games, 52 goals.

COACHING CAREER: Carlton, 1956-58, 55 games, 29 wins, 25 losses, 1 draw, 1 final. Winning percentage – 53. St Kilda, 1959-60, 36 games, 18 wins, 18 defeats, 0 draws, 0 finals. Winning percentage – 50.

A wonderfully versatile footballer, Francis already was a VFL star when he left Hawthorn to join Carlton. On retirement as a player he became coach of the Carlton Under 19s and then the reserves. Francis was seen as the natural successor to the senior job when Perc Bentley retired at the end of 1955 and Francis held the job for three seasons, with Carlton finishing fifth, fourth and seventh. At the end of the 1958 season, there was a push to replace him with good friend, Ken Hands. Francis and Hands had clashed during the 1957 season and although club president Lew Holmes tried to reconcile the pair, the split deepened. Although Francis seemed to be the supporters' choice as coach, senior players gave their support to Hands. Carlton therefore was a divided club in 1958 and Hands' supporters eventually won the day. Hands was appointed non-playing coach for 1959 and St Kilda immediately swooped to name Francis coach in place of Alan Killigrew. The Saints finished eighth in 1959 and then sixth, with Allan Jeans taking over as coach in 1961.

FRANKLIN, Tony

PLAYING CAREER: South Melbourne, 1974-75, 32 games, 11 goals.

COACHING CAREER: Sydney Swans, 1984, 1 game, 0 wins, 1 loss, 0 draws, 0 finals. Winning percentage – 0.

Franklin, an underrated defender with South Melbourne after being recruited from Tasmanian club Penguin, was the Swans' chairman of selectors when coach Rick Quade fell seriously ill during the 1984 season and was hospitalised. Franklin therefore took over as interim coach for one match (a loss to Collingwood), with South Australian Bob Hammond then taking over for the rest of the season. When appointed caretaker coach, Franklin said he did not want the job permanently and, besides, he was based in Melbourne at that time.

FRAWLEY, Danny

PLAYING CAREER: St Kilda, 1984-95, 240 games, 13 goals.

COACHING CAREER: Richmond, 2000-04, 113 games, 45 wins, 68 losses, 0 draws, 3 finals. Winning percentage – 40.

After a hugely successful playing career with St Kilda in which he was one of

Danny Frawley leads Carlton's Earl Spalding to the ball.

the best full-backs in the competition, Frawley joined Collingwood as an assistant coach in 1996 and, after three seasons with the Magpies was appointed Richmond coach to succeed Jeff Gieschen in 2000. Frawley, renowned for his honesty and integrity, lifted the Tigers off the bottom to finish ninth in his debut season and then to a preliminary final in 2001. They were heady days for the success-starved Tigers but their joy was short-lived as they crashed to fourteenth the following season. Frawley was unable to lift the Tigers again and supporters eventually turned on him, booing him off the ground at half-time in one match at Docklands. Frawley announced during 2004 that he would finish as Richmond coach at the end of the season. The Tigers lost their last 14 matches of the season to collect the wooden spoon.

FROUDE, Fred

PLAYING CAREER: Collingwood, 1930-39, 148 games, 41 goals.

COACHING CAREER: St Kilda, 1948-50, 56 games, 14 wins, 41 losses, 1 draw, 0 finals. Winning percentage – 25.

Froude made a name for himself as a dashing half-back flanker for Collingwood and played in the Magpies' 1935-36 premiership sides. A keen student of the game, he was appointed coach of the St Kilda reserves in 1946 and when senior coach Allan Hird stepped down at the end of the 1947 season, Froude was waiting in the wings. However, the Saints wanted a playing coach and set their sights on Collingwood's Phonse Kyne, who was just 32 years of age at the time. Kyne might have been flattered by St Kilda's invitation, but he declined to apply for the vacant position and the Saints, in turn, appointed Froude non-playing coach. Froude, who was described as a "quiet achiever" and a "great organiser", had coached VFA club Brighton before guiding St Kilda to a VFL reserves premiership. He said when he was appointed senior St Kilda coach that he wanted to bring "Collingwood methods" to training, with twice weekly practice matches and an emphasis on fitness. The Saints collected the wooden spoon in Froude's first season of 1948 and although they improved slightly to finish eleventh the following year and then ninth in 1950, the former Magpie stepped down and was replaced by Fred Green.

GARVIN, Reg

PLAYING CAREER: St Kilda, 1937-46, 130 games, 33 goals.

COACHING CAREER: St Kilda, 1942-43, 24 games, 7 wins, 16 losses, 1 draw, 0 finals. Winning percentage – 29.

Sydneysider Garvin had played soccer at school before playing rugby league with the Canterbury-Bankstown club and Australian football with Newtown. A fine key position defender, he won the 1941 C.T. Suhr Memorial Trophy as St Kilda's best and fairest and was appointed the Saints' captain-coach in 1942, replacing former Collingwood player Jack Knight. A fitness fanatic, Garvin introduced a tougher training regime and lifted the Saints to seventh position in his first season as coach. However, the Saints then slid to eleventh position in 1943 and he was replaced as senior coach by Hugh Thomas, who had guided the Saint reserves to two premierships, Although VFA club Brunswick sought Garvin's services as captain-coach in 1944, he continued playing with St Kilda and retired in 1946. He later coached VFA club Prahran and Federal League club Camden.

GAUDION, Charlie

PLAYING CAREER: Footscray, 1926-29, 63 games, 7 goals. North Melbourne, 1931-37, 77 games, 9 goals.

COACHING CAREER: North Melbourne, 1956-57, 36 games, 11 wins, 25 losses, 0 draws, 0 finals. Winning percentage – 31.

Although Gaudion started his VFL career with Footscray, he played his best football with North Melbourne and captained Victoria. A key position defender, he coached West Adelaide in 1940 and returned to North as coach in 1956, replacing Jock McCorkell. A former decathlon champion, Gaudion initiated a strict training regime at Arden Street and, on his appointment as coach, wrote in the Argus: "I'm not saying North Melbourne is a premiership side this year ... but watch us all the same. We'll be a much better combination than last season – and we will do well. I have the talent at North this year to do well. I have planned training this year so that all players will be at their peak for the opening match against St Kilda." North thrashed St Kilda by 57 points at Arden Street, but the Shinboners won only two more matches to collect the wooden spoon. Although North improved to finish in eighth position (with eight wins) in 1957, Gaudion was replaced by Wally Carter, who returned to the club after a successful stint with VFA club Williamstown. Remarkably, one of Gaudion's charges as coach in 1957 was son Mick, who played 152 games with North from 1957-67 and, like his father, represented Victoria. Charlie Gaudion became a players' advocate at the VFL Tribunal.

GELLIE, Graeme

PLAYING CAREER: St Kilda, 1978-83, 32 games, 12 goals.

COACHING CAREER: St Kilda, 1984-86, 48 games, 6 wins, 42 losses, 0 draws, 0 finals. Winning percentage – 13.

A clever rover recruited from Redan, Gellie's career was ruined by knee injuries and, on retirement, became an assistant coach. When St Kilda sacked coach Tony Jewell 18 rounds into 1984, Gellie stepped up as senior coach. The Saints won only one of their final four games of the season, but Gellie was so impressive that he was given the senior coaching position for 1985 after club legend Darrel

Baldock had accepted the job and then pulled out because of commitments in his native Tasmania. Gellie held the position for two seasons, with St Kilda finishing on the bottom with three wins in 1985 and then last again in 1986, with just two wins. Gellie then was replaced by Baldock.

GIESCHEN, Jeff

PLAYING CAREER: Richmond, 1974-78, 24 games, 1 goal.

COACHING CAREER: Richmond, 1997-99, 49 games, 25 wins, 24 losses, 0 draws, 0 finals. Winning percentage – 51.

Footscray recruited Gieschen from country zone club Maffra and although he played just 24 senior games, he twice was runner-up in the Gardiner Medal count for reserves best and fairest. He returned to Maffra as coach in 1979 and then was in charge at Wodonga before moving to West Perth as non-playing coach. Gieschen was appointed Geelong reserves coach in 1994 and left at the end of 1996 to join Richmond. Then, when senior coach Robert Walls was dumped after a 137-point thrashing by Adelaide in round 17, 1997 the Tigers named Gieschen as interim coach. The Tigers defeated the Western Bulldogs by 15 points in Gieschen's first game in charge and Richmond fans immediately launched a campaign for him to continue as coach into the next season, with banners demanding that the Tiger hierarchy "unleash the Giesch". Richmond ended the season with a two-point defeat of Carlton, giving Gieschen four wins in five games. He therefore was handed the job in his own right for 1998 and the Tigers finished ninth, only to slump to twelfth in 1999. Gieschen then was replaced by former St Kilda captain Danny Frawley and later became boss of the AFL's umpiring department.

GOGGIN, Bill

PLAYING CAREER: Geelong, 1958-71, 248 games, 279 goals.

COACHING CAREER: Footscray, 1976-78, 46 games, 21 wins, 23 losses, 2 draws, 1 final. Winning percentage – 46. Geelong 1980-82, 71 games, 41 wins, 30 losses, 0 draws. 5 finals. Winning percentage – 58.

One of the best rovers of his era, Goggin was Geelong captain from 1968-71 and on his retirement from VFL football at the end of the 1971 season, joined VFA club Geelong West as captain-coach. He won two flags with the VFA Roosters and was appointed Footscray coach to replace Bob Rose in 1976. He immediately took the Bulldogs to a finals series, only for his team to go down to Geelong by seven points in the elimination final. Footscray fell to seventh position in 1977 and when the Bulldogs sold star key forward Bernie Quinlan to Fitzroy in 1978, Goggin

resigned just six days into the new season in protest. He said at the time: "I feel that the club is going nowhere. I'm not prepared to be the scapegoat for the lack of administration and recruiting." Goggin was appointed Geelong coach to replace Rod Olsson in 1980 and took the Cats to preliminary finals in his first two seasons, losing both to Collingwood. After the Cats finished ninth in 1982, Goggin was replaced by Tom Hafey. The great Cat favourite then became coach of Victorian State of Origin sides.

GOODE, Frank

PLAYING CAREER: North Melbourne, 1961-67, 73 games, 107 goals.

COACHING CAREER: Footscray, 1981, 1 game, 0 wins, 1 loss, 0 draws, 0 finals. Winning percentage – 0.

A fine key position player with North Melbourne, Goode could play at full-forward or full-back. He led North's goalkicking with 38 in 1966 and later was appointed coach of the Footscray reserves. Goode took over as senior coach for one game, against Melbourne at the Western Oval in round 3, 1981, when regular coach Royce Hart was ill in hospital. Footscray went into the match without injured star Kelvin Templeton, but pushed the Demons all the way to go down by just one point. Melbourne star Robert Flower kicked the winning goal to

Mick Grace pulls in a chest mark against Collingwood.

deny Goode a win in his only match as a senior coach. Hart was released from hospital two days later.

GRACE, Mick

PLAYING CAREER: Fitzroy, 1897-1900, 65 games, 55 goals. Carlton, 1903-07, 86 games, 133 goals. St Kilda, 1908, 16 games, 26 goals.

COACHING CAREER: St Kilda, 1908, 19 games, 10 wins, 9 losses, 0 draws, 1 final. Winning percentage – 53.

A hugely-talented follower/forward, Grace starred with Fitzroy in its earliest VFL years, crossed to Carlton and then St Kilda. He ended his VFL playing career during the 1900 season and he joined VFA club Brighton. However, Carlton recalled him from the 1903 season and he played in the Blues' premiership side in 1906. He was appointed playing St Kilda coach (with Jack Wells as club captain) in 1908, but even then was dogged by ill-health. The Saints made the finals under Grace's coaching in 1908, but were thrashed by Carlton (58 points) in a semi-final. Grace then moved to Sydney and coached the NSW state side at the 1911 Carnival in Adelaide. He already was terminally ill with tuberculosis and special testimonial matches, including one between the VFL and VFA umpires, raised more than 300 pounds ($600) for Grace and his family. He eventually returned to Melbourne but died in the Austin Hospital, Heidelberg, in May, 1912. Grace, who also was a talented cricketer, was just 38 years of age and left a widow and three children.

GRAVENALL, Sam

PLAYING CAREER: St Kilda, 1903, 1906 and 1910, 30 games, 15 goals.

COACHING CAREER: Essendon, 1922, 12 games, 7 wins, 4 losses, 1 draw, 0 finals. Winning percentage – 58.

Gravenall was a fine forward for St Kilda but had a sporadic VFL career as he spent two years playing in Western Australia. The 1910 St Kilda captain was a surprise choice as non-playing Essendon coach in 1922. Essendon that season returned to its roots, moving from playing its home games at the East Melbourne Cricket Ground to the Essendon Recreation Reserve. Gravenall therefore had the distinction of being the first Essendon coach at the club's new ground. The Dons defeated Carlton by 18 points in front of 22,000 fans. When the Dons won just seven of their first 12 games,

the committee decided the players needed more discipline and Gravenall was replaced by Syd Barker. Gravenall, a schoolteacher and sports writer, moved to England in the late 1930s and served as an air raid warden during World War II. He died in London in March, 1948, at 72 years of age.

GREEN, Fred

PLAYING CAREER: Essendon, 1939-41, 1943 and 1946, 49 games, 7 goals. St Kilda, 1947-51, 66 games, 9 goals.

COACHING CAREER: St Kilda, 1951, 18 games, 5 wins, 13 losses, 0 draws, 0 finals. Winning percentage – 28.

A powerful ruckman/defender, Green's VFL playing career with Essendon was interrupted by war service and, after returning to the Dons in 1946, joined St Kilda the following year. He was appointed St Kilda captain in 1949 and in 1951 was named senior coach to replace Fred Froude. Green originally intended being a non-playing coach, but kept himself fit through training by himself and decided after a brilliant performance in an intra-club practice match to continue playing. However, he played just eight games in his final VFL season and when the Saints finished tenth in 1951, he did not apply for the coaching position for 1952 and was replaced by Col Williamson. St Kilda was so impressed with Green's efforts, however, that the club asked him to continue with the club as a "coach's advisor".

GRIGGS, Les

PLAYING CAREER: Essendon, 1933-35 and 1939-44, 99 games, 52 goals.

COACHING CAREER: Essendon, 1941, 1 game, 1 win, 0 losses, 0 draws, 0 finals. Winning percentage – 100.

Griggs, a brilliant centreman or centre half-forward, started with Essendon at 19 years of age and would have played many more than his 99 games had he not been transferred to the country in his professional career as a schoolteacher. He therefore missed three seasons from 1936-38. Griggs coached Essendon in one game when regular captain-coach Dick Reynolds was unavailable because of interstate duties with Victoria against South Australia and club vice-captain Hugh Torney was selected for a Big Vee game against NSW. Griggs later coached the Essendon and South Melbourne reserves, as well as various country clubs (including Mildura) in his moves around Victoria as a schoolteacher.

GUY, Eric

PLAYING CAREER: St Kilda, 1957-62, 93 games, 0 goals.

Eric Guy stood in as St Kilda coach for Allan Jeans.

COACHING CAREER: St Kilda, 1972 and 1974, 6 games, 2 wins, 4 losses, 0 draws, 0 finals. Winning percentage – 33.

One of the toughest footballers of his era, defender Guy had been a star player with VFA club Oakleigh before joining the Saints at 24 years of age. Guy was an assistant coach with the Saints when he twice stepped in for senior coach Allan Jeans, including five games at the end of the 1974 season when Jeans was ill with hepatitis. Guy died on May 3, 1991, at just 58 years of age.

HAFEY, Tom

PLAYING CAREER: Richmond, 1953-58, 67 games, 10 goals.

COACHING CAREER: Richmond, 1966-76, 248 games, 173 wins, 73 losses, 2 draws, 20 finals, 4 premierships. Winning percentage – 70. Collingwood, 1977-82, 138 games, 89 wins, 47 losses, 2 draws, 18 finals. Winning percentage – 68. Geelong, 1983-85, 66 games, 31 wins, 35 losses, 0 draws, 0 finals. Winning percentage – 47. Sydney Swans, 1986-88, 70 games, 43 wins, 27 losses, 0 draws, 4 finals. Winning percentage – 61.

Tom Hafey.

Although Hafey had a modest career as a back pocket specialist with Richmond, he made a name for himself in coaching country club Shepparton to three premierships. He therefore was an obvious choice as senior Richmond coach after former champion Jack "Skinny" Titus had been interim coach in 1965. Hafey immediately laid down the law at Tigerland and introduced the toughest fitness demands in the competition. The Tigers under Hafey became one of the most feared teams in the VFL, renowned for their fitness, ferocity and strength. Hafey even insisted that his wingers be tall and powerful and Francis Bourke and Dick Clay became the scourge of rival wingers. Hafey lifted the Tigers to their first premiership since 1943 in guiding them to a Grand Final victory over Geelong in 1967 and also took Richmond to the 1969 and 1973-74 premierships. In fact, the Tigers missed the finals only three times (1965, 1970 and 1976) in Hafey's tenure at Tigerland. Yet, inexplicably, he was sacked when the Tigers finished seventh in 1976 and replaced by Barry Richardson.

Hafey immediately was snapped up by Collingwood after the Magpies had collected the wooden spoon under Murray Weideman in 1976. Hafey again introduced a tough training regime and won the respect of the playing list. The Magpies reached the 1977 Grand Final but, after a draw with North Melbourne, were well beaten in the replay. Criticism was levelled at Hafey for pushing his team too hard at training in the lead-up to the replay, but he insisted his methods were correct. Collingwood made each Grand Final from 1979-81 under Hafey, but was defeated each time, in turn, by Carlton, Richmond and Carlton again. Fate had been cruel to Hafey at Victoria Park and, when the Magpies slipped in 1982, he was replaced mid-season by Mick Erwin.

The Tiger premiership coach was out of football only briefly as Geelong snapped him up to replace Bill Goggin in 1983. Hafey failed to take the Cats to a finals series in his three seasons at Kardinia Park and, in 1986, Sydney Swan owner Dr Geoffrey Edelsten appointed him coach after missing out on Essendon coach Kevin Sheedy. The Swans embarked on one of the biggest recruiting campaigns in football history, but success eluded them, despite a wealth of talent. The Swans crashed out of both the 1986 and 1987 finals series in straight sets and when talented players started leaving the club in 1988, they started slipping down the ladder. Hafey was dumped at the end of that season and was replaced by Colin Kinnear. It was an inglorious end to one of the greatest coaching careers in VFL/AFL history. Hafey coached in a total of 522 games for an overall winning percentage of 64.

HAGGER, Lloyd

PLAYING CAREER: Geelong, 1917-27 and 1929, 174 games, 389 goals.

COACHING CAREER: Geelong, 1924, 16 games, 8 wins, 8 losses, 0 draws, 0 finals. Winning percentage – 50.

A high-marking centre half-forward from Barwon, Hagger was appointed Geelong captain-coach in 1924 to replace Bert Taylor as coach and Bert Rankin as captain. Ironically, Rankin had recruited Hagger, but had been dropped from the Geelong side for the 1923 first semi-final and brother Cliff refused to accept the captaincy. Geelong slipped to fifth position under Hagger in 1924 and Cliff Rankin not only accepted the captain-coach position for 1925 but guided Geelong to its first VFL premiership that season. Hagger remained loyal to the Cats and played at full-forward in the 10-point defeat of Collingwood in the Grand Final.

HAINES (HEINZ), George

PLAYING CAREER: Geelong, 1909-14, 87 games 71 goals. Melbourne 1919-25, 106 games, 97 goals. St Kilda, 1927, 1 game, 1 goal.

COACHING CAREER: Melbourne, 1919, 16 games, 0 wins, 16 losses, 0 draws, 0 finals. Winning percentage - 0. St Kilda, 1927, 18 games, 8 wins, 10 losses, 0 draws, 0 finals. Winning percentage – 44.

A talented rover who represented Victoria, Haines moved from Geelong to captain-coach Melbourne in 1919. However, he had changed his name from Heinz during World War I because of anti-German sentiment in Australia. He had the dubious distinction of not coaching Melbourne to a single victory and he was replaced in 1920 by former Fitzroy star Gerald Brosnan. However, Haines defeated four other applicants for the St Kilda coaching position in 1927 and made an abortive playing comeback in the 20-point opening round defeat of Hawthorn at the Junction Oval. The 35-year-old realised his playing days were behind him and was St Kilda's non-playing coach over the rest of the season. Although St Kilda finished seventh, Haines was replaced by George Sparrow for the 1928 season.

HALE, Jack

PLAYING CAREER: Carlton, 1933-41, 123 games, 78 goals.

COACHING CAREER: South Melbourne, 1948-49, 28 games, 9 wins, 19 losses, 0 draws, 0 finals. Winning percentage – 32. Hawthorn, 1952-59, 148 games, 61 wins, 86 losses, 1 draw, 2 finals. Winning percentage – 41.

A courageous rover with Carlton, Hale's career was cut short by a severely broken leg. He joined South Melbourne as an assistant coach and was handed the senior job in 1948 when "Bull" Adams resigned over controversial comments

Jack Hale.

he had made about his players on radio. Hale immediately made changes to the South team and, for example, switched club captain Jack Graham from the ruck to centre half-forward. When the Swans won two of their last four games of the season, Hale was reappointed for 1949. But, when the Swans won just one of their final 10 games that season to finish tenth, Hale was replaced by Gordon Lane. Hale then became an assistant coach with Hawthorn and assumed the senior position in 1952 when Bob McCaskill died following a long illness. Hale already had assumed many of the coaching duties, so the promotion was seamless. Hale immediately set about to harden Hawthorn's image and rid the club of its loser mentality. He succeeded where others had failed and, in 1957, guided the Hawks to their first finals series. They defeated Carlton in the first semi-final before going down to eventual premier Melbourne in the preliminary final. It represented the rebirth of Hawthorn and Hale, who coached the Hawks until the end of the 1959 season and was regarded as an extremely tough task master, will always be regarded as one of the club's greatest identities.

HALL, Alex

PLAYING CAREER: Essendon, 1898-1900, 19 games, 8 goals. St Kilda, 1906, 1 game, 0 goals.

COACHING CAREER: St Kilda, 1906, 13 games, 4 wins, 9 losses, 0 draw, 0 finals. Winning percentage – 31. Melbourne, 1907-09, 53 games, 24 wins, 28 losses, 1 draw, 0 finals. Winning percentage – 45. Richmond, 1910, 18 games, 7 wins, 10 losses, 1 draw, 0 finals. Winning percentage – 39. Hawthorn, 1925, 17 games, 3 wins, 14 losses, 0 draws, 0 finals. Winning percentage – 18.

Hall had a remarkable career as he was the first man to coach St Kilda, Melbourne and Hawthorn. He also was Richmond's second VFL coach, after Dick Condon (1908-09). A dashing defender or rover in his playing career, which started with Essendon in the VFA, Hall was an itinerant footballer who wandered from club to club and even country to country. Apart from playing with VFA clubs Preston and Williamstown (as captain-coach), he moved to South Africa after coaching St Kilda in 1906, coached in the country and served overseas with the AIF during World War I. Although regarded as a master tactician, Hall had a poor coaching record as he did not take any of his four clubs into a finals series.

HAMMOND, Bob

PLAYING CAREER: Did not play at VFL/AFL level, but played 234 games for SAFL club South Adelaide and 14 for Norwood.

COACHING CAREER: Sydney Swans, 1984, 8 games, 3 wins, 5 losses, 0 draws, 0 finals. Winning percentage – 38.

The Sydney Swans were forced to find a replacement coach when Rick Quade fell seriously ill in 1984 and turned to South Australian Bob Hammond, who was involved in the liquor industry at the time. Hammond was an iconic football identity in South Australia and had played seven games for his state in a stellar playing career. He also had coached Norwood to two premierships and was seen as an ideal replacement for Quade. The Swans might have won just three games under Hammond, but he was highly-regarded and the Swans were hopeful he would continue as coach. However, Hammond's business commitments saw him return to South Australia. He later joined the Norwood board and was the Adelaide Crows' chairman from 1991-2000 before serving as an AFL Commissioner from 2001-11.

HAMPSHIRE, Ian

PLAYING CAREER: Geelong, 1968-75, 113 games, 22 goals. Footscray , 1976-82, 111 games, 73 goals.

COACHING CAREER: Footscray, 1982-83, 33 games, 12 wins, 21 losses, 0 draws, 0 finals. Winning percentage – 36.

Ian Hampshire.

A powerful ruckman who was surplus to requirements at Geelong, Hampshire gave Footscray wonderful service and found himself coaching the side when former Richmond champion Royce Hart was pushed aside after 10 rounds in 1982. The Bulldogs had just one win on the board to that stage of the season, but stunned the football world when it announced Hampshire would take over as coach, with Kelvin Templeton as captain. Hampshire, a popular figure at the Western Oval, guided the Bulldogs to just two wins over the final

12 rounds, landing the wooden spoon in the process. Hampshire retained the coaching position for 1983 with Jim Edmond as club captain and the Bulldogs improved dramatically to finish seventh. Hampshire resigned just three months before the start of the 1984 season and was replaced by former Richmond defender Mick Malthouse.

HANDS, Ken

PLAYING CAREER: Carlton, 1945-57, 211 games, 188 goals.

COACHING CAREER: Carlton, 1959-64, 114 games, 60 wins, 51 loses, 3 draws, 6 finals. Winning percentage – 53.

A tough, relentless ruckman who played in two Carlton premiership sides (1945 and 1947), Hands captained the Blues from 1952-57 and, after just one year of retirement, was appointed Carlton coach to replace good friend Jim Francis. Hands had wanted the coaching position when Francis was appointed coach in 1956 and indicated he was more than happy to play under the man who had been best man at his wedding. Although Carlton finished fourth in 1957, internal rumblings which had existed for two seasons, came to a head. The club committee backed Francis, but most of the players indicated they wanted Hands as coach. Then, when Carlton slid to seventh position the

Ken Hands at training.

following year, it was obvious Francis' days were numbered and Hands took over for the 1959 season. Carlton lifted immediately and, after finishing third in 1959, made the 1962 Grand Final. Carlton went down to Essendon by 42 points and slid to sixth and then tenth over the following two years. Carlton, desperate for on-field success, then turned to Melbourne's Ron Barassi as captain-coach from 1965.

HARDWICK, Damien

PLAYING CAREER: Essendon, 1994-2001, 153 games, 13 goals. Port Adelaide, 2002-04, 54 games, 1 goal.

COACHING CAREER: Richmond, 2010-, 66 games, 22 wins, 42 losses, 2 draws, 0 finals. Winning percentage – 33.

A hard-hitting defender, Hardwick played in the 2000 Essendon and 2004 Port Adelaide premiership sides. He was assistant coach to Alastair Clarkson at Hawthorn for three years before winning the senior Richmond job late in 2009. Hardwick immediately set about correcting the Tigers' faults and told the club it would be back on its feet within a couple of years. Richmond had finished above only Melbourne in 2009. It had been a dramatic time for the Tigers as Jade Rawlings replaced coach Terry Wallace 11 games into the season. Although the Tigers again finished fifteenth in Hardwick's first season of 2010, there were definite signs of improvement. Richmond then finished twelfth in 2011 and it was obvious from early in 2012 that the Tiger army was on the march again.

HARDY, Charlie

PLAYING CAREER: Essendon, 1921-25, 36 games, 21 goals.

COACHING CAREER: Essendon, 1928-30, 54 games, 30 wins, 23 losses, 1 draw, 0 finals. Winning percentage – 55. St Kilda, 1931-32, 25 games, 9 wins, 16 losses, 0 draws, 0 finals. Winning percentage – 36.

Hardy had one of the most unusual careers in football history as he was a coach well before he made his VFL playing debut at 34 years of age. A good country footballer, he arrived in Melbourne to train with Melbourne but, instead, ended up as playing coach of VJFA club Williamstown Juniors. He also starred in the VFA with North Melbourne and was lured to the VFL with Essendon in 1921. The tiny (just 157cm) Hardy played in the 1923-24 Essendon premiership sides before being appointed non-playing coach of VFA club Coburg. He made such an impression in the VFA, taking Coburg to the 1926-27 flags that Essendon appointed him coach to replace Frank Maher for the 1928 season. Maher remained as club captain and Hardy lifted Essendon from eighth to fifth in his first season. The Dons marked time from there, finishing sixth in both 1929 and 1930. Hardy was replaced by Garnet Campbell as captain-coach for 1931, with St Kilda swooping for his services. St Kilda made the announcement on January 9, 1931, with Hardy's appointment following a committee meeting. St Kilda had finished eighth under Bill Cubbins' coaching in 1930 and, when the Saints finished one rung lower in Hardy's first season, there were rumblings among fans. Hardy continued in 1932, but was dumped just seven rounds into the season and replaced by club captain Stuart King. Hardy immediately announced that he would take legal action against St Kilda for "unjustifiable termination" of his agreement to coach throughout the 1932 season. The matter eventually was settled and Hardy later coached VFA club Williamstown.

HARRIS, Dick

PLAYING CAREER: Richmond, 1934-44, 196 games, 548 goals.

COACHING CAREER: Richmond, 1964, 6 games, 3 wins, 3 losses, 0 draws, 0 finals. Winning percentage – 50.

One of Richmond's greatest goalkickers after being recruited from Warrnambool, Harris ended his VFL career in 1944 and then played in the VFA with Williamstown. From there he was captain-coach of VFA rival Yarraville and then suburban club Mordialloc. Harris was assistant coach at Tigerland from 1956-65 and, at one stage, made a one-match comeback with the reserves and kicked four goals. He took over as Richmond coach for six games after Len Smith had a heart attack during the 1964 season.

HARRIS, Jack

PLAYING CAREER: Collingwood, 1925-29, 88 games, 48 goals. Hawthorn, 1930-31, 34 games, 10 goals.

COACHING CAREER: Hawthorn, 1930-31, 36 games, 9 wins, 27 losses, 0 draws, 0 finals. Winning percentage – 25.

A dashing winger, Harris walked out on Collingwood after missing selection for the 1929 premiership side and went to Hawthorn as captain-coach the following year. Harris had played in the 1927-28 flag sides and Hawthorn made him an offer he could not refuse – of seven pounds 10 shillings a week, plus his three pound per match playing fee. Harris years later explained that Hawthorn did not know how to win matches in its earliest VFL years, but it improved from four wins and tenth position in 1929 to six wins and the same position in 1930. However, the Mayblooms slipped to eleventh (with just three wins) in 1931 and Harris was replaced by Hawthorn's first VFL captain, Jim Jackson.

HART, Royce

PLAYING CAREER: Richmond, 1967-77, 187 games, 369 goals.

COACHING CAREER: Footscray, 1980-82, 53 games, 8 wins, 45 losses, 0 draws, 0

Royce Hart.

finals. Winning percentage – 15.

Footscray believed it had pulled off a major coup in appointing former Richmond champion Royce Hart as coach from 1980. Hart had been an inspirational Tiger captain in the 1973-74 flag successes and also played in Richmond's 1967 and 1969 triumphs. Hart replaced Bulldog stalwart Don McKenzie and immediately implemented a youth policy, as well as a heavy emphasis on track work. Hart in 1980 dumped more than 20 players and gave 12 their VFL debuts. The Bulldogs, light

on for experience, finished tenth with just five wins. They slipped to eleventh in 1981 amid player concerns that there was too much emphasis on running long distances at training, especially around the Flemington racecourse. When the Bulldogs won only one of their first 10 matches, Hart was demoted to the position of reserves coach and ruckman Ian Hampshire was given the senior job.

HARVEY, Mark

PLAYING CAREER: Essendon, 1984-97, 206 games, 170 goals.

COACHING CAREER: Fremantle, 2007-11, 97 games, 39 wins, 58 losses, 0 draws, 2 finals. Winning percentage – 40.

Harvey had a wonderful playing career with Essendon, being a member of three premiership sides, and then seemed to be a permanent fixture at Windy Hill as an assistant to senior coach Kevin Sheedy. He held this position for eight years before becoming an assistant coach with Fremantle in 2006. Harvey was appointed senior coach with seven rounds to play in 2007 when Chris Connolly resigned. The Dockers won four of those seven games and Harvey was appointed coach in his own right for 2008. They won just six games in each of 2008 and 2009, but made the finals in 2010 defeating Hawthorn in an elimination final before going down to Geelong in a semi-final. Although the Dockers slipped to eleventh in 2011, the football world was shocked when Harvey was dumped in favour of St Kilda coach Ross Lyon. There had been no hint of Harvey's demise and, in fact, he had been regarded as a good coach. He immediately joined the Brisbane Lions as an assistant coach.

HICKINBOTHAM, Dave

PLAYING CAREER: Did not play at VFL/AFL level.

COACHING CAREER: Geelong, 1910-11, 36 games, 18 wins, 16 losses, 2 draws, 0 finals. Winning percentage – 48.

Hickinbotham had the distinction of being Geelong's first official coach, appointed in 1910. Henry "Tracker" Young had been club captain and unofficial coach from 1901-09, but Geelong turned to its past in appointing Hickinbotham coach as he had played with the Pivotonians in their VFA days. A shrewd tactician as Geelong captain, he insisted on fast, open football. He played with Geelong until 1894 and on his appointment as coach in 1910, "Markwell" in The Australasian wrote: "Whilst looking around for a coach, the executive bethought them of Dave Hickinbotham, formerly a player of fine ability and a leader of the tactful order."

Geelong finished fifth in 1910 and then sixth in 1911; he then relinquished his position in favour of Bill Eason.

HICKEY, Reg

PLAYING CAREER: Geelong, 1926-40, 245 games, 24 goals.

COACHING CAREER: Geelong, 1932, 1936-40 and 1949-59, 304 games, 184 wins, 117 losses, 3 draws, 18 finals, 3 premierships. Winning percentage – 61.

There are few more revered Geelong identities than Reg Hickey, who gave the Cats a lifetime of service as a great centre half-back and then a highly-successful coach. Yet Hickey came from a Fitzroy family as uncles Pat and Con Hickey were early stars with the Maroons. Hickey, recruited from Cressy, had three stints as Geelong coach, the first being in 1932. Geelong had won the 1931 premiership under the coaching of Charlie Clymo, but when he resigned the club was left in limbo. Hickey took over as captain-coach for the 1932 season but, after the Cats slipped to fifth position, he was replaced by Arthur Coghlan as coach while retaining the captaincy. Hickey then had a second stint as coach following the resignation of former Collingwood champion Charlie Dibbs in 1936. The Cats responded so well under Hickey that they finished fifth and he found

R. HICKEY,
GEELONG.

himself again captain-coach in 1937. Hickey had installed a new regime of discipline and, after a stuttering start to the season, the Cats won their last 12 games of the season and then defeated Collingwood by 32 points in the Grand Final. Hickey produced a winning move in the Grand Final by switching centre half-forward Les Hardiman into defence against the dangerous Ron Todd. The move worked to perfection and the Cats celebrated long and hard.

Geelong finished third under Hickey in 1938 before slipping to seventh the following season. The 34-year-old Hickey retired four games into the 1940 season and was replaced as coach by Les Laver and then Allan Everett, with Everett as club captain. However, Hickey returned to Geelong as non-playing coach in 1949 and presided over one of the Cats' greatest eras. They won the 1951-52 flags under Hickey, who was a stickler for discipline and keeping the ball moving. The Cats from round nine, 1952, to round 13 the following season went 26 games undefeated (including a draw with Essendon). Hickey used pace to destroy rivals and although he was not regarded as a brilliant tactician, he had the respect of all his players as he had the rare ability of playing them in their correct positions and keeping faith with them even though they might have had a poor game. Hickey stepped down as coach at the end of 1959 and was replaced by Bob Davis. Hickey still holds the record for most games (304) as Geelong coach, with Mark Thompson next on 260 games from 2000-10. Hickey died on December 13, 1967, at 67 years of age. Grandson Matthew Primus played with Fitzroy and Port Adelaide before being appointed Power coach in 2010.

HILLARD, Norm

PLAYING CAREER: Hawthorn, 1933-37, 32 games, 57 goals. Fitzroy, 1939-46, 95 games, 12 goals.

COACHING CAREER: Fitzroy, 1945, 1

game, 1 win, 0 losses, 0 draw, 0 finals. Winning percentage – 100.

A reliable centre half-back, Hillard was rated one of the best players on the ground in Fitzroy's 1944 Grand Final defeat of Richmond. He coached the Maroons in one game in 1945 while captain-coach Fred Hughson was on interstate duty as captain of Victoria.

HINKLEY, Ken

PLAYING CAREER: Fitzroy, 1987-88, 11 games, 20 goals. Geelong, 1989-95, 121 games, 59 goals.

COACHING CAREER: Port Adelaide, 2013-. No senior AFL coaching record to start of 2013 season.

From Camperdown, Hinkley won Geelong's best and fairest in 1992 and was a Cat co-captain in 1995. He spent the 2004-09 seasons as an assistant coach with Geelong and worked with the Gold Coast Suns before being appointed Port Adelaide's senior coach from 2013.

HIRD, Allan

PLAYING CAREER: Hawthorn, 1938-39, 14 games, 12 goals. Essendon, 1940-45, 102 games, 2 goals. St Kilda, 1946-47, 38 games, 5 goals.

COACHING CAREER: St Kilda, 1946-47, 38 games, 5 wins, 32 losses, 1 draw, 0 finals. Winning percentage – 13.

Grandfather of Essendon champion and coach James Hird, he started his football career in the VFA with Williamstown before progressing to the VFL with Hawthorn. A utility who was best suited to the defence, Hird played on a half-back flank in Essendon's 1942 Grand Final defeat of Richmond. He was appointed captain-coach of St Kilda in 1946 to replace Hugh Thomas, but had two unsuccessful seasons with the Saints. In fact, they won just four games in 1946 to finish above only Hawthorn and won just once the following season to collect the wooden spoon, Hird, who was one of the fastest players of his era, returned to Essendon as reserves coach and later served the Bombers as club president. A schoolteacher and later a lecturer at the Melbourne Teachers' College, he once was a semi-finalist in the Stawell Gift. His son Allan Jnr played four games with Essendon over the 1966-67 seasons.

HIRD, James

PLAYING CAREER: Essendon, 1992-2007, 253 games, 343 goals.

COACHING CAREER: Essendon 2011-, 45 games, 22 wins, 22 losses, 1 draw, 1 final. Winning percentage – 50.

One of the greatest players of the modern era, Hird was drafted from ACT club Ainslie and, after playing in the 1993 Essendon premiership side, went on to captain the Bombers in their 2000 Grand Final defeat of Melbourne. The Essendon administration pulled off a coup at the end of the 2010 season when it appointed Hird coach to replace former Richmond midfielder Matthew Knights. Bomber membership soared and Essendon further fanned the expectation of fans when it appointed dual Geelong premiership coach and 1993 Bomber premiership captain Mark Thompson as an assistant coach. Essendon improved from fourteenth in 2010 to eighth in Hird's first season as coach, only for Carlton to thrash the Bombers in an elimination final. Hird realised that his young Bomber squad needed more bulk and concentrated on developing strength and stamina for future success. The Bombers at first continued their improvement in 2012, but then had to contend with a plague of soft-tissue injuries.

HISKINS, Arthur

PLAYING CAREER: South Melbourne, 1908-15 and 1919-23, 185 games, 56 goals.

COACHING CAREER: South Melbourne, 1920, 16 games, 7 wins, 9 losses, 0 draws, 0 finals. Winning percentage – 44.

An attacking half-back from Rutherglen, brother Stan also played for South, while other brothers in Fred (Essendon) and Rupert (Carlton) also played in the VFL. Hiskins, known as "Poddy" because he was regarded as the "poddy" (small) calf in a large dairy farming family, had a distinguished career with South before enlisting in the AFL and missing three seasons while serving on the Western Front. He was appointed playing coach in 1920 to replace Herb Howson, with Vic Belcher as his captain. However, South slipped from third to fifth and Hiskins was replaced as coach by Artie Wood. Hiskins, who had played in South's 1909 premiership side, remained loyal to the Southerners and remained with them to the end of the 1923 season. He then officiated in 52 games as a VFL goal umpire from 1930-32.

HOCKING, Garry

PLAYING CAREER: Geelong, 1987-2001, 274 games, 243 goals.

COACHING CAREER: Port Adelaide, 2012- 4 games, 0 wins, 3 losses, 1 draw, 0 finals. Winning percentage – 0.

A wonderfully committed on-baller in a long career with Geelong, Hocking assumed control as interim coach at Port Adelaide when the Power parted company with coach Matthew Primus with just four rounds to play in 2012. He had joined the Power in 2010 as a development coach after coaching WA club Peel Thunder in 2005 and then TAC Cup club Geelong Falcons from 2006-09. He had a tough initiation as senior coach, with the Power going down to Hawthorn.

HOLDEN, George

PLAYING CAREER: Fitzroy, 1908-19, 164 games, 37 goals.

COACHING CAREER: Fitzroy 1916-19, 54 games, 24 wins, 28 losses, 2 draws, 6 finals, 1 premiership. Winning percentage – 44.

A quick winger who starred with Fitzroy after being recruited from West Melbourne, Holden was appointed the Maroons' coach in 1916, with Wal Johnson as captain. Because of World War I, there were only four competing teams – Fitzroy, Carlton, Collingwood and Richmond – in 1916 and The Winner newspaper reported that Holden was to succeed Percy Parrat, who had resigned at the end of the 1915 season. It added: "The club is fortunate to be able to secure such a worthy successor." The newspaper hinted that Holden, who had announced his retirement as a player in 1915, might play again. He did, but only after missing Fitzroy's first five matches. Fitzroy finished on the bottom of the ladder but, amazingly, there was a final four and the Maroons then defeated Collingwood in a semi-final and then Carlton in a preliminary final. Carlton, as minor premier, had right of challenge in a Grand Final and Holden's Maroons defeated the Blues by 29 points. Fitzroy finished fourth the following season and fifth in 1918. Holden's playing career was wrecked by a knee injury in the opening round of the 1919 season and he was replaced as coach by Ted Melling. He later coached Victorian Junior Football association club Northcote Diggers.

HOPKINS, Allan

PLAYING CAREER: Footscray, 1925-34, 151 games, 205 goals.

COACHING CAREER: Footscray, 1930, 18 games, 4 wins, 14 losses, 0 draws, 0 finals. Winning percentage – 22.

One of the finest players of his era, "Banana-legs" Hopkins was Footscray captain in 1929 and was equal second in that season's Brownlow Medal count. When Footscray was looking to replace Alec Eason at the end of the season, Hopkins was one of the applicants. Footscray initially wanted Collingwood's Syd Coventry as coach, but it has been suggested that Hopkins offered to coach

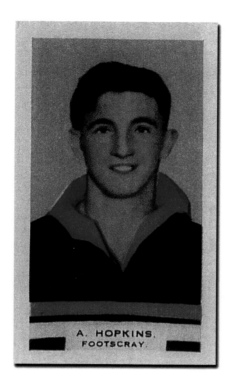

A. HOPKINS,
FOOTSCRAY.

HOWELL, Verdun

PLAYING CAREER: St Kilda, 1958-68, 159 games, 55 goals.

COACHING CAREER: Richmond, 1971, 1 game, 0 wins, 1 loss, 0 draws, 0 finals. Winning percentage – 0.

Tasmanian Howell shared Brownlow Medal honours (retrospectively) with South Melbourne's Bob Skilton and was a wonderfully reliable full-back who played in the Saints' 1966 premiership. He was Richmond reserves coach in 1971 when senior coach Tom Hafey was unavailable for the round 12 match against Fitzroy at the MCG because he was coaching Victoria. The Lions defeated the Tigers by 18 points and Howell later coached in Western Australia.

HOWSON, Bert (or Herb)

PLAYING CAREER: South Melbourne, 1897-1908, 152 games, 2 goals.

COACHING CAREER: South Melbourne, 1918-19, 33 games, 27 wins, 6 losses, 0 draws, 3 finals, 1 premiership. Winning percentage – 82.

A star winger who played with South Melbourne for six years before it was one of the inaugural VFL clubs in 1897, Howson, who sometimes was referred

the Tricolours for a lower fee. Although Footscray slipped from ninth position to eleventh under Hopkins as captain-coach, he had a wonderful individual season and tied with Richmond's Stan Judkins and Collingwood's Harry Collier for the Brownlow Medal. Judkins won on a countback, but Hopkins and Collier later were awarded retrospective medals. Hopkins was replaced as captain-coach by St Kilda's Bill Cubbins in 1931. He retired as a player in 1934 as the last of those who had played with the club in the VFA. Hopkins also coached VFA club Yarraville.

to as Herb Howson, captained the club in 1906 and was appointed coach for the 1918 season, with Henry "Sonny" Elms his co-coach or assistant. The Southerners swept all before them, being defeated only once – by St Kilda. South defeated Collingwood by five points in the Grand Final and although the Elms-Howson partnership continued into 1919, when the Southerners finished third, the dual coaches were replaced by Arthur Hiskins for the 1920 season. Howson served South as a committeeman from 1901-03 and as club secretary from 1904-21. He died in 1948.

HUGHES, Frank 'Checker'

Frank Hughes.

PLAYING CAREER: Richmond, 1914-15 and 1919-23, 87 games, 41 goals.

COACHING CAREER: Richmond 1927-32, 120 games, 87 wins, 31 losses, 2 draws, 12 finals, 1 premiership. Winning percentage – 73. Melbourne, 1933-41, 1943-48 and 1965, 258 games, 157 wins, 99 losses, 2 draws, 17 finals, 4 premierships. Winning percentage – 61.

A classy rover in his playing days with Richmond, his career was severely interrupted by service in World War I in which he won a Military Service Medal. Hughes briefly coached the Tiger reserves before spending three seasons as coach of Tasmanian club Ulverstone and made such a good impression that he was appointed senior Richmond coach from 1927. A master tactician and a wonderful motivator, Hughes guided the Tigers to every finals series over six seasons, including five Grand Final appearances for one flag, in 1932. He ended his reign at Tigerland when he elected to follow Tiger secretary Percy Page to Melbourne in 1933. Many thought it was an unwise move, but Hughes relished the challenge and even wore a Richmond guernsey at his first session in charge to let the Melbourne players know of what he had achieved with the Tigers.

Hughes also changed the Melbourne nickname from the Fuchsias to the Demons when, in one match, he implored his men to "play like demons".

A printer who often wore his overalls to training, Hughes started slowly with Melbourne but, after finishing tenth in 1933, the Demons started climbing the ladder to play in preliminary finals in both 1936 and 1937. He then achieved his greatest triumph, leading the Demons to triple premiership success from 1939-41. The "Old Fox", as Hughes was known, stepped down at the end of the 1941 season, with Percy Beames captain-coach from 1942-44. Hughes resumed coaching duties in 1945. The Demons were runners-up to Essendon the following season and, two years later, defeated the Bombers in the Grand Final replay after the first one had been drawn. Hughes, who had masterminded four Melbourne premierships, again stepped down and was replaced by Allan La Fontaine. However, Hughes remained with Melbourne as a selector and worked closely with legendary Demon coach Norm Smith. He even coached Melbourne for one game in 1965 following the sensational temporary sacking of Smith.

HUGHSON, Fred

PLAYING CAREER: Fitzroy, 1938-47, 164 games, 95 goals.

COACHING CAREER: Fitzroy, 1943-47, 95 games, 58 wins, 35 losses, 2 draws, 6 finals, 1 premiership. Winning percentage – 61.

Hughson for ever will be known as the last man to guide Fitzroy to premiership glory, in 1944. A champion full-back, he was recruited from VFA club Preston as a full-forward and once kicked 10 goals in a match (against Essendon in 1938). However, he was moved to full-back in 1940 and his long kicking usually sent Fitzroy well into attack. When Fitzroy was looking to replace Dan Minogue as coach at the end of the 1942 season, it turned to Hughson. Hughson accepted the position but insisted on telling the players that he had not back-stabbed anyone to get the job. Enormously popular with players and fans at Brunswick Street, Hughson guided the Maroons to third position in 1943 but, after defeating Carlton by 51 points in the first semi-final, Fitzroy went down to Richmond by 25 points in the preliminary final. Hughson and his Maroons had their revenge the following year when they defeated the Tigers by 11 points in the second semi-final and then by 15 points in the Grand Final at the Junction Oval. Hughson had missed the semi-final because of a hip injury, but was at full-back in the Grand Final win. Hughson continued as captain-coach to the end of the 1947 season, when he again led the Maroons to third position. Fitzroy in 1948 replaced him with former North Melbourne and Fitzroy winger Charlie Cameron. Hughson was appointed captain-coach of Hampden Football League club South Warrnambool in 1948 and became a legend at the country club, playing until he was 41 years of age. Hughson died in 1986 at 72 years of age.

HUNTER, HARRY

PLAYING CAREER: Essendon, 1921-27 and 1929, 109 games, 9 goals.

COACHING CAREER: Essendon, 1939, 12 games, 6 wins, 6 losses, 0 draws, 0 finals. Winning percentage – 50.

Hunter, a powerful defender, had played in the VFA with Footscray before joining Essendon and played in the Dons' 1924 premiership side. He spent the 1928 season as captain-coach of West Albury and returned to Essendon for the 1929 season. Hunter then coached VFA clubs Yarraville (1930-31) and Preston (1932) before returning to Essendon as chairman of selectors. When Jack Baggott was coach in 1939, Essendon suggested the former Richmond star should change his training methods, culminating in Baggott's resignation. Hunter was appointed co-coach with champion rover Dick Reynolds, mainly to help "King Richard" settle into the job. Hunter also served Essendon as a committeeman and club treasurer.

HUTCHISON, Greg

PLAYING CAREER: Melbourne 1975-84, 96 games, 21 goals.

COACHING CAREER: Melbourne 1997, 13 games, 3 wins, 10 losses, 0 draws, 0 finals. Winning percentage – 23.

A solid utility in his 10 seasons as a Melbourne player, he later coached VFA club Prahran and coached Melbourne when Neil Balme was sacked during the 1997 season. Melbourne won just three of its 13 games under Hutchison and he was replaced at the end of the season by Neale Daniher. Hutchison later was an assistant coach with Richmond, coached VFL club the Casey Scorpions and appointed St Kilda's Football Operations Manager.

INCIGNERI, Len

PLAYING CAREER: South Melbourne, 1903 and 1905, 2 games, 0 goals. Richmond, 1908-11, 62 games, 5 goals. Melbourne, 1913-15, 32 games 7 goals.

COACHING CAREER: Richmond, 1911, 18 games, 7 wins, 11 losses, 0 draws, 0 finals. Winning percentage – 39.

A powerful and rugged defender, Incigneri joined South Melbourne from Mornington Peninsula club Tyabb, but played just one game in each of his two seasons with the Southerners. Incigneri, a blacksmith, returned to the country, but was wooed to Richmond in 1908 and was appointed captain-coach for the 1911 season. Richmond won just seven games to finish above only St Kilda and University and former Collingwood and Richmond winger Charlie H. Pannam was named non-playing coach for 1912. Incigneri played in a premiership side with Hastings and also was captain-coach of Somerville and Oakleigh. He later became a stipendiary steward with the Queensland Turf Club.

Len Incigneri (inset, with Richmond), was with South Melbourne when it played this match against Fitzroy at the SCG in 1905.

JACKSON, Jim

PLAYING CAREER: St Kilda, 1909, 1 game 0 goals. Collingwood, 1910-15 and 1920, 93 games, 22 goals. Hawthorn, 1925-26, 22 games, 1 goal.

COACHING CAREER: Hawthorn, 1932, 18 games, 3 wins, 15 losses, 0 draws, 0 finals. Winning percentage – 17.

A clever and dashing winger, Jackson joined Hawthorn in 1921 and was club vice-captain in its final VFA season of 1924. He then became the Mayblooms' first VFL captain in 1925 and retired at the end of the following season. Jackson became Hawthorn's sixth VFL coach in 1932 when he replaced another former Magpie in Jack Harris. However, Hawthorn won just three games that season – against Melbourne, Footscray and St Kilda – to collect the wooden-spoon. Jackson then was replaced as coach by St Kilda's Fred Phillips. Tragically, however, Phillips died of blood poisoning on the eve of the 1933 season and Hawthorn had to make a new appointment. As Phillips had been appointed captain-coach, Hawthorn wanted another on-field leader and settled on Collingwood's Bill Twomey. While negotiations took place between Collingwood and Hawthorn, former Hawthorn VFA captain and 1918 South Melbourne premiership defender Arthur Rademacher stood in as caretaker coach over the first four rounds of the 1934 season.

JEANS, Allan

PLAYING CAREER: St Kilda, 1955-59, 77 games, 26 goals.

COACHING CAREER: St Kilda, 1961-76, 332 games, 194 wins, 137 losses, 1 draw, 18 finals, 1 premiership. Winning percentage – 58. Hawthorn, 1981-87 and 1989-90, 221 games, 159 wins, 61 losses, 1 draw, 23 finals, 3 premierships. Winning percentage – 72. Richmond, 1992, 22 games, 5 wins, 17 losses, 0 draws, 0 finals. Winning percentage – 23.

Jeans was a more than handy half-forward or ruck-rover with St Kilda who trained with Carlton before signing with the Saints after being recruited from

Allan Jeans.

A coaching legend was born and Jeans was appointed senior coach to replace Jim Francis in 1961 – at just 27 years of age. Jeans grew into the job and took the Saints to fourth position in his debut season; it was the Saints' first finals appearance since 1939. Jeans in 1965 guided St Kilda to its first Grand Final appearance since going down to Fitzroy in 1913, but the Saints went down by 35 points. Learning from that experience, the Saints defeated Collingwood by a point in the memorable and historic 1966 Grand Final. Jeans also coached St Kilda in the losing (to Hawthorn) 1971 Grand Final and, during his tenure, took the Saints to nine finals series. He stepped down at the end of 1976 and spent four years out of senior football and, during this period, coached the NSW state side.

Jeans was appointed Hawthorn coach in 1981 and took the Hawks to the 1983, 1986 and 1989 premierships. His reign was punctuated by a serious brain illness, with Alan Joyce taking over for the 1988 season, and winning the flag. Jeans was a fierce disciplinarian at both St Kilda and Hawthorn, with simple football philosophies, including the basic tenet that either his team had the ball, the opposition had it or it was in dispute. He was a father-figure during his years at Hawthorn and was regarded as one of the club's greatest identities when he stepped down at the end of 1990 in favour of

NSW club Finley. He was promised six senior games and thought he would be lucky to get an extension and was prepared to head back to the country. However, Jeans performed better than he expected and became a St Kilda regular until he was forced into premature retirement because of a ribs injury in 1959. He then was appointed coach of Sandhurst but could not get a transfer as a police officer and decided to play reserves football with St Kilda. Then, when reserves coach Brian Gleeson was forced to stand down because of work commitments, Jeans was offered the position.

Joyce. However, Jeans had just one year in retirement before Richmond knocked on his door. He spent just one unsuccessful year with the Tigers before declaring that his coaching days were over. Jeans died during the 2011 season of a lung disease and was deeply mourned by the entire football world.

JENKINS, Ern

PLAYING CAREER: Fitzroy, 1897-1908 and 1910, 182 games, 16 goals.

COACHING CAREER: Richmond, 1913, 18 games, 6 wins, 12 losses, 0 draws, 0 finals. Winning percentage – 33.

Jenkins played in Fitzroy's 1899 and 1904 premiership sides and captained the Maroons over the 1906-07 seasons. A regular Victorian representative, the tough and reliable defender coached Scotch College on his retirement before being appointed Richmond coach for 1913, replacing Charlie H. Pannam. The Tigers finished seventh and he was replaced after just one season by 1909 South Melbourne captain-coach Charlie Ricketts.

JESAULENKO, Alex

PLAYING CAREER: Carlton, 1967-79, 256 games, 424 goals. St Kilda, 1980-81, 23 games, 20 goals.

COACHING CAREER: Carlton, 1978-79 and 1989-90, 76 games, 53 wins, 22 losses, 1 draw, 1 premiership. Winning percentage – 70. St Kilda, 1980-82, 64 games, 13 wins, 49 losses, 2 draws, 0 finals. Winning percentage – 20.

Jesaulenko, born in Austria, was an exceptional football talent who became a legend with Carlton after being recruited from the ACT. He played in Carlton's 1968, 1970 and 1972 premiership sides and captained the Blues over the 1975-76 seasons. When Ian Stewart resigned as non-playing coach early in 1978 because of health reasons, Carlton unexpectedly named Jesaulenko playing coach and he seemed to change his persona overnight and introduced a severe training and disciplinarian regime. Carlton finished fourth in 1978 and Jesaulenko the

Alex Jesaulenko.

following year guided the Blues to the premiership with a nail-biting five point defeat of Collingwood in the Grand Final. Jesaulenko broke an ankle during the match and had to be helped on to the podium to receive the premiership trophy. It might have been the pinnacle of his career and Carlton fans might have celebrated long and hard, but it was the last time they would see their idol in the famous old dark navy blue. Jesaulenko sided with club president George Harris in a power struggle at Princes Park and when Harris lost the presidency to Ian Rice, Jesaulenko's tenure as Carlton coach was over.

Jesaulenko crossed to St Kilda the following season and although he had no coaching ambitions at the time, he found himself in the hot seat at Moorabbin when the Saints dumped Mike Patterson during the 1980 season. Jesaulenko continued as playing coach the following year and then as non-playing coach in 1982. However, he was unable to lift the Saints and they finished eleventh, tenth and then eleventh again in his two and a half seasons in charge. St Kilda replaced him with Tony Jewell for the 1983 season, but Jesaulenko's coaching career was far from over. Carlton surprisingly recalled him in 1989 to replace Robert Walls following a shock loss to the Brisbane Bears at Princes Park. Jesaulenko's second stint as Carlton coach started controversially,

against the Sydney Swans at the SCG. Carlton's David Rhys-Jones and Sydney's Greg Williams were involved in a couple of nasty altercations and although the Blues defeated the Swans, they finished the season in eighth position. Jesaulenko retained the coaching position for the 1990 season but when the Blues again finished eighth he was replaced by David Parkin, who also was recalled to Princes Park for a second stint as coach.

JEWELL, Tony

PLAYING CAREER: Richmond, 1964-70, 80 games, 16 goals.

COACHING CAREER: Richmond, 1979-81 and 1986-87, 113 games, 53 wins, 59 losses, 1 draw, 3 finals, 1 premiership. Winning percentage – 47. St Kilda, 1983-84, 40 games, 9 wins, 31 losses, 0 draws. Winning percentage – 23.

A ferociously competitive ruckman who had been recruited from VFA club Oakleigh, Jewell had barracked for Richmond as a boy and played in the Tigers' 1967 premiership side. After leaving Richmond at the end of the 1970 season, he was captain-coach of VFA club Caulfield and led the Bears to a Second Division premiership. He was with Caulfield for six years before being invited to coach the Richmond reserves. Jewell took them to three finals series for one flag and was appointed senior coach to replace Barry Richardson in 1979. The Tigers had a mediocre 1979 season, finishing eighth, but improved dramatically the following season to defeat Collingwood by 81 points in the Grand Final. Jewell was so determined to remember the celebrations that he refused to have a drink until well after midnight. The 1980 premiership triumph followed a dramatic incident in the qualifying final at Waverley Park when Jewell was involved in a dust-up with Carlton coach Peter Jones.

Amazingly, Richmond dispensed with the services of its premiership coach at the end of the next season when the Tigers finished seventh. They replaced him with club favourite son Francis

Tony Jewell.

Bourke, but Jewell was not lost to coaching as he was appointed to the St Kilda position in 1983 to replace Alex Jesaulenko. They were turbulent times for the Saints and, in 1983, they even played South Melbourne's Silvio Foschini and Paul Morwood without a clearance. The Saints had finished last in 1983 and, when there was no improvement in 1984, Jewell was dumped 18 rounds into the season and replaced by Graeme Gellie. Richmond, probably regretting its hasty decision in sacking Jewell at the end of the 1981 season, invited him back in 1986, but the Tigers by then were a spent force and finished tenth in 1986 before collecting the wooden spoon the following season, with former champion Kevin Bartlett replacing him at the end of that season. The Tigers who played under Jewell in the 1980 premiership season still say they had the utmost faith in their mentor.

JOHN, Graeme

PLAYING CAREER: South Melbourne, 1964-69, 77 games, 97 goals.

COACHING CAREER: South Melbourne, 1973-75, 66 games, 15 wins, 50 losses, 1 draw, 0 finals. Winning percentage – 23.

An outstanding centre half-forward who represented both Western Australia and Victoria, John joined South from East Perth. He was appointed the

Graeme John addresses the South players at Kardinia Park.

Swans' coach in 1973 to replace the legendary Norm Smith in controversial circumstances. South in 1973 wanted to appoint former Richmond ruckman Mike Patterson as coach, with John to be appointed his assistant. But, when Patterson decided to stick with North Adelaide, John was given the senior job. It was a poisoned chalice as John was told there was no money to buy name players from other clubs and he therefore had to rely on developing talent from within. South collected the wooden-spoon in 1973 and when it improved to ninth the following year John was named the VFL coach of the season. John in 1974 had to deal with what was known as the John Pitura saga, with the Swan forward wanting to be cleared to Richmond. South stood firm while John masterminded a trade in 1975, landing ruckman Brian Roberts, defender Francis Jackson and future Brownlow Medal winning ruckman/forward Graham Teasdale from Tigerland. John resigned to concentrate on his business career after the Swans again collected the wooden spoon in 1975. John later became South president and was heavily involved in the club's move to Sydney

Dennis Jones.

in 1982. His business career flourished and he became CEO of Australia Post. John, who was named in the Swans' Hall of Fame in 2011, also became an AFL Commissioner.

JONES, Dennis

PLAYING CAREER: Melbourne, 1956-60 and 1962, 62 games, 4 goals.

COACHING CAREER: Melbourne, 1978, 22 games, 5 wins, 17 losses, 0 draws, 0 finals. Winning percentage – 23.

Jones, a dour Demon defender who played in Melbourne's 1959 premiership side, coached South Australian club Central District before being appointed Melbourne coach to replace Bob Skilton in 1978. However, the Demons won just five games to collect the wooden spoon (two games behind Footscray) and Jones resigned because of business commitments and was replaced by St Kilda's Carl Ditterich.

JONES, Peter

PLAYING CAREER: Carlton, 1966-79, 249 games, 294 goals.

COACHING CAREER: Carlton, 1980, 24 games, 17 wins, 7 losses, 0 draws, 2 finals. Winning percentage 71.

Carlton was split down the middle soon after it won the 1979 premiership when, on December 5, coach Alex Jesaulenko resigned in support of embattled club president George Harris. At an extraordinary meeting of members early the following year, Ian Rice took control as president, leaving Jesaulanko in limbo. The Blues therefore were left without a coach and turned to former ruckman Peter "Percy" Jones, a Tasmanian who had given the club tremendous service. Most observers saw it as a temporary measure and although Jones guided the Blues to second position (behind Geelong), they lost their two finals matches. One, the qualifying final against Richmond at

Waverley Park, was highly controversial as Jones and Tiger coach Tony Jewell were involved in a dust-up at quarter time. Carlton turned to Hawthorn premiership coach David Parkin in 1981, but Jones remained intensely loyal to the Blues and became a club director.

JORDON, Ray

PLAYING CAREER: Did not play at VFL/ AFL level.

COACHING CAREER: North Melbourne, 1976, 1 game, 0 wins, 1 loss, 0 draws, 0 finals. Winning percentage – 0.

Jordon was a Victorian state wicketkeeper who toured India and South Africa with Australian teams and also played football with VFA club Coburg. He was regarded as the finest junior football coach of his era when in charge of the Richmond, North Melbourne and Melbourne Under 19s. Jordon was a key figure in the spectacular development of Irishman Jim Stynes with the Demons. While with the Roos, he coached North Melbourne in one senior game in 1976 when Ron Barassi was unavailable following a motor accident. Jordon died in August, 2012.

JOYCE, Alan

PLAYING CAREER: Hawthorn, 1961-65, 49 games, 7 goals.

COACHING CAREER: Hawthorn, 1988 and 1991-93, 93 games, 67 wins, 26 losses, 0 draws, 7 finals, 2 premierships. Winning percentage – 72. Western Bulldogs, 1994-96, 57 games, 25 wins, 30 losses, 2 draws, 3 finals. Winning percentage – 44.

Joyce, a hard-hitting ruck-rover in his playing days with Hawthorn after joining the club from Glen Iris, left VFL ranks at just 22 years of age and became a dual VFA premiership coach with Preston. He also coached East Fremantle, NSW club Newtown, the NSW state side and Perth. On returning to Victoria, he wrote to Hawthorn asking if there were any coaching vacancies and although there was no position available at that time, he eventually was appointed a match committee advisor and later became the Hawks' director of football. Then, when senior coach Allan Jeans underwent emergency surgery to seal a leaking blood vessel at the base of his brain before the start of the 1988 season, Joyce was appointed senior Hawthorn coach.

A quiet achiever, Joyce was a seamless replacement for the highly-regarded Jeans and guided the Hawks to the 1988 premiership, with Jeans returning the following year to land another flag for the Hawks. Joyce returned as senior coach when Jeans stepped down at the end of the 1990 season and won another flag, in 1991. He spent another two seasons as Hawthorn coach and, after being replaced by Peter Knights in 1994, joined the ABC's team for football broadcasts. Then, in 1994, he was appointed Footscray coach when the Bulldogs sacked Terry Wheeler just a couple of games into the season. Bulldog legend Doug Hawkins later quipped that Joyce did not know the names of many of his players, but Footscray pushed Collingwood to one point in Joyce's first game in charge. Footscray played disciplined and consistent football under Joyce in 1994 and was rewarded with a finals berth, only to go down to Geelong and then Melbourne. Footscray made the finals again in 1995 but, after struggling early the following season, sacked Joyce in favour of reserves coach Terry Wallace.

JUDGE, Ken

PLAYING CAREER: Hawthorn, 1983-86, 72 games, 158 goals. Brisbane Bears, 1987-88, 17 games, 18 goals.

COACHING CAREER: Hawthorn, 1996-99, 89 games, 37 wins, 50 losses, 2 draws, 1 final. Winning percentage – 42. West Coast, 2000-01, 44 games, 12 wins, 31 losses, 1 draw, 0 finals. Winning percentage – 27.

A gifted half-forward, Judge joined Hawthorn from East Fremantle and played in the Hawks' 1983 premiership side. He succeeded Peter Knights as Hawthorn coach in 1996 and lifted the Hawks from second-last to eighth in his first year. The Hawks went down by just six points to Sydney in a qualifying final at the SCG and then fell back into a trough over the next couple of seasons, although they went within half a game of making the finals under Judge in 1999. Judge then was lured to his home state of Western Australia to take over from Mick Malthouse as coach of the West Coast Eagles. However, the Eagles finished a modest thirteenth in 2000 and slipped a further rung the following year when Judge was replaced by John Worsfold.

K

KELLY, Harvey

PLAYING CAREER: South Melbourne, 1902 and 1913-14, 49 games, 50 goals. Carlton, 1907-9, 43 games, 75 goals.

COACHING CAREER: South Melbourne, 1913, 19 games, 14 wins, 4 losses, 1 draw, 1 final. Winning percentage – 74.

Kelly, recruited locally to play with South Melbourne, was a football itinerant as, after just one season with the Southerners, he moved to Western Australia to play with South Fremantle. He returned to Victoria to play with Carlton before moving to Tasmania to be captain-coach of Lefroy. Then, when he wanted to return to South Melbourne in 1912, Carlton blocked his release. He therefore accepted the position as captain-coach of Gippsland club Traralgon. When Carlton relented, he was appointed South coach (with Vic Belcher as captain) in 1913. He guided the Southerners to second position, but they went down to St Kilda in a semi-final. Although the South players voted to replace him with Belcher as captain-coach for 1914, Kelly spent that season as the club vice-captain.

KELLY, Joe

PLAYING CAREER: Carlton, 1926-34, 137 games, 15 goals.

COACHING CAREER: Footscray, 1937-40, 69 games, 29 wins, 40 losses, 0 draws, 1 final. Winning percentage – 42. South Melbourne, 1941-44, 68 games, 35 wins, 33 losses, 0 draws, 2 finals. Winning percentage – 51.

A quick and brilliant winger, Kelly was a star with Carlton from the time he was recruited from Thornbury and Xavier College. He played in Carlton's losing 1932 Grand Final side, but retired at just 28 years of age with the express ambition of coaching at VFL level. He therefore accepted a position as captain-coach of suburban club South Caulfield before replying to an advertisement for the position as captain-coach of the Footscray reserves. Kelly won the position and guided the young Bulldog reserves to the 1936 premiership before being the right man at the right time for the senior position the following season.

Former Collingwood great Syd Coventry,

J.KELLY

scheduled to play Collingwood in the first semi-final and Kelly implored his players to push the ball into the open to counter the Magpies' expected tactic of clogging up play. However, the Magpies won by 41 points to ruin the Footscray dream. Footscray slumped to eleventh the following season and although it climbed to sixth the following year, Kelly believed he could do no more with the Bulldogs and resigned to accept the South Melbourne coaching position for 1941, replacing former Richmond and Essendon player Jack Baggott. The Swans finished eighth in Kelly's first season and then third in 1942. Ironically, the Swans defeated Footscray by 27 points in the first semi-final before going down to Essendon by 28 points in the preliminary final.

Kelly, who insisted on fast, attacking football, spent another two seasons with the Swans, but they failed to make the finals over the 1943-44 seasons and he resigned his position to take over as club secretary, with Bill "Bull" Adams taking over as coach in 1945. Kelly, who also played District cricket with Northcote and Collingwood, later coached amateur club Ormond with great success and was in charge of the All-Australian Amateurs for the exhibition match against a combined VFL/VFA amateur side during the 1956 Melbourne Olympics.

who had been Footscray coach from early in the 1935 season, resigned after just a few rounds in 1937 and the Bulldogs called on Kelly to take over. It was a wholly understandable decision as Kelly's reserves were undefeated and he had won himself an admirable reputation as a man-manager and as a tactician. Although the Bulldogs finished above only North Melbourne in 1937, Kelly lifted them to the finals the following year for the first time since the club was admitted to the competition in 1925. The western suburbs went wild with delight.

Footscray, which had finished third, was

KENNEDY, John

PLAYING CAREER: Hawthorn, 1950-59, 164 games, 29 goals.

COACHING CAREER: Hawthorn, 1957, 1960-63, and 1967-76, 299 games, 181 wins, 116 losses, 2 draws, 15 finals, 3 premierships. North Melbourne, 1985-89, 113 games, 55 wins, 55 losses, 3 draws, 3 finals. Winning percentage – 49.

John Kennedy.

The man in the gabardine overcoat is regarded as one of Hawthorn's iconic identities. He not only was a talented, even if awkward, ruckman for the Hawks, but in 1961 coached the club to its first VFL premiership. Kennedy at one stage had stood in for Jack Hale when the coach was unavailable during the 1957 season and had impressed several committeemen with his ability to draw the best from his players. There therefore was a succession plan for Kennedy to succeed Hale and, when Kennedy retired as a player at the end of 1959, he was appointed non-playing coach. Hale told him: "It's now your baby". Hawthorn had finished seventh in 1959 and there were high hopes during the following season that Kennedy would guide the Hawks to the finals. They finished fifth, behind fourth-placed Collingwood only on percentage. Kennedy in 1961 had his side fitter than any of their rivals and the press took note of a team described as "Kennedy's Kommandoes". The Hawks finished on top of the ladder with 14 wins and just four defeats and then defeated Melbourne by seven points to march straight into the

Grand Final. When Hawthorn thrashed Footscray by 43 points in the Grand Final, Glenferrie Road became a hub of wild celebrations. The easybeats had become premiers under Kennedy.

The Hawks slumped to ninth the following year but made the Grand Final in 1963, only to go down to Geelong. Even worse for the Hawks, schoolteacher Kennedy resigned because he had been transferred to Stawell. Graham Arthur took over as playing coach over the 1964-65 seasons and Peter O'Donohue in 1966. The Hawks then welcomed Kennedy back with open arms in 1967 as he was regarded as one of the most innovative football thinkers of his era and was able to win the respect of everyone associated with the club. Kennedy's mantra was "team before the individual", and he built a new era of success at the Glenferrie Oval, culminating in the 1971 Grand Final defeat of St Kilda. Then, after taking Hawthorn to another premiership in 1976, Kennedy stood down in favour of David Parkin. However, he was far from finished with coaching as he joined North Melbourne in 1985 and immediately lifted the Roos from eleventh to fourth. The Roos made the finals again under Kennedy when they finished fifth in 1987, but he called it quits at the end of the 1989 season. Kennedy later became chairman of the AFL Commission, a position he held from 1993-97.

Alan Killigrew.

KILLIGREW, Alan

PLAYING CAREER: St Kilda, 1938-41 and 1943-45, 78 games, 75 goals.

COACHING CAREER: St Kilda, 1956-58, 54 games, 19 wins, 34 losses, 1 draw, 0 finals. Winning percentage – 35. North Melbourne, 1963-66, 70 games, 27 wins, 43 losses, 0 draws, 0 finals. Winning percentage – 39.

Originally rejected by St Kilda because he was considered too small, Killigrew went on to become a Saints legend. His playing career was interrupted by service in the navy during World War II and he was forced into retirement because of tuberculosis of the spine. Killigrew was coaching country club Golden Point when St Kilda invited him to replace Les Foote in 1956. It was an inspired choice as Killigrew was passionate about St Kilda, having barracked for the club as a boy, and desperately wanted to lift his old side. He became famous as football's "hot orator" and he often took his side to the boundary fence to be near St Kilda supporters during his three-quarter time addresses. Killigrew lifted the Saints from being perennial easybeats to being at least competitive. They finished eleventh, ninth and eighth in his three seasons in charge before he was replaced by Jim Francis. Killigrew in 1963 was lured to North Melbourne, where he again adopted an evangelical approach. The Kangaroos finished seventh, eighth, ninth and seventh in Killigrew's four years as coach. Killigrew, a devout Catholic who even frowned on swearing, was so passionate in defence of his players that while he was with North he was involved in a punch-up in a players' race at Geelong.

KING, Stuart

PLAYING CAREER: St Kilda, 1931-33, 43 games, 14 goals.

COACHING CAREER: St Kilda, 1932, 11 games, 2 wins, 9 losses, 0 draws, 0 finals. Winning percentage – 18.

Recruited from University Blacks, King also

was a brilliant cricketer who represented Victoria as a batsman. He was 25 years of age when he joined St Kilda in 1931 and was appointed vice-captain the following season. Then, when captain-coach Charlie Hardy was sacked during the 1932 season, King took over for the remaining 11 games. St Kilda won just two of the games to finish above only Hawthorn and King was pushed into the background the following season when St Kilda lured former Melbourne champion Colin Deane from Tasmania as captain-coach. King played with the Saints in 1933, but then retired to concentrate on his legal career. As Flying Officer King, he was aboard a Catalina on an anti-submarine mission off the north-east coast of Australia on February 28, 1943, when the plane went missing. No trace was ever found.

KINNEAR, Colin

PLAYING CAREER: Did not play at senior VFL/AFL level.

COACHING CAREER: Sydney Swans, 1989-91, 66 games, 23 wins, 42 losses, 1 draw, 0 finals. Winning percentage – 35.

Although Kinnear did not play football at the elite level, he had a fine football pedigree as father Joe had played 47 games with Melbourne from 1932-37. Kinnear first made an impression as a coach with VFA club Coburg before stints as assistant coach with North Melbourne and then Carlton. He guided the Blues reserves to four consecutive Grand Final appearances and his appointment as Sydney coach in 1989 was seen as a bold initiative. Kinnear had the unenviable task of replacing coaching legend Tom Hafey and also had to contend with the loss of key players during his three-year tenure with the Swans. Although the Swans finished seventh in 1989, they slid to thirteenth the following year and Kinnear resigned three weeks before the end of the 1991 season. He said: "The young players were being questioned about it (the coaching position) and it was better to get out of the way." The Swans finished twelfth in that final Kinnear season.

Matthew Knights.

KNIGHT, Jack

PLAYING CAREER: Collingwood, 1934-40, 104 games, 85 goals. St Kilda, 1941-42, 24 games, 16 goals.

COACHING CAREER: St Kilda, 1941, 18 games, 3 wins, 15 losses, 0 draws, 0 finals. Winning percentage – 17.

"Cracker" Knight was a tough and fearless ruckman who played in Collingwood's 1936 premiership side. He was appointed St Kilda captain-coach to replace Ansell Clarke in 1941, but the Saints won only three games that season and he was replaced by Reg Garvin. Knight remained as a player in 1942 and later coached VFA club Yarraville.

KNIGHTS, Matthew

PLAYING CAREER: Richmond, 1988-2002, 279 games, 141 goals.

COACHING CAREER: Essendon, 2008-10, 67 games, 25 wins, 41 losses, 1 draw, 1 final. Winning percentage – 37.

Following a highly distinguished career, champion midfielder Knights joined SANFL club Port Adelaide in 2004 before moving to Essendon as an assistant coach the following season and made a big impression as a lateral thinker. When the Bombers parted company with Kevin Sheedy after 27 years, Knights was an obvious candidate for the senior position, but had to beat a hot field to clinch the job. Knights in 2008 had Essendon playing with a much more attacking style and Bomber fans revelled in their team's new-found flair, even though Essendon finished twelfth. Knights lifted the Bombers into the finals in 2009, but they crashed badly in the finals, going down to Adelaide by 96 points in an elimination final at AAMI Stadium. When the Bombers slumped to finish above only Richmond and West Coast in 2010, Bomber fans lost patience with their coach and the club reacted by replacing Knights with club legend James Hird. Knights helped coach at Xavier College while out of AFL ranks, but then accepted an invitation to join the Geelong coaching staff, in charge of the Cats' VFL side.

Peter Knights.

KNIGHTS, Peter

PLAYING CAREER: Hawthorn, 1969-85, 267 games, 202 goals.

COACHING CAREER: Brisbane Bears, 1987-89, 59 games, 17 wins, 42 losses, 0 draws, 0 finals. Winning percentage – 29. Hawthorn, 1994-95, 45 games, 20 wins, 25 losses, 0 draws, 1 final. Winning percentage – 44.

One of the greatest centre half-backs to have played the game, Knights played in three Hawthorn premiership sides and seemed destined to coach. He was invited to coach the Brisbane Bears in their inaugural season of 1987 and although he took charge of what was described as a team of misfits, he guided them to victory in their first two matches, against North Melbourne at the MCG and Geelong at Kardinia Park. Knights, however, was on a hiding to nothing as the Bears had limited resources and little squad depth. Regardless, they won six games in their inaugural season to finish above Richmond. Seven more wins followed in 1988 and although the Bears were doing better than most pundits expected, Knights was dumped midway through the 1989 season and replaced by former North Melbourne centreman Paul Feltham. The football world sympathised with Knights and it was no surprise when he was appointed Hawthorn coach in 1994. Knights guided the Hawks to the finals in his first season in charge only for them to go down to North Melbourne in a qualifying final. When Hawthorn slumped to finish above only Fitzroy the following season, Hawthorn replaced Knights with Ken Judge.

KYNE, Phonse

PLAYING CAREER: Collingwood, 1934-44 and 1946-50, 245 games, 237 goals.

COACHING CAREER: Collingwood, 1950-63, 272 games, 161 wins, 109 losses, 2 draws, 20 finals, 2 premierships. Winning percentage – 59.

Phonse Kyne.

Although Alphonsus "Phonse" Kyne was a Collingwood man to his bootlaces, his father had wanted him to play with Melbourne. Kyne was a champion centre half-forward or ruckman who played in the Magpies' 1935 and 1936 premiership sides and therefore was accustomed to Collingwood success. When the great Jock McHale stepped down as Magpie coach at the end of the 1949 season, it was assumed that Kyne would take over. When the Magpies inexplicably overlooked him in favour of another former player in Bervyn Woods, Collingwood fans expressed their disapproval at an intra-club practice match. The Magpie hierarchy within a week replaced Woods with Kyne and reaped a handsome reward. Although Collingwood slumped from fourth to seventh in Kyne's first season in charge, he lifted the Magpies to the 1953 premiership. Collingwood under Kyne was runner-up in 1955-56 before he achieved his greatest coaching triumph in 1958. Although Melbourne was an almost unbackable favourite in this Grand Final, Kyne was determined that the Demons would not equal the Magpies'record of four consecutive premierships from 1927-30 and implored his men to "bleed for Collingwood". The Magpies defied the odds to defeat Melbourne by 18 points. Collingwood missed the finals in all of Kyne's final three seasons and he stepped down at the end of 1963 in favour of another club legend in Bob Rose.

LA FONTAINE, Allan

PLAYING CAREER: Melbourne, 1934-42 and 1945, 171 games, 77 goals.

COACHING CAREER: 1949-51, 56 games, 25 wins, 31 losses, 0 draws, 1 final. Winning percentage – 45.

Although La Fontaine was a champion centreman with Melbourne after being recruited from Old Paradians and University Blacks, this success did not carry into his coaching career. La Fontaine captained Melbourne in its 1939-41 flag sides and was the logical successor when Frank "Checker" Hughes retired as coach at the end of 1948. The Demons had won the 1948 flag, but slipped to fifth in La Fontaine's first season in charge. They might have made the finals in 1950, but crashed out to Geelong (by 44 points) in the first semi-final. The mighty Demons then slipped to bottom position, with just one win in 1951 and La Fontaine was replaced by Norm Smith. La Fontaine told the Melbourne committee on September 21, 1951, that he would not seek reappointment, but it was a mutual decision.

LAHIFF, Tom

PLAYING CAREER: Essendon, 1935-37, 49 games, 67 goals. South Melbourne, 1942, 6 games, 10 goals. Hawthorn, 1942-44, 19 games, 23 goals.

COACHING CAREER: Hawthorn, 1944, 18 games, 2 wins, 15 losses, 1 draw, 0 finals. Winning percentage – 11.

One of the game's most loved characters, Lahiff was former umpire Harry Beitzel's sidekick on radio broadcasts for many years after a long and distinguished playing and coaching career. Short, but pugnacious, he was a clever rover who made a name for himself with VFA club Port Melbourne. After playing with Essendon for three seasons, he returned to Port Melbourne and was captain-coach of its 1940-41 flag sides. When the VFA went into recession because of World War II, Lahiff bobbed up as a player with South Melbourne and Hawthorn. Hawthorn, believing it needed the toughness of a club like Port Melbourne, appointed Lahiff non-playing coach in 1944. However, Hawthorn had so many injuries that Lahiff made a one-game comeback. When the VFA resumed competition, Lahiff moved back to his beloved Port Melbourne. He also coached country club Albury and was an assistant to Bob Skilton when the South Melbourne champion was captain-coach of the Swans over the 1965-66 seasons.

LAIDLEY, Dean

PLAYING CAREER: West Coast, 1987-90 and 1992, 52 games, 10 goals. North Melbourne, 1993-97, 99 games, 5 goals.

COACHING CAREER: North Melbourne, 2003-09, 149 games, 72 wins, 75 losses, 2 draws, 5 finals. Winning percentage – 48.

Known as "the Junkyard Dog" for his relentless playing style from a half-back flank, Laidley played in North's 1996 premiership side and, on retirement, coached ACT club Weston Creek before becoming an assistant coach to Mick Malthouse at Collingwood. He replaced Denis Pagan as North coach before the start of the 2003 season and won himself a reputation as a dour, yet sometimes feisty mentor. Although Laidley took the Kangaroos into three finals series, in 2005 (seventh), 2007 (third) and 2008 (eighth) in his six full seasons as North coach, his intensity never helped him endear himself to fans. Laidley resigned following a round 12 loss to Adelaide in 2009 and stated that he felt he could not take the playing group any further. He was replaced by former teammate Darren Crocker as interim coach. Laidley later became as assistant coach with Port Adelaide.

LANE, Gordon

PLAYING CAREER: Essendon, 1940-49, 131 games, 256 goals. South Melbourne, 1950-52, 47 games, 92 goals.

COACHING CAREER: South Melbourne 1950-52, 55 games, 24 wins, 29 losses, 2 draws, 0 finals. Winning percentage – 44.

A hugely-talented key forward, Lane kicked six goals in Essendon's 1942 Grand Final triumph over Richmond and seven goals in the Bombers' 1946 Grand Final defeat of Melbourne, but later was troubled by knee injuries. When South parted company with coach Jack Hale at the end of 1949, it declared it wanted a playing coach and settled on "Whoppa" Lane. The Swans finished eleventh in Lane's first season in charge, but improved to finish eighth the following year and then fifth in 1952. In fact, South missed the finals by just two match points after inexplicably going down to lowly Footscray in a final round match at the Western Oval, with Carlton snatching fourth position. It had been South's best season since making the 1945 Grand Final, but it was not enough for the Swans and Lane was asked to resign. He was replaced by former club champion Laurie Nash, but the Swans slumped to eighth position in 1953.

LAVER, Les

PLAYING CAREER: Geelong, 1926, 1928 and 1931-32, 8 games, 0 goals.

COACHING CAREER: Geelong, 1940, 2 games, 1 win, 1 loss, 0 draws, 0 finals. Winning percentage – 50.

Although Laver had a modest playing career with Geelong, he coached the Cats in two games in 1940. Captain-coach Reg Hickey retired just three games into the season and vice-captain Tommy Quinn was dropped to the reserves and also announced his retirement. Laver assumed the coaching position until new captain Allan Everett took charge for the rest of the season. He later coached the Geelong Under 19s.

LEONARD, Johnny

PLAYING CAREER: South Melbourne, 1932, 12 games, 17 goals.

COACHING CAREER: South Melbourne, 1932, 19 games, 13 wins, 6 losses, 0 draws, 1 final. Winning percentage – 68.

When South Melbourne recruited 1926 Sandover Medal winner Leonard as captain-coach in 1932, it had in mind the start of the most ambitious recruiting campaign in the VFL to that stage. Leonard, a champion rover who had won consecutive best and fairest awards with Subiaco from 1926-30, had spent the 1931 season as captain-coach of Maryborough and South realised he could tap into an enormous reservoir of talent in WA. Leonard helped South recruit fellow Sandgropers Brighton Diggins, Bill Faul and

Gilbert Beard, as well as other interstate stars. Leonard, a brilliant rover, missed the start of the 1932 season because of illness, but then lifted the Southerners into their first finals series since 1924. Collingwood defeated South by 26 points in the first semi-final and Leonard then shocked the South committee when he informed them that he had to return to Western Australia in his employment with a football manufacturing company. Leonard had laid the foundations for South's 1933 premiership triumph under captain-coach Jack Bisset and, when Bisset retired at the end of the 1936 season, South unsuccessfully tried to lure their 1932 leader back to the Lake Oval.

LETHBRIDGE, Chris

PLAYING CAREER: Fitzroy, 1913-22, 148 games, 19 goals.

COACHING CAREER: Fitzroy, 1925, 17 games, 12 wins, 5 losses, 0 draws, 0 finals. Winning percentage – 71.

When Lethbridge offered his playing services to Fitzroy in 1913, the Maroons had no idea that the well-built defender already had represented NSW. Lethbridge went on to become a Fitzroy stalwart and also represented Victoria. He played in the Maroons' 1913 flag side and was captain of the 1922 premiership side, in his last VFL game. Lethbridge coached Fitzroy in 1925 and although the Maroons missed the finals behind fourth-placed Collingwood by just

1.4 in percentage, he was replaced as coach by 1922 premiership coach Vic Belcher. Lethbridge later became a vice-president of the Fitzroy Football Club and also served as a Victorian selector.

LEWIS, Johnny

PLAYING CAREER: North Melbourne 1925-35, 150 games, 142 goals. Melbourne 1936-38, 46 games, 18 goals.

COACHING CAREER: North Melbourne, 1930, 18 games, 1 win, 17 losses, 0 draws, 0 finals. Winning percentage – 6.

A champion ruckman, Lewis started with North Melbourne in the VFA in 1921. Bigger (194cm) than most players of his era, Lewis was appointed captain-coach in 1930, but the Shinboners won only one game and

he was replaced at season's end by former Carlton star Norman Clark. Lewis continued as North captain, but lost this position to Dick Taylor in 1932. Lewis crossed to Melbourne in 1936 and, after three seasons with the Redlegs, was appointed captain-coach of Murtoa at a reported six pounds ($12) a week. He resigned during a team form slump during the 1939 season.

LONGMIRE, John

PLAYING CAREER: North Melbourne, 1988-99, 200 games, 511 goals.

COACHING CAREER: Sydney Swans, 2011-, 49 games, 32 wins, 16 losses, 1 draw, 5 finals, 1 premiership. Winning percentage – 65.

A champion full-forward with North

Melbourne who played in the Roos' 1999 premiership side in his last AFL game, he joined the Swans as an assistant coach in 2002 and, from 2007, was coaching co-ordinator as second in charge to senior coach Paul Roos. Longmire played a pivotal role in the Swans' 2005 premiership success and, from there, was seen as Roos' natural successor. He then was handed the senior job when Roos stepped down at the end of the 2010 season. Longmire immediately tinkered with the Swans' game plan, with longer kicking and less emphasis on grinding tactics. The Swans finished sixth in his first season in charge and further emphasised the change in tactics with more free-flowing football in 2012. The Swans then shocked the football world in defeating Hawthorn by 10 points in the 2012 Grand Final.

LYON, Ross

PLAYING CAREER: Fitzroy, 1985-94, 127 games, 112 goals. Brisbane Bears, 1995, 2 games, 0 goals.

COACHING CAREER: St Kilda, 2007-11, 121 games, 76 wins, 41 losses, 4 draws, 11 finals. Winning percentage – 63. Fremantle, 2012-, 24 games, 15 wins, 9 losses, 0 draws, 2 finals. Winning percentage – 63.

A hard-hitting utility as a player, Lyon was forced into retirement because of a knee injury and started his coaching career as an assistant with Richmond. He spent four years at Punt Road before spending another four years in a similar role with Carlton and then joining former Fitzroy teammate Paul Roos with the Sydney Swans. When Lyon was an assistant coach with the Swans, AFL boss Andrew Demetriou criticised Sydney for its playing style and Lyon reacted by telling club supporters that Demetriou did not know what was required to win a flag. Lyon's comment was proved accurate when the Swans won the 2005 flag. Lyon crossed to St Kilda as senior coach in 2007 and he immediately implemented a controversial game plan of strangling the opposition and scoring on the rebound. This playing style required enormous discipline and levels of fitness, but it worked and St Kilda made the 2009-10 Grand Finals, only to go down to Geelong by just 12 points in 2009 and playing a draw with Collingwood the following season before going down by 56 points in the replay. Lyon's Saints were desperately unlucky in the drawn 2010 Grand Final as a fickle bounce for opportunist forward Steve Milne probably cost the club the premiership. St Kilda went down to the Swans in an elimination final in 2011, but Lyon then shocked the football world when he announced that he would be leaving St Kilda to take over from Mark Harvey at Fremantle. Lyon's Dockers shocked hot favourite Geelong in a 2012 elimination final, but then crashed to Adelaide in a semi-final.

MAHER, Frank

PLAYING CAREER: Essendon, 1921-28, 137 games, 124 goals.

COACHING CAREER: Essendon, 1925-27, 56 games, 32 wins, 23 losses, 1 draw, 3 finals. Winning percentage – 57. Fitzroy, 1932-33, 36 games, 14 wins, 21 losses, 1 draw, 0 finals. Winning percentage – 39. Carlton, 1935-36, 38 games, 26 wins, 11 losses, 1 draw, 2 finals. Winning percentage – 68.

Maher, a talented winger/forward, originally wanted to play with Carlton but was tied to Essendon and played in the Dons' 1923-24 premiership sides. He took over from Syd Barker as captain-coach in 1925, but saw his side go down to Collingwood in the first semi-final. In 1926, Essendon went down to eventual premier Melbourne by just three points in the preliminary final and, the following year, the Maher-led Dons slid to eighth position. Although Maher remained as Essendon captain in 1928, he was replaced as coach by Charlie Hardy. It was Maher's last season with Essendon as he became captain-coach of VFA club Oakleigh. He made such a good impression with the Oaks in winning the 1930-31 flags that he was appointed non-playing coach of Fitzroy in 1932, only for the Maroons to finish tenth. Maher lifted the Maroons to fifth position in 1933 but then relinquished the position. In a surprising twist, Fitzroy in October, 1934, named Maher coach for the following season, even though he had not applied for the position. Instead, he had applied for the Carlton coaching position and won it. Maher took Carlton to the finals in two seasons in charge, but the Blues went down to Richmond in the 1935 first semi-final and to Melbourne in the 1936 first semi-final. He was replaced in 1937 by former Collingwood player Percy Rowe.

MALTHOUSE, Mick

PLAYING CAREER: St Kilda, 1972-76, 53 games, 5 goals. Richmond, 1976-83, 121 games, 10 goals.

COACHING CAREER: Footscray, 1984-89, 135 games, 67 wins, 66 losses, 2 draws, 3 finals. Winning percentage – 50. West Coast – 1990-99, 243 games, 156 wins, 85 losses, 2 draws, 25 finals, 2 premierships. Winning percentage – 64. Collingwood – 2000-11, 286 games, 163 wins, 121 losses, 2 draws, 22 finals. 1 premiership. Winning percentage – 57.

Malthouse joined St Kilda from North Ballarat and, after being told by coach Allan Jeans that he would struggle to win a regular spot, he crossed to Richmond. A tough back pocket, he played in the Tigers' 1980 premiership side and, following retirement as a player, joined Footscray as non-playing coach in 1984. Malthouse was just 31 years of age, but relished his new position and gave the Bulldogs a far more professional edge. He insisted on doing things his way, even though it caused some players to resent his authority. He fell out with defender Brad Hardie and had run-ins with other players as he lifted the Bulldogs to respectability. After finishing seventh in Malthouse's first season of 1984, they reached the finals the next year, only to go down by just 10 points to Hawthorn in the preliminary final. It was the Bulldogs' best finish under Malthouse and, when West Coast indicated it would be seeking a new coach to replace John Todd at the end of the 1989 season, Malthouse applied for the position and won it.

The wily Malthouse lifted the Eagles from eleventh in 1989 to a losing preliminary final the following year and, in 1991, into their first Grand Final, against Hawthorn. The big match was played at Waverley

Mick Malthouse won flags with West Coast and Collingwood.

Park as the MCG was unavailable because of a rebuilding program and the Eagles went down by 53 points. Although the Eagles finished the home and away ladder in fourth position in 1992, they defeated Hawthorn in an elimination final and then Geelong in the second semi-final to march straight into the Grand Final. Malthouse's men defeated Geelong by 28 points to become the first non-Victorian team to win the AFL premiership. Western Australia went wild with delight and, when Malthouse guided the Eagles to the 1994 premiership, the former back pocket player was regarded as one of the finest coaches of the modern era, even if some of his comments and coaching decisions left critics bewildered. For example, he once told the media "the ox is slow but the earth is patient", a line which became the title of one of his books.

By the time Malthouse had been in Perth for the best part of a decade, he sought a return to Victoria and Collingwood snapped him up as coach from 2000. Malthouse, with his trademark emphasis on defence, had his Magpies playing tight, contested football with run down one wing or the other instead of through the centre. His match tactics and strict discipline paid dividends, but only after heartbreaking Grand Final defeats by the Brisbane Lions in 2002 and 2003. Malthouse twice had to rebuild his Magpie side but, in 2010, he led them to glory with a Grand Final victory over St Kilda after the two clubs had played a draw the previous week. It was Collingwood's first premiership for 20 years, yet Malthouse had just one more season with the Magpies as there was a plan for former star Nathan Buckley to replace him as team coach and for Malthouse to assume a role as director of coaching. But, after the Magpies went down to Geelong in the 2011 Grand Final, Malthouse stepped aside and spent a year in the media. He said at the time: "I will not be at any other club, in any other role, next year." Malthouse was as good as his word, but there were suggestions late in the 2012 season that the Blues would dump Brett Ratten and appoint Malthouse as his replacement. Malthouse insisted he would not take over at any club during a season but, when the Blues failed to make the finals, Carlton announced the week before the end of the home and away season that Ratten would not be reappointed for 2013. Malthouse was named Carlton coach the following week.

MANN, Neil

PLAYING CAREER: Collingwood, 1945-56, 179 games, 155 goals.

COACHING CAREER: Collingwood, 1967 and 1972-74, 71 games, 48 wins, 22 defeats. 1 draw, 5 finals. Winning percentage – 68.

Mann gave Collingwood a lifetime of loyal service, as player, coach and committeeman. Mann was a strong-marking key forward or ruckman who played in the Magpies' 1953 premiership side. On retirement as a player he spent 14 years as reserves coach and was in charge in one game in 1967 when Bob Rose was unavailable. Mann took over from Rose in 1972 and Collingwood finished fourth after going down to St Kilda in the first semi-final. Collingwood topped the ladder under Mann with just three defeats in 1973, but crashed out of the premiership race in straight sets, with losses to Carlton in the second semi-final and to Richmond in the preliminary

Neil Mann guided the Magpies to three finals series.

final. Collingwood defeated Footscray in an elimination final in 1974, but then went down to Hawthorn in a semi-final. Mann, who coached Victoria in 1974, resigned and was replaced by former Magpie star Murray Weideman. He served Collingwood as a committeeman from 1976-82.

MATTHEWS, Herbie

PLAYING CAREER: South Melbourne, 1932-45, 191 games, 17 goals.

COACHING CAREER: South Melbourne, 1939 and 1954-57, 90 games, 27 wins, 62 losses, 1 draw, 0 finals. Winning percentage – 30.

One of South Melbourne's greatest identities, Matthews played in the 1933 premiership side and won a Brownlow Medal in 1940. Matthews was Swan captain-coach in 1939 but stepped down when the club decided it wanted him to concentrate on his playing career and replaced him with Jack Baggott. Matthews played his last game for South in the 1945 "Bloodbath" Grand Final against Carlton and became captain-coach of VFA club Oakleigh and then suburban club Ringwood before returning to the Lake Oval as reserves coach. He then took over as senior coach when South parted company with Laurie Nash at the end of the 1953 season. The Swans originally were keen on luring Essendon champion Bill Hutchison to the Lake Oval as captain-coach, but believed the Bombers would refuse to clear their star rover. Matthews had the respect of all South players, but did not have the talent for team success and, in four seasons in charge, the Swans finished no higher than ninth. Ron Clegg took over as captain-coach in 1958.

MATTHEWS, Leigh

PLAYING CAREER: 1969-85, 332 games, 915 goals.

COACHING CAREER: Collingwood, 1986-95, 224 games, 125 wins, 94 losses, 5 draws, 9 finals, 1 premiership. Winning percentage – 56. Brisbane Lions, 1999-2008, 237 games, 142 wins, 92 losses, 3 draws, 18 finals, 3 premierships. Winning percentage – 61.

Matthews had a phenomenal playing career with Hawthorn after being recruited from Chelsea. He won eight Hawk best and fairest awards, topped their goalkicking six times, captained

the club from 1981-85 and played in four premiership sides. Matthews joined Collingwood as an assistant coach and was appointed senior coach when Magpie legend Bob Rose stood aside just three rounds into the 1986 season. Collingwood finished sixth that season and, after slumping to finish above only the Brisbane Bears and Richmond the following season, Matthews' non-negotiable discipline started to pay dividends in 1988 when the Magpies finished fourth. After being eliminated by Melbourne in an elimination final in 1989, Collingwood the following season finished behind only Essendon on the ladder and then defeated the Bombers by 48 points in a spiteful Grand Final. Matthews was the uncrowned king of Collingwood as he had guided the Magpies to their first premiership in 32 years. The Magpies failed to capitalise on that success and

Leigh Matthews.

even missed the finals the following year and in 1993. When Collingwood finished tenth in 1995 he was replaced as coach by 1990 premiership captain Tony Shaw.

Matthews spent three years in the media before being lured back into coaching, with the Brisbane Lions, who had finished on the bottom of the ladder in 1998. Matthews again instilled his insistence on discipline and lifted the Lions to the finals in his first season in charge. They defeated Carlton by 73 points in the second qualifying final and then the Western Bulldogs by 53 points in the second semi-final before going down by 45 points to North Melbourne in a preliminary final. The Lions again made the finals in 2000, only to crash out of the premiership race in going down by 82 points to Carlton in the second semi-final. Matthews by now had built an imposing squad and, after finishing second on the home and away ladder in 2001, went on to defeat Essendon by 26 points in the Grand Final. The Lions under Matthews also won the 2002-03 flags and were trying to equal Collingwood's four consecutive flags (1927-30) when defeated by Port Adelaide in the 2004 Grand Final. He resigned as the Lions' coach in September, 2008, suggesting "the time is right". He since has been involved in media work, regarded as one of football's most incisive commentators. The AFL Players' Association Award each season is the Leigh Matthews Trophy.

MAY, Charlie

PLAYING CAREER: Essendon, 1922-26, 83 games, 3 goals.

COACHING CAREER: Essendon, 1934-35, 36 games, 12 wins, 24 losses, 0 draws, 0 finals. Winning percentage – 33.

"Chooka" May was a tough centreman who gave Essendon many years of service on and off the field. He coached both the Essendon reserves (at one time in tandem with Len Webster) and seniors, along with South Australian club Glenelg. May was appointed Essendon coach after the Dons collected the wooden spoon under Garnet Campbell in 1933. Despite lifting Essendon to tenth in his first season in charge and then eighth in 1935, May was replaced by Richmond's Jack Baggott, as captain-coach, for 1936. May later served the Bombers for many years as a trainer.

MAYBURY, Percy

PLAYING CAREER: Richmond, 1910-19, 128 games, 61 goals.

COACHING CAREER: Richmond, 1917, 15 games, 3 wins, 11 losses, 1 draw, 0 finals. Winning percentage – 20.

A talented but erratic small forward, Maybury was a local product who was appointed Tiger captain-coach for the 1917 season. However, Richmond won just three games (plus a draw) to finish on the bottom in a six-team competition (because of World War I). Maybury continued to play with Richmond and football writer "Rover", in the Weekly Times of May 29 that year, suggested the club vice-captain was ideally suited to serving the club as a committeeman. Maybury did just that from 1927-33 but, in the interim, played in the VFA with Footscray (including the 1920 flag side), captained the Tricolours in 1921 and was captain-coach of Mornington Peninsula club Frankston. Maybury also was a long-standing Richmond Cricket Club secretary.

McALPINE, Ivan

PLAYING CAREER: Footscray, 1927-33, 112 games, 24 goals. Hawthorn, 1934-37, 67 games, 27 goals.

COACHING CAREER: Hawthorn, 1935-38, 72 games, 22 wins, 50 losses, 0 draws, 0 finals. Winning percentage – 31.

McAlpine developed into a brilliant winger after joining Footscray from Longwarry and won the Bulldogs' best and fairest three times. McAlpine joined Hawthorn as captain-coach in 1935 and said his aim was not necessarily to win matches, but to "build a team". Unfortunately for McAlpine he did not have the playing material for success and Hawthorn's best season in his four years at the Glenferrie Oval was its eighth finish of 1937. Even though that represented Hawthorn's best finish to a season since it joined the competition in 1925, McAlpine was asked to take a pay cut. He agreed and although he continued with Hawthorn in 1938 for a finish of eleventh, he was replaced as captain-coach by Len Thomas the following season. McAlpine later coached Murray League club St James and Ballarat club Sebastopol.

McCARTHY, Con

PLAYING CAREER: Collingwood, 1915-21, 101 games, 22 goals. Footscray, 1925-26, 30 games, 17 goals.

COACHING CAREER: Footscray, 1925, 17 games, 4 wins, 13 losses, 0 draws. Winning percentage – 24.

With Footscray desperate to move from the VFA to the VFL in the early 1920s, it decided it wanted the best possible coach. The Tricolours in 1922 therefore made a momentous decision in naming Collingwood ruckman John Cornelius "Con" McCarthy as captain-coach. McCarthy, the Magpies' 1919 premiership captain, was one of the best big men of his era and was handed the Footscray job ahead of former club captain Johnny Craddock at a reported 400 pounds a season – a mammoth payment in that era – plus a job with a local soft drink company run by club president George Sayer.

McCarthy crossed to the VFA without a clearance and guided Footscray to the 1923 (he also won the Recorder Cup as the VFA's best and fairest that season) and 1924 VFA flags and masterminded the defeat of 1924 VFL premier Essendon in a special match at the MCG in aid of a returned soldiers' charity run by famous opera singer Dame Nellie Melba. Footscray the following season was admitted to the VFL, along with Hawthorn and North Melbourne, and McCarthy therefore was the red, white and blues' first VFL coach. The Sporting Globe suggested that McCarthy would "handle the players in a shrewd and strong manner" and Footscray did well in its first League match to push Fitzroy to nine points at Brunswick Street. Then, in round two, Footscray defeated South Melbourne by 10 points at the Western Oval.

Footscray won four games in 1925, with McCarthy missing just one game. He might have been a tireless worker for his team, but had turned 32 before the start of the season and knew he had little football left in him. He therefore stood down as coach while retaining the captaincy for the 1926 season. Former Footscray player, coach and head trainer Jim Cassidy was appointed non-playing coach, but resigned during the season because of ill-health. McCarthy played 14 of Footscray's 18 games in 1926 and then retired, at 33 years of age.

McCARTNEY, Brendan

PLAYING CAREER: Did not play at senior VFL/AFL level.

COACHING CAREER: Western Bulldogs, 2012-, 22 games, 5 wins, 17 losses, 0 draws, 0 finals. Winning percentage – 23.

Although McCartney never played at the elite level, he built himself an admirable coaching CV. He coached Bellarine League club Ocean Grove to consecutive premierships from 1994-97 before joining Richmond as a development coach in 1998. McCartney spent two years with the Tigers before spending 11 seasons (2000-10) in a similar role at Geelong and then spent the 2011 season as an assistant to Essendon coach James Hird. Soon after his appointment to the senior Bulldog job, McCartney said he wanted the Bulldogs to play "tough, uncompromising football" with a tough edge.

McCASKILL, Bob

PLAYING CAREER: Richmond, 1923-25, 35 games, 0 goals.

COACHING CAREER: North Melbourne, 1941-42 and 1944-47, 103 games, 43 wins, 60 losses, 0 draws, 1 final. Winning percentage – 42. Hawthorn, 1950-51, 36 games, 4 wins, 32 losses, 0 draws, 0 finals. Winning percentage – 11.

Although McCaskill had a modest VFL career with Richmond as a centreline player, he made a name for himself as the first coach to take North Melbourne to a finals series. McCaskill, who had a tremendous coaching record with Victorian country club Sandhurst (nine premierships, including six in a row), was appointed North coach in 1941 and immediately implemented a new training regime which included gymnasium work to help flexibility. The Shinboners finished ninth in both 1941 and 1942, but McCaskill missed the 1943 season because of army duties. He resumed in 1944 and took North to sixth position and then third in 1945 before going down to Carlton in the first semi-final. North finished ninth and then tenth under McAskill over the 1946-47 seasons before he was replaced by Wally Carter. However, the tough disciplinarian was snapped up as Hawthorn's coach in 1950. Hawthorn that season was racked by internal problems and finished on the bottom of the ladder. Hawthorn's poor run continued in 1951 but, by then, McCaskill was seriously ill. Assistant coach Jack Hale had to take over at many training sessions and Hawthorn finished above only Melbourne. Despite this, Hawthorn had the utmost respect for McAskill, who died in June, 1952, at 55 years of age.

McCONNELL, Alan

PLAYING CAREER: Footscray, 1980-82, 37 games, 5 goals.

COACHING CAREER: Fitzroy, 1995-96, 11 games, 0 wins, 11 losses, 0 draws, 0 finals. Winning percentage – 0.

McConnell will always be remembered as Fitzroy's last coach. A defender in his playing days with the Bulldogs, he took over as Fitzroy coach for three games when Bernie Quinlan was sacked in 1995 and then for eight games the following season when Mick Nunan quit. He never tasted success as a senior coach and joined the Geelong coaching panel in 1997. McConnell later became a coach at the Australian Institute of Sport before becoming a development coach with GWS.

McCORKELL, Jock

PLAYING CAREER: North Melbourne, 1940-42 and 1946-53, 167 games, 5 goals.

COACHING CAREER: North Melbourne, 1954-55, 37 games, 14 wins, 22 losses, 1 draw, 1 final. Winning percentage – 38.

A superb full-back, McCorkell's playing career was interrupted by three years of army service during World War II. After retiring at the end of 1953, he was appointed North's non-playing coach to replace Wally Carter in 1954. McCorkell guided North to the final four, only for the Shinboners to go down by 30 points to Melbourne in the first semi-final. The future looked bright for North, but the club was involved in a bitter power struggle before the start of the new season. North won just one of its first six games in 1955 and, in the lead-up to the round 12 clash with Carlton, the club was engulfed in controversy when it sacked popular stars Laurie Icke and Mick Grambeau. North had gone down to bottom side St Kilda the previous Saturday and, as it turned out, it was the Saints' only win of the season. The North players were so angry they held a protest meeting at Unity Hall, Bourke Street, the morning after the 17-point defeat by the Blues at Arden Street. Grambeau the next week said: "North has not been a happy club all season." He said in another interview: "One reason why North aren't doing as well as expected is that the players have lost all team spirit. Can you blame them? So many have been dropped without explanations that everyone is wondering who is next." McCorkell had argued with Icke in the training rooms on the Thursday night before the Carlton match and although the club refused to give reasons for the sackings, it was hinted that both Icke and Grambeau had been suspected (incorrectly) of "playing dead" against St Kilda. However, Icke had played with back and thigh injuries, while Grambeau said he had "two pounds on North, with five goals in". The row was the beginning of the end for McCorkell as North coach and he was replaced by Charlie Gaudion at the end of the season.

McDONALD, Alan

PLAYING CAREER: Richmond, 1939-41 and 1943, 49 games, 8 goals.

COACHING CAREER: Richmond, 1957-60, 72 games, 22 wins, 48 losses, 2 draws, 0 finals. Winning percentage – 31

A clever winger recruited from Leongatha, McDonald became Richmond's third coach in three years when given the job in 1957. McDonald had coached VFA club Camberwell and South Bendigo after he left Tigerland as a player at just 25 years of age. He succeeded Max Oppy as senior coach and it was such a surprise appointment that Oppy said he had no idea that he had been replaced until the day after McDonald's appointment. McDonald coached the Tigers at their lowest ebb and, in four seasons in charge, could lift them no higher than seventh – in his first season as coach. He was replaced by Des Rowe after the Tigers collected the wooden spoon in 1960.

McDONALD, Donald

PLAYING CAREER: North Melbourne, 1982-92, 155 games, 165 goals.

COACHING CAREER: Hawthorn, 2004, 5 games, 2 wins, 3 losses, 0 draws, 0 finals. Winning percentage – 40.

A handy ruckman/forward, McDonald

moved to VFA club Werribee at the end of his playing career and guided the club to a premiership in his first season as coach. He was an assistant coach with Hawthorn when it parted company with senior coach Peter Schwab with five rounds to play in 2004. McDonald was appointed interim coach and took the Hawks to two wins from the final five rounds. He later became North's Chief of Football Operations.

McHALE, James 'Jock'

PLAYING CAREER: Collingwood, 1903-18 and 1920, 261 games, 18 goals.

COACHING CAREER: Collingwood, 1912-49, 714 games, 467 wins, 237 losses, 10 draws, 59 finals, 8 premierships. Winning percentage – 65.

J. McHALE

McHale fully deserves his title as "the Prince of Coaches". His 714 games as coach of Collingwood is an AFL record, along with his eight premierships in charge at Victoria Park. McHale, educated at St Brigid's, North Fitzroy, and Christian Brothers' College, East Melbourne, made his Collingwood playing debut in 1903 and he developed into one of the most durable footballers of his era. He played in Collingwood's 1910 premiership side and was appointed captain-coach to succeed George Angus in 1912. No one was to know that it would be the start of football's most enduring relationship.

Although Collingwood finished a modest seventh in McHale's first season, he soon developed a playing style to lift the Magpies to the top – and to stay there. McHale said in an interview in 1935 that football success depended on tradition, club spirit and harmony. He added that he developed Collingwood's short-passing and handball style after it was first introduced by Dick Condon and other early Magpie stars. Collingwood was on a trip to Tasmania when the players started chipping balls around for fun and later decided to use this style in a match against Geelong, with devastating effect. "It was the men who played about 1902 who deserve the credit for Collingwood's success," McHale said in that 1935 interview.

McHale landed his first premiership as coach in 1917, with another one in 1919 and, from 1927-30, the Magpies won four consecutive premierships. McHale, however, did not take charge of the Magpies for their 1930 Grand Final triumph over Geelong as he was ill in bed and Bob Rush coached the side that day. Regardless, McHale is credited with being Collingwood's premiership coach that season. Further flags followed over the 1935-36 seasons and, over his long reign as Magpie coach, Collingwood invariably was at or near the top of the ladder. McHale was a stickler for team discipline and had the rare knack of knowing when his players were at their peak or on the slide. He had no favourites and had a tremendously loyal band of advisors. His methods became known as "the Collingwood way" but, after 38 years in charge, McHale knew his time as Collingwood coach was about to end. He eventually stood down at the end of the 1949 season and, at first, was replaced by Bervyn Woods. But, when Magpie fans vented their disapproval, Collingwood gave the job to Phonse Kyne, who guided the Magpies to the 1953 flag. The emotion of the victory proved too much for McHale, who had a heart attack the following day and died on October 4, at 71 years of age. The AFL premiership coach each season is presented with the Jock McHale Medal.

McKENNA, Guy

> **PLAYING CAREER:** West Coast, 1988-2000, 267 games, 28 goals.
>
> **COACHING CAREER:** Gold Coast, 2011-12, 44 games, 6 wins, 38 losses, 0 draws, 0 finals. Winning percentage – 14.

McKenna was one of the finest defenders of his era, with impeccable poise and skills. He played in the 1992 and 1994 Eagle premiership sides and, because of his excellent leadership skills, was seen as a fine appointment when named Gold Coast coach for its development seasons. He coached the Suns in the TAC Cup in 2009 and then in the VFL in 2010, preparing the team for its AFL debut in 2011. Although the Suns won only three games, they showed great determination and pulled off the shock of the season in defeating Richmond at Cairns. The Suns struggled early in 2012, but were given a fillip when club director and experienced mentor Malcolm Blight started sitting in the coach's box from mid-season. Gold Coast showed more poise and structure over the second half of the season and claimed the big scalp of early season premiership favourite Carlton at Metricon Stadium in round 22.

McKENZIE, Don

PLAYING CAREER: Footscray, 1962-70, 137 games, 128 goals.

COACHING CAREER: Footscray, 1978-79 and 1982, 44 games, 14 wins, 29 losses, 1 draw, 0 finals. Winning percentage – 32.

McKenzie, a great Footscray loyalist, was a talented half-forward who later moved to local club Spotswood. He was coaching the Footscray reserves in 1978 when senior coach Bill Goggin stepped down just six days into the new season. McKenzie's earliest days as coach were

Don McKenzie.

troubled ones as the players passed a vote of no confidence in the board. Although the internal problems eased, Footscray finished above only Melbourne in 1978. McKenzie coached the Bulldogs to ninth position the following year but was replaced by former champion Richmond centre half-forward Royce Hart. McKenzie, quiet and unassuming, also coached the Bulldogs in one game in 1982 following the demotion of Hart and later the appointment of Ian Hampshire as coach.

McKENZIE, Jack 'Dookie'

PLAYING CAREER: Essendon, 1901-02, 1904-06, 81 games, 90 goals. Melbourne, 1915, 16 games, 10 goals.

COACHING CAREER: Melbourne, 1915, 17 games, 9 wins, 8 losses, 0 draws, 1 final. Winning percentage – 53.

McKenzie started his senior playing career with VFA club Brunswick and became a wonderful ruckman with Essendon in its 1901 premiership season. However, he moved to Western Australia in 1903 to play with the White Feather club. Essendon lured him back in 1904 and he was club captain in 1906. However, McKenzie was an itinerant footballer and moved back to Brunswick in 1907 as captain-coach. He guided the Wickers to the 1909 premiership, even though he missed the Grand Final victory over Prahran because of concussion. McKenzie was lured to Melbourne as captain-coach for the 1914 season, but could not win a clearance and again played for Brunswick. Then, in 1915, he won his release and replaced Alec Hall as coach. McKenzie was 32 years of age but guided the Fuchsias to fourth position. Melbourne crashed out of the premiership race in going down to eventual premier Carlton in a semi-final and, the following year, Melbourne pulled out of the competition because of World War I. McKenzie later coached Hawthorn in the VFA.

McKENZIE, Keith

PLAYING CAREER: North Melbourne, 1944-51, 130 games, 12 goals.

COACHING CAREER: North Melbourne, 1966-70, 82 games, 23 wins, 57 losses, 2 draws, 0 finals. Winning percentage – 28. Carlton, 1972 and 1975, 2 games, 2 wins, 0 losses, 0 draws, 0 finals. Winning percentage – 100.

McKenzie had a delayed entry to the VFL because of service with the RAAF during World War II. Recruited locally, he was a brilliant winger who won North's best and fairest in 1947. He was assistant coach when he stood in for Alan Killigrew in two games in 1966 and was appointed senior coach in his own right the following season. In four seasons in charge at Arden Street, the Kangaroos had a best finish of

Keith McKenzie.

eighth, in 1967 and in 1969. McKenzie, who later was secretary of the Carlton Football Club, also stood in as Carlton coach in one game in 1972 and another in 1975.

McLAREN, George

PLAYING CAREER: Footscray, 1944-51, 139 games, 24 goals.

COACHING CAREER: Footscray, 1951, 1 game, 1 win, 0 losses, 0 draws, 0 finals. Winning percentage – 100.

"Binga" McLaren was a talented winger who represented Victoria. He coached the Bulldogs in one game (for a win) in 1951 when regular coach Charlie Sutton was unavailable. McLaren, as captain-coach of Hampden Football League club Colac won two premierships and also coached Sunshine, but was killed in a motor accident at Bunyip in September, 1956. Footscray and a combined local Gippsland team played a benefit match for McLaren's family and raised 450 pounds ($900).

McMAHEN, Noel

PLAYING CAREER: Melbourne, 1946-56, 175 games, 28 goals.

COACHING CAREER: South Melbourne, 1962-64, 54 games, 9 wins, 45 losses, 0 draws, 0 finals. Winning percentage – 17.

A tough, hard-hitting half-back, McMahen captained Melbourne's 1955-56 premiership sides. He coached Victorian country club Rochester on retirement and was appointed South Melbourne coach in 1962 to replace the retired Bill Faul. McMahen made a stunning start to his VFL coaching career, with the Swans defeating North Melbourne and St Kilda in his first two games in charge. However, reality eventually hit and South won just one more game that season (against Fitzroy) to finish last. South improved one position in 1963 and again finished eleventh the following season. McMahen did not seek reappointment for the 1965 season and Bob Skilton took charge as captain-coach.

McMASTER, Bill

PLAYING CAREER: Geelong, 1951-54, 61 games, 75 goals.

COACHING CAREER: 1971-72, 44 games, 12 wins, 32 losses, 0 draws, 0 finals. Winning percentage – 27.

Although McMaster spent just four seasons playing with Geelong before being forced into retirement because of a severe ankle injury, he had an enormous impact at Kardinia Park. A strong-marking ruckman, he played in the 1951-52 premiership sides. McMaster succeeded Peter Pianto as senior coach in 1971 but, in his two seasons in charge, the Cats finished tenth both years. McMaster served the Cats in recruiting for more than a quarter of a century.

McNAMARA, Dave

PLAYING CAREER: St Kilda, 1905-09, 1914-15, 1918-19 and 1921-23, 122 games, 187 goals.

COACHING CAREER: St Kilda, 1913-1914 and 1922-23, 68 games, 33 wins,

33 losses, 2 draws, 0 finals. Winning percentage – 50.

One of the greatest players of the early years of the VFL, McNamara was a 194cm giant who excelled at centre half-forward or in the ruck. He was just 22 years of age when he and several other players had a dispute with the St Kilda hierarchy and he crossed to VFA club Essendon Town. He returned to St Kilda in 1913 as captain-coach, only for the VFA to block his clearance because it believed he had been made an illegal inducement (in the form of a hotel licence) to play with the Dreadnoughts. McNamara became non-playing coach but, on the eve of the finals, had yet another row with the St Kilda committee and resigned. His place was taken by George Sparrow, who took the Saints to a Grand Final defeat by Fitzroy. It now is a matter of conjecture whether St Kilda would have won the flag with McNamara in its side. McNamara returned to the Saints as captain-coach in 1914 and, in his first game back, kicked six of his team's eight goals. However, he then copped a 10-match suspension for elbowing an opponent and, without its leader for much of the season, St Kilda finished seventh. McNamara was replaced by Jimmy Smith in 1915 and, when St Kilda went into recess because of World War I over the 1916-17 seasons, he was left without a club. St Kilda returned to the competition in 1918 and McNamara the following season announced his playing retirement. He made a comeback in 1921 and was St Kilda's playing coach over the 1922-23 seasons. The Saints finished seventh in 1922 and eighth the following year. McNamara later played with Victorian amateur club Ormond until he was 45 years of age. He also served St Kilda as a committeeman and as club chairman. He died on August 14, 1967, at 80 years of age.

MELLING, Ted

PLAYING CAREER: Did not play at senior VFL/AFL level.

COACHING CAREER: Fitzroy, 1919, 9 games, 4 wins, 4 losses, 1 draw, 0 finals. Winning percentage – 50.

Melling was a star rover with Fitzroy in its VFA days, but was seriously injured in 1895 and spent several months in the St Vincent's Hospital. Fitzroy ran special benefits to help Melling and his family as he was seen as one of the club's great identities. Melling coached Fitzroy over the second half of the 1919 season when George Holden had to relinquish the position because of business commitments. Fitzroy finished fifth and missed the finals by just two match points. Star forward Percy Parratt took over as captain-coach in 1920.

MERRETT, Roger

PLAYING CAREER: Essendon, 1978-87, 149 games, 146 goals. Brisbane, 1988-96, 164 games, 287 goals.

COACHING CAREER: Brisbane, 1998, 11 games, 3 wins, 7 losses, 1 draw, 0 finals. Winning percentage – 27.

Merrett became one of the most feared key forwards in the game after Essendon recruited him from Victorian club Kaniva.

He played in the 1984-85 Essendon premiership sides, but accepted an offer to join the fledgling Brisbane Bears in 1988. Merrett captained the Bears from 1990 to his retirement in 1996 and then was an assistant coach with the Brisbane Lions when Fitzroy and the Bears merged for the 1997 season. He then took over as senior coach during the 1998 season when John Northey was dumped. The Lions had won just two games under Northey that season and although they won three of their 11 games under Merrett, they finished on the bottom of the ladder. The Lions the following year appointed 1990 Collingwood premiership coach and former Hawthorn champion Leigh Matthews as coach.

METHERELL, Len

PLAYING CAREER: Geelong, 1930-36, 110 games, 117 goals.

COACHING CAREER: Geelong, 1941, 18 games, 3 wins, 15 losses, 0 draws, 0 finals. Winning percentage – 17.

Metherell and brother Jack gave Geelong wonderful service after joining the Cats from WA club Subiaco. Len Metherell, a powerful ruckman, was appointed Geelong coach in 1941 after the Cats had chewed through three coaches – Reg Hickey, Les Laver and Allan Everett – the previous season. He had taken charge of training for a short period when Everett had the flu, but the Cats slid from fourth to tenth in Metherell's only season in charge and won only three games – against St Kilda, North Melbourne and Hawthorn.

MILLER, Allan

PLAYING CAREER: Did not play senior football at VFL/AFL level.

COACHING CAREER: South Melbourne, 1967-68, 38 games, 11 wins, 25 losses, 2 draws, 0 finals. Winning percentage – 29.

South Melbourne shocked the football world when it named its senior coach for the 1967 season following the resignation of captain-coach Bob Skilton. The Swans appointed an "unknown" in Allan Miller, whose coaching experience had been limited to local club Albert Park (for two premierships) and the Swan Under 19s. The South committee believed Miller was the right man to develop young talent, but the Swans finished ninth in both 1967 and 1968 and Miller was replaced by the legendary Norm Smith.

MILLS, Bert

PLAYING CAREER: Hawthorn, 1930-42, 196 games, 60 goals.

COACHING CAREER: Hawthorn, 1940-41, 36 games, 10 wins, 26 losses, 0 draws, 0 finals. Winning percentage – 28.

A great Hawthorn stalwart who played in the ruck or at centre half-back, Mills captained the club several times and won the best and fairest three times. Mills was so loyal to Hawthorn that he rejected offers to play with St Kilda or Fitzroy on the promise of employment in tough times. After winning a newspaper "most popular player" award in 1939, he defeated a field of six candidates to be appointed captain-coach for the 1940 season and guided the Mayblooms to seven wins, equalling their previous best, of 1937. However, the Hawks slid back to the bottom in 1941 with just three win and Mills was replaced by the legendary Roy Cazaly. Mills did not seek reappointment for 1942 and stated that he felt the burden of playing and coaching a weak side was too much for him.

MINOGUE, Danny

PLAYING CAREER: Collingwood, 1911-16, 85 games, 37 goals. Richmond, 1920-25, 95 games, 38 goals. Hawthorn, 1926, 1 game, 2 goals.

COACHING CAREER: Richmond, 1920-25, 105 games, 59 wins, 45 losses, 1 draw, 8 finals, 2 premierships, Winning percentage – 56. Hawthorn, 1926-27, 36 games, 4 wins, 31 losses, 1 draw, 0 finals. Winning percentage – 11. Carlton, 1929-34, 117 games, 85 wins, 32 losses, 0 draws, 9 finals. Winning percentage – 73. St Kilda, 1935-38, 62 games, 34 wins,

28 losses, 0 draws, 0 finals. Winning percentage – 55. Fitzroy, 1940-42, 51 games, 25 wins, 26 losses, 0 draws, 0 finals. Winning percentage – 49.

It is part of football folklore that when Minogue left Collingwood to join Richmond as captain-coach in 1920 that the Magpies turned his photograph at Victoria Park to the wall. Minogue left Collingwood over what he saw as poor treatment to a former teammate and fellow World War I Digger, Jim Sadler. A powerful follower, Minogue captained Collingwood from 1914-16 before serving on the Western Front. Richmond saw him as an ideal leader for its young team and Minogue lived up to all expectations. Former Carlton star Norman Clark had taken the Tigers to the 1919 Grand Final, only for them to go down to Collingwood and Richmond believed Minogue's on-field presence would have made all the difference. Minogue, a man of strict principles and a fierce disciplinarian, lived up to all expectations. He guided Richmond to the 1920-21 premierships and, most galling of all for Collingwood, was that the Tigers defeated the Magpies by 17 points in the 1920 Grand Final. Minogue then was among Richmond's best when the Tigers defeated Carlton by four points in the 1921 Grand Final.

Minogue had four more seasons in charge at Tigerland, with only one of them involving the finals – in 1924 when the Tigers were runners-up to Essendon in a round-robin series. Minogue in 1925 was 34 years of age and although he was restricted to just seven games that season, it did not stop Hawthorn hunting him as captain-coach for 1926. Unfortunately, Minogue was injured in his first match with Hawthorn and forced into playing retirement, with Paddy Burke taking over the club captaincy. Although Minogue worked tirelessly to improve the Hawthorn players' skills, the Mayblooms finished above only the winless North Melbourne in 1926 and collected the wooden spoon the following season. Minogue then spent a season coaching Tasmanian club Newtown before returning to the VFL as non-playing coach of Carlton. He took the Blues into consecutive finals from 1929-31 before they went down to Richmond in the 1932 Grand Final. Carlton's lowest finish in Minogue's six seasons in charge was fifth in 1934 – a tremendous record.

A career coach by then, Minogue crossed to St Kilda in 1935 and went within four match points of taking the Saints into the finals that year, missing out to Richmond. Minogue continued as St Kilda coach to the end of the 1937 season and then was an assistant to former Carlton rover Ansell Clarke. But when Clarke seriously broke a leg and missed several games as coach while in hospital following surgery, Minogue again took charge. Minogue's final VFL coaching position was with Fitzroy, from 1940-42 and many contemporary judges suggested he laid the groundwork for the Maroons' 1944 flag triumph. Minogue, who was a football writer with the Sun-News Pictorial for many years, died in September, 1961, at 69 years of age.

MORIARTY, Geoff

PLAYING CAREER: Fitzroy, 1898-1907, 106 games, 0 goals.

COACHING CAREER: Fitzroy, 1911-12, 36 games, 20 wins, 16 losses, 0 draws, 0 finals. Winning percentage – 56.

Fitzroy's first official coach, Moriarty played in the Maroons' 1899 and 1905 flag sides as a winger/centreman. He won the job following the election of a new administration at the end of 1910. And, in an amazing move, he also was appointed club secretary, a position he held for two years. Fitzroy narrowly missed the finals in Moriarty's two seasons in charge, finishing fifth both times. He was replaced in 1913 by Percy Parratt, who took the Maroons to the 1913 premiership with a Grand Final victory over St Kilda. Moriarty's son Jack became one of the greatest goalkickers on his era, once kicking 12 goals in a match against North Melbourne in 1928.

MORRIS, Mel

PLAYING CAREER: Richmond, 1921-26, 89 games, 148 goals.

COACHING CAREER: Richmond, 1926, 18 games, 9 wins, 9 losses, 0 draws, 0 finals. Winning percentage – 50.

Morris, a talented centreman recruited from Elsternwick and Wesley College, won Richmond's best and fairest in 1922 and was named captain-coach in 1926 after Dan Minogue stepped down. The Tigers finished seventh and Morris was replaced by non-playing coach Frank "Checker" Hughes. Morris later created football history by becoming one of the game's first radio broadcasters. After a successful ABC broadcast of the 1925 Geelong-Collingwood Grand Final, the national broadcaster teamed Morris with former Carlton star Rod McGregor to call games in 1926. Morris ended his football broadcasting career in 1950.

MORRISON, Alby

PLAYING CAREER: Footscray, 1928-38, 1941-42 and 1946, 224 games, 369 goals.

COACHING CAREER: Footscray, 1934-35, 16 games, 4 wins, 12 losses, 0 draws. Winning percentage – 25.

Morrison, a big-hearted key position and ruck utility recruited locally from Kingsville, gave the Bulldogs many years of splendid service and was one of their earliest VFL superstars. He was always willing to put

A. MORRISON.

the club before himself and was appointed captain-coach early in the 1934 season when Footscray replaced Bill Cubbins. The Bulldogs finished ninth and although Morrison started the following season as captain-coach, he was replaced as coach by former Collingwood champion Syd Coventry. Morrison gracefully stepped aside and, despite retaining the captaincy, did not show his hurt and continued to give the Bulldogs great service in a variety of positions. He left the Bulldogs to be captain-coach of VFA club Preston over the 1941-42 seasons and, after enlistment in the RAAF during World War II, returned to Footscray in 1946 for a final VFL season

– at 37 years of age. However, he was far from finished with football as he became captain-coach of Mornington Peninsula club Sorrento and guided this club to the flag in the same year as the Bulldogs won its only VFL flag, in 1954.

MURRAY, Kevin

PLAYING CAREER: Fitzroy, 1955-64 and 1967-74, 333 games, 51 goals.

COACHING CAREER: Fitzroy, 1963-64, 34 games, 0 wins, 34 losses, 0 draws, 0 finals. Winning percentage – 0.

Murray, one of football's greatest identities, is an Australian Football Hall of Fame legend who won the 1969 Brownlow Medal. A wonderfully committed half-back or ruck-rover, Murray took over as Fitzroy coach in 1963, but his two-year tenure coincided with Fitzroy's leanest years. The Lions won only one game in 1963, but Murray missed the victory over Geelong at Brunswick Street because he was on interstate duties and the team that day was coached by Wally Clark. Fitzroy did not win a game in 1964 and Murray was replaced as coach by Bill Stephen. Murray joined East Perth as captain-coach, but returned to the Lions as club captain in 1967 and held this position to 1972 before retiring in 1974. Murray later was captain-coach of VFA club Sandringham.

NASH, Laurie

PLAYING CAREER: South Melbourne, 1933-37 and 1945, 99 games, 246 goals.

COACHING CAREER: South Melbourne, 1953, 18 games, 9 wins, 9 losses, 0 draws, 0 finals. Winning percentage – 50.

A superb centre half-forward or centre half-back, Nash had coached VFA club Camberwell and guided country clubs Wangaratta and Greta to premierships in the one season (1946) before returning to the Swans as coach in 1953. South initially wanted West Australian Johnny Leonard, who had coached the club in 1932, to return after an absence of more than 20 years, but Nash got the job when Leonard indicated he would not leave the west. Nash, told players soon after his appointment: "I learned the game the hard way, boys, and that's the way I intend to teach it to you." Nash, unfortunately, allowed his ego to get the better of him and he told the South committee he expected to guide the club to its first premiership since he was a member of the 1933 flag side. He told the Herald: "I was in South's

last premiership side in 1933; now I expect to be the first old player to coach them to a premiership. With specialised training, I will improve every player 33 and one third per cent." South won nine games in 1953 to finish eighth and the club committee advertised the coaching position for 1954. Although Nash applied for the job, he was overlooked and the position went to another former player, Herbie Matthews.

NEELD, Mark

PLAYING CAREER: Geelong, 1990-93, 48 games, 17 goals; Richmond, 1994-96, 26 games, 16 goals.

COACHING CAREER: Melbourne 2012-, 22 games, 4 wins, 18 losses, 0 draws, 0 finals. Winning percentage – 18.

Neeld was appointed Melbourne coach from the 2012 season and immediately declared that he wanted the Demons to be the "hardest team" in the competition. A teacher, he started his coaching career with Victorian amateur club Old Geelong and, after three years, coached Bellarine League club Ocean Grove to four consecutive premierships from 2000-03. Neeld also coached local Geelong club St Joseph's before being appointed coach of TAC Cup club Western Jets. Neeld was an assistant coach with Collingwood from 2008-11 before winning the senior Melbourne position. His stint with the Demons started disastrously and there was media speculation that the Demons had rushed his appointment. However, Melbourne clarified this by stating it had interviewed Neeld six times. The Demons suffered a string of losses under Neeld in 2012 until they broke through with a six-point victory over Essendon in round 10.

NEESHAM, Gerard

PLAYING CAREER: Sydney Swans, 1982, 9 games, 1 goal.

COACHING CAREER: Fremantle, 1995-98, 88 games, 32 wins, 56 losses, 0 draws, 0 finals. Winning percentage – 36.

Although Neesham played just nine senior AFL games, with the Sydney Swans in 1982, he played 218 games in the WAFL with Swan Districts, East Fremantle and Claremont. He coached Claremont to four premierships and was an obvious choice as Fremantle coach when the Dockers entered the VFL in 1995. Despite having a mediocre playing list, Neesham's possession-type tactics bamboozled many rival coaches and he won himself a reputation as an innovative and daring coach. However, Fremantle's best season

Gerard Neesham.

under Neesham was in 1997 when the Dockers finished twelfth. When the Dockers finished above only the Brisbane Lions in 1998, he was replaced by Damian Drum.

NICHOLLS, John

PLAYING CAREER: Carlton, 1957-74, 328 games, 307 goals.

COACHING CAREER: 1972-75, 95 games, 61 wins, 31 losses, 3 draws, 9 finals, 1 premiership. Winning percentage – 64.

It is part of football folklore that when Carlton officials went to Maryborough to sign Don Nicholls, the family told them they also had to sign younger brother John. It proved to be a wonderful coup as John Nicholls went on to become a Carlton legend and one of the greatest ruckmen the game has seen. Nicholls was captain of the 1968 and 1970 Carlton premiership sides under the coaching of Ron Barassi and was appointed captain-coach when Barassi stepped down at the end of 1971. Nicholls, who won five Carlton best and fairest awards, was a strict disciplinarian and he could stare down any opponent or denigrator. He landed a premiership in his first season in charge, with the Blues defeating Richmond by 27 points in a high-scoring Grand Final. It was a personal triumph for Nicholls as the Tigers had defeated the Blues by 41 points in fhe second semi-final and

John Nicholls.

the Carlton captain-coach subsequently switched his side around to confuse Richmond. And Nicholls kicked six goals. Richmond had its revenge in defeating Nicholls' Carlton in the next year's Grand Final and the Blues slipped to seventh in 1974. Nicholls, who retired as a player during that season, guided the Blues to second position at the end of the 1975 home and away season, but saw his side crash out of the premiership race in going down to North Melbourne by 20 points in a qualifying final. Carlton was shocked on the eve of the 1976 season when Nicholls resigned as coach. He told the

Blues: "I have lost the drive to be coach." He resigned just six days before the start of the season and he was replaced by former Melbourne premiership player Ian Thorogood. Nicholls later coached VFA club Coburg.

NIVEN, Colin

PLAYING CAREER: Fitzroy, 1929-32, 59 games, 26 goals. Melbourne, 1933-35, 44 games, 13 goals.

COACHING CAREER: Fitzroy, 1930-31, 36 games, 11 wins, 25 losses, 0 draws, 0 finals. Winning percentage – 31.

Niven, a fearless follower, joined Fitzroy from Maryborough and was appointed captain-coach in 1930 after just one season and 18 games with the Maroons; he replaced Doug Ringrose, who won just three games as coach in 1929. Niven lifted Fitzroy from eleventh to ninth in his first season, but the Maroons finished tenth in 1931 and Niven was replaced by former Essendon star and coach Frank Maher. Niven continued as a player with Fitzroy in 1932, but then moved to Melbourne and was the Fuchsias' captain over the 1934-35 seasons. Niven, whose brother Ray also played with both Fitzroy and Melbourne, later coached a number of Victorian country clubs, winning a premiership with Donald in 1937 and then coaching Wesburn.

NOLAN, Bernie

PLAYING CAREER: Melbourne, 1904-12, 84 games, 10 goals.

COACHING CAREER: Richmond, 1918, 14 games, 5 wins, 9 losses, 0 draws, 0 finals. Winning percentage – 36.

Nolan was a serviceable ruckman with Melbourne and captained the Fuchsias in 1909. He bobbed up as Richmond coach in 1918 and, after the Tigers finished sixth in an eight-team competition was replaced by former Carlton star Norman Clark. Nolan later became secretary of the Richmond Cricket club.

NOONAN, Paddy

PLAYING CAREER: Fitzroy, 1897-99, 36 games, 7 goals. Carlton, 1901-02, 19 games, 5 goals.

COACHING CAREER: North Melbourne, 1929, 13 games, 1 win, 12 losses, 0 draws, 0 finals. Winning percentage – 8.

Noonan, a small but clever rover, moved to VFA club North Melbourne at the end of his VFL career and played in North's 1903 premiership side. He later coached VFA cub Williamstown and took over as North coach when the Shinboners parted company with former Collingwood star Charlie Tyson early in the 1929 season. North won just one game under Noonan, by 13 points, against Footscray at Arden Street in round 14. North appointed former North star Johnny Lewis as captain-coach for 1930.

NORTHEY, John

PLAYING CAREER: Richmond, 1963-70, 118 games, 192 goals.

COACHING CAREER: Sydney Swans, 1985, 22 games, 6 wins, 16 losses, 0 draws, 0 finals. Winning percentage – 27. Melbourne, 1986-92, 167 games, 90 wins, 76 losses, 1 draw, 13 finals. Winning percentage – 54. Richmond, 1993-95, 67 games, 32 wins, 34 losses, 1 draw, 3 finals. Winning percentage – 48. Brisbane Bears/Lions – 1996-98, 59 games, 29 wins, 28 losses, 2 draws, 4 finals. Winning percentage – 49.

A gifted half-forward, Northey won himself the nickname "Swooper" while playing with Richmond. The Tigers signed him from Western Districts club Derrinallum and he played in Richmond's 1967 and 1969 premiership sides. Northey left the Tigers to coach Sydney club Western Suburbs and also coached in Ballarat as well as a two-year stint as assistant coach at St Kilda. When the Sydney Swans were looking for a senior coach to replace the reluctant Bob Hammond at the end of the 1984 season, they chose Northey, a renowned football teacher with a solid coaching background. The Swans made a good impression in their first games under Northey, but fell away by the end of the 1985 season to finish tenth, with six wins.

Northey, who was popular with players and fans, then became the sacrificial lamb in the competition's first foray into private ownership. After Dr Geoffrey Edelsten's group bought the club licence, Northey was considered too unfashionable and was dumped in favour of former Richmond premiership coach Tom Hafey. However, Northey was too good a coach to be out of a job for long and he was appointed Melbourne coach from 1986. He spent seven seasons with the Demons, taking them to the 1988 Grand Final, only for his young side to be thrashed by a ruthless Hawthorn. Northey had only a handful of stars at Melbourne, but he worked wonders with the material available and, over his seven seasons, took the Demons to five finals series. In fact, their 1987 finals appearances were their first since they won the 1964 flag and there were wild scenes among Melbourne supporters when their side defeated Footscray at the Western Oval to clinch their finals berth.

Northey perhaps is best remembered for waving a finger at ruckman Jim Stynes after an unfortunate incident in the 1987 preliminary final against Hawthorn at Waverley Park. Stynes ran across the mark as Hawthorn's Gary Buckenara was lining up for goal after the final siren and had a 15-metre penalty awarded against him.

The mistake allowed Buckenara to goal for the Hawks to march into the Grand Final and Northey bellowed at the forlorn Stynes "never do that again". His next port of call as a senior coach was his old club Richmond, taking over from Allan Jeans in 1993. Northey in 1995 guided the Tigers to their first finals series since 1982, but then was lured north to coach the Brisbane Bears. Although Northey coached Brisbane from 1996-98, he again was handicapped by lack of player talent, but guided them to third position in 1996, going down to eventual premier North Melbourne (by 38 points) in a preliminary final. The Lions finished eighth the following season, crashing out to St Kilda in the finals. However, Northey then was sacked during the following season and replaced by former Bear player Roger Merrett.

NUNAN, Mick

PLAYING CAREER: Richmond, 1971, 1 game, 3 goals.

COACHING CAREER: Fitzroy, 1996, 14 games, 1 win, 13 losses, 0 draws, 0 finals. Winning percentage – 7.

Although Nunan played just one VFL game with Richmond while on National Service in 1971, he was a champion footballer in South Australia in 259 games with Sturt, Norwood and North Adelaide. He was a highly successful coach and after landing

two premierships with North Adelaide was appointed Fitzroy coach for the 1996 season. The Lions the previous season had sacked club favourite Bernie Quinlan, with Alan McConnell taking over for the rest of the season. Nunan therefore assumed the Fitzroy position at a time when the Lions were down on their heels. They won just one game (against Fremantle) under Nunan amid suggestions the club would be unable to continue. The Lions were declared insolvent and there even was talk that the club would merge with North Melbourne. Nunan claimed he had been "torpedoed" by the merger talk and resigned following a round 14 defeat by Essendon at Optus Oval. He was replaced by McConnell, who assumed caretaker duties for a second time.

Michael Nunan presents Matthew Primus with his Fitzroy jumper.

O'BRIEN, Paddy

PLAYING CAREER: Carlton, 1913-25, 167 games, 7 goals. Footscray, 1925-26, 15 games 0 goals.

COACHING CAREER: Carlton, 1925, 2 games, 0 wins, 2 losses, 0 draws, 0 finals. Winning percentage – 0. Footscray, 1926, 1 game, 0 wins, 0 losses, 0 draws, 0 finals. Winning percentage – 0.

A champion centre half-back, O'Brien was recruited from Yarraville and described as one of the toughest players of his era. He was a regular Victorian representative who captained the Blues in 1920 and 1924 and was appointed the Blues' coach in 1925, with Maurie Beasy as club captain. The players at that time elected the captain and vice-captain and because they overlooked O'Brien for both positions, the Blues decided after two rounds that they felt they had to replace him as coach and the job went to former South Melbourne coach Jim Caldwell. Carlton explained that it could not have a playing coach who did not fill either of the two on-field leadership positions. O'Brien, also a champion heavyweight boxer,

Paddy O'Brien.

played just five games with the Blues in 1925 before moving to Footscray and he coached the Tricolours in one game after coach Jim Cassidy resigned through illness. O'Brien had taken his captaincy duties with Carlton so seriously in 1920 that he took elocution lessons so that he could better address the players. He won medals at the prestigious South Street competition for a Shakespeare recital and was fond of reciting Lord Tennyson's epic poem "The Charge of the Light Brigade" at Carlton functions.

O'DONNELL, Gary

PLAYING CAREER: Essendon, 1987-98, 243 games, 88 goals.

COACHING CAREER: Essendon, 2006, 1 game, 0 wins, 0 losses, 1 draw, 0 finals. Winning percentage – 0.

A wonderfully reliable player after being recruited from North Ringwood, he started his career as a half-back and developed into a fine midfielder. He won Essendon's best and fairest award in the 1993 premiership season and he captained the Bombers over the 1996-97 seasons, O'Donnell on retirement joined the Brisbane Lions' coaching staff, but returned to Windy Hill as an assistant coach in 2005. He took charge of the senior side in a match against Carlton in 2006 when coach Kevin Sheedy was unavailable following a training accident. O'Donnell therefore holds the unique distinction of being the only coach in VFL/AFL history to coach in only one match for a draw. He returned to the Brisbane Lions as an assistant coach late in 2010.

O'DONOHUE, Peter

PLAYING CAREER: Hawthorn, 1942-43 and 1946-52, 109 games, 24 goals.

COACHING CAREER: Hawthorn, 1966, 18 games, 5 wins, 13 losses, 0 draws, 0 finals. Winning percentage – 28.

Recruited from Hawthorn CYMS, O'Donohue was a solid and reliable defender who missed the 1944-45 seasons because of service in the navy. He coached West Perth, Deniliquin and Northcote before being Hawthorn reserves coach and then taking over as Hawthorn coach in 1966 after Graham Arthur had stepped down after two years in charge. Hawthorn at that time was a club in transition as 1961 premiership coach John Kennedy had moved to Stawell in his profession as a schoolteacher in 1964. Hawthorn finished ninth in O'Donohue's only season in charge, with Kennedy returning in 1967.

OGDEN, Percy

PLAYING CAREER: Collingwood, 1905, 4 games, 0 goals. Essendon, 1910-15 and 1918-21, 161 games, 91 goals.

COACHING CAREER: Essendon, 1920-21, 20 games, 3 wins, 15 losses, 2 draws, 0 finals. Winning percentage – 15.

Although rejected by Collingwood after just a handful of games, Ogden played in the

VFA with Essendon Town and Preston before he became a star rover with Essendon. He played in the 1911-12 Essendon premiership sides and represented Victoria. He also was involved in one of football's biggest sensations in 1911 when Fitzroy's George Holden was charged with assault and fined three guineas after punching the Essendon star to the head in a match at Brunswick Street. Ogden went back to Preston when Essendon went into recess during World War I, but returned in 1918 and was appointed captain-coach in 1920 when Jack Worrall stepped down. Essendon finished sixth, but slid to ninth under Ogden in 1921 – the Dons' last season at the East Melbourne Cricket Ground. Ogden therefore had the distinction of being Essendon's captain-coach in its last game at its old home ground. The match, against Fitzroy, was a draw. Ogden later coached VFA club Northcote and had a third stint with Preston, this time as captain-coach.

OLLIVER, Arthur

PLAYING CAREER: Footscray, 1935-50, 272 games, 354 goals.

COACHING CAREER: Footscray, 1943-46 and 1948-50, 131 games, 68 wins, 62 losses, 1 draw, 2 finals. Winning percentage – 52.

A champion ruckman recruited from Footscray Technical School Old Boys, Olliver shared best and fairest honours with

Arthur Olliver.

Norman Ware in 1941 and won it outright in 1944. He was appointed captain-coach to succeed Ware in 1943, but only after his employers blocked his decision to join the RAAF. Footscray finished sixth in his first season in charge, but made the final four in 1944, only to be defeated by Essendon in the first semi-final. Olliver guided the Bulldogs to another series in 1946 and, this time, they went down to Melbourne in the first semi-final. Incredibly, Footscray gave the coaching job to former Carlton and Collingwood player Jim Crowe the following season and the bitterly disappointed Olliver applied for a clearance to Hawthorn. The Bulldogs blocked this move and, after they slipped to ninth in 1947, reappointed Olliver captain-coach for 1948. He again took them into the finals, going down to Essendon in the first semi-final. This was followed by finishes of ninth and tenth, but Olliver was replaced as captain-coach by Charlie Sutton in 1951. Olliver moved to Tasmania and coached New Norfolk before moving to Western Australia and coaching West Perth to a WAFL premiership. He died in May, 1988, at 69 years of age.

OLSSON, Rod

PLAYING CAREER: Hawthorn, 1962-69, 116 games, 64 goals.

COACHING CAREER: Geelong, 1976-79, 91 games, 45 wins, 46 losses, 0 draws, 3 finals. Winning percentage – 49.

Recruited from Old Scotch, Olsson was a tough ruck-rover or half-forward who left Hawthorn to be captain-coach of Tasmanian club Sandy Bay and landed the 1971-72 flags.

Rod Olsson.

He was appointed Geelong's non-playing coach in 1976 to replace Graham Farmer and immediately launched a stricter code of discipline. The Cats finished the home and away season in fourth position and then defeated Footscray by seven points in an elimination final before going down to North Melbourne in the first semi-final. Olsson also took the Cats to the finals in 1978, but they went down to Carlton in an elimination final. When Geelong missed the finals the following season Olsson was replaced as coach by club favourite Bill Goggin.

OPPY, Max

PLAYING CAREER: Richmond, 1942-54, 185 games, 29 goals.

COACHING CAREER: Richmond, 1956, 18 games, 6 wins, 12 losses, 0 draws, 0 finals. Winning percentage – 33.

A tough and relentless defender, Oppy was recruited from Kew Amateurs and was rated best on the ground in Richmond's 1943 Grand Final defeat of Essendon. He had grown up barracking for Essendon as his cousin was Bomber champion Dick Reynolds. When the Tigers sacked Alby Pannam as coach at the end of the 1955 season, they turned to Oppy. The Tiger stalwart later joked that he won the coaching position because no one else wanted it. In many ways, Oppy was an interim coach and was replaced by Alan McDonald after just one season in which the Tigers won six games and finished tenth.

Max Oppy, a Tiger trough and through.

ORCHARD, Billy

PLAYING CAREER: Geelong, 1906 and 1908-15, 112 games, 67 goals.

COACHING CAREER: Geelong, 1914, 19 games, 11 wins, 7 losses, 1 draw, 1 final. Winning percentage – 58.

Orchard, recruited from Geelong Grammar School, was a highly skilled centreman or small forward who succeeded Bill Eason as captain-coach in 1914. The Geelong players elected Orchard their leader just before the opening round match against Essendon at the Corio Oval and he immediately appealed to them to "pull together and to always play the game". Geelong finished the home and away season in fourth position and then went down to South Melbourne in a semi-final. Orchard continued as captain (with Geelong not having a coach) in 1915, but enlisted in the AIF in July and played just eight games. Orchard might have enlisted as a private, but quickly rose through the ranks to become a captain. He twice was wounded in action, once by a bayonet to the leg and the other a shrapnel splinter in his right eye. The eye wound severely affected Orchard's sight. South Melbourne's Les Turner, in one of his regular letters to the Emerald Hill Record, wrote about Orchard's wound and described the former Geelong star as "a fine chap among the boys". Orchard, who won a Military Cross for bravery, returned to Australia in 1919 and later became a VFL umpire.

PAGAN, *Denis*

PLAYING CAREER: North Melbourne, 1967-74, 120 games, 6 goals. South Melbourne, 1975-76, 23 games, 0 goals.

COACHING CAREER: North Melbourne, 1993-2002, 240 games, 150 wins, 90 losses, 0 draws, 22 finals, 2 premierships. Winning percentage – 63. Carlton, 2003-07, 104 games, 25 wins, 77 losses, 2 draws, 0 finals. Winning percentage – 24.

Pagan started his career with the Carlton Under 19s but failed to win promotion to the senior side and crossed to North Melbourne and developed into a reliable back pocket. After he played in North's losing 1974 Grand Final side he crossed to South Melbourne for two seasons and later played suburban football with Oakleigh Districts before coaching VFA club Yarraville. Pagan served a long coaching apprenticeship, guiding North Under 19s to five flags and the Essendon reserves to the 1992 premiership. He was appointed North's senior coach when the Roos dumped Wayne Schimmelbusch during the pre-season series and immediately took North

to third position, only to crash out of the premiership race in an elimination final defeat by West Coast. Pagan, a strict disciplinarian but a wonderful football teacher and communicator, took the Roos to a preliminary final defeat by Geelong the following season and repeated this effort in 1995 when Carlton defeated North in a preliminary final. However, Pagan's greatest triumph was just around the corner as North defeated the Sydney Swans by 43 points in the 1996 Grand Final – the Roos' first premiership since 1977.

Pagan was able to keep North at or near the top over the following seasons and, in 1999, landed another premiership when the Roos defeated Carlton by 35 points in the Grand Final. North, under Pagan's coaching, played tight, disciplined football and used champion centre half-forward Wayne Carey to perfection in allowing him plenty of room. The tactic was known as "Pagan's Paddock". North's only poor season under Pagan was in 2001 when it missed the finals for the only time in a decade. Pagan left North at the end of the 2002 season and, in a shock football move, was snapped up as Carlton coach to replace Wayne Brittain.

Denis Pagan celebrates a North flag.

Pagan immediately launched a clean-sweep of the Blues' playing personnel, but was hamstrung by draft restrictions imposed by salary cap breaches. Pagan, despite impeccable credentials, struggled to lift the Blues. His only success was guiding the Blues to the 2005 pre-season title, with a best season's finish of eleventh in 2004. Carlton collected the wooden spoon in both 2005 and 2006 and he was dumped after the Blues suffered a string of losses in 2007 and was replaced by Brett Ratten. Pagan was never fully accepted by Carlton fans and he once suggested that coaching Carlton was "the worst job" he'd ever had.

After a brief stint on the North Melbourne board, Pagan walked away from football and went into real estate with son Ryan, who played three games for the Roos under his father's coaching in 2000.

PANNAM, Albert

PLAYING CAREER: Collingwood, 1933-43 and 1945, 181 games, 453 goals. Richmond, 1947, 2 games, 6 goals.

COACHING CAREER: Richmond, 1953-55, 54 games, 22 wins, 31 losses, 1 draw, 0 finals. Winning percentage – 41.

A member of the famous Pannam football family, his father Charles E. Pannam played for Collingwood and coached South. He was one of the best rovers of his era and played in the Magpies' 1935-36 premiership sides and captained Collingwood in 1945. Pannam crossed to Richmond as reserves coach and made a two-game comeback with the Tigers in 1947. He played more than 100 games for the Richmond reserves and was the logical successor to Jack Dyer when Captain Blood stood down as coach at the end of the 1952 season. The Tigers finished tenth, fifth and sixth in three seasons under Pannam and he was replaced by Max Oppy in 1956. He also guided the Tigers to a 1954 lightning premiership and he later coached VFA club Oakleigh to a premiership.

Charlie E. Pannam.

PANNAM, Charlie E.

PLAYING CAREER: Collingwood, 1917-22, 97 games, 12 goals. South Melbourne, 1926-28, 45 games, 31 goals.

COACHING CAREER: South Melbourne, 1923-28, 108 games, 54 wins, 54 losses, 0 draws, 5 finals. Winning percentage – 50.

The son of early Collingwood legend Charlie H. Pannam, he was a fine centreman, but rocked Victoria Park to its foundations when he announced that he had been appointed captain-coach of South Melbourne from 1923. He was just 25 years of age and Collingwood was so horrified it blocked his move. Pannam therefore spent three years on the sidelines before Collingwood eventually relented and cleared him to play with South from 1926. With Pannan as non-playing coach over his first three seasons with South, star utility Paddy Scanlan captained the Southerners. South made the finals in 1923 (third) and 1924 (fourth under a round-robin finals series) and eighth in

1925. With Pannam eventually cleared to play in 1926, Scanlan agreed to step down as captain and said: "It is only right that the coach be captain of the side." South improved slightly when Pannam returned to the playing field in 1926 to finish fifth. South slid to sixth in 1927 and tenth the following season before Pannam was replaced by Jim Caldwell and then, late in the 1929 season, by Fred Fleiter. Pannam, a strict disciplinarian, was the first man to coach South for more than three years and held the club's record for games as coach (108) until Ian Stewart coached the club in 111 games from 1976-77 and 1979-81. The record now is held by Paul Roos, with 202 games from 2002-10.

PANNAM, Charlie H.

PLAYING CAREER: Collingwood, 1897-1907, 179 games, 111 goals. Richmond, 1908, 14 games, 22 goals.

COACHING CAREER: Richmond, 1912, 18 games, 3 wins, 15 losses, 0 draws, 0 finals. Winning percentage – 17.

Pannam, recruited locally, was one of Collingwood's earliest champions after starting with the Magpies in its VFA days, in 1894. A clever winger/forward, Pannam played in Collingwood's 1902-03 premiership sides and captained the Magpies in 1905. He retired after just two games in 1907 but was lured to then VFA club Richmond. He also coached a combined Ballarat side against the VFL that season and, when it was announced Richmond would join the VFL in 1908, Pannam expected to be named coach. The job went to former Collingwood teammate Dick Condon and Pannam walked out on the Tigers and later coached VFA club Preston. His turn at Richmond came in 1912 when he was appointed non-playing coach but, with just three wins that season, Pannam was replaced by former Fitzroy star Ern Jenkins. Pannam's sons Charlie and Albert and grandsons Lou and Ron Richards played for the Magpies.

PARKIN, David

PLAYING CAREER: Hawthorn, 1961-74, 211 games, 21 goals.

COACHING CAREER: Hawthorn, 1977-80, 94 games, 57 wins, 37 losses, 0 draws, 6 finals, 1 premiership. Winning percentage – 61. Carlton, 1981-85 and 1991-2000, 355 games, 219 wins, 134 losses, 2 draws, 27 finals, 3 premierships. Winning percentage – 62. Fitzroy, 1986-88, 69 games, 30 wins, 39 losses, 0 draws, 3 finals. Winning percentage – 43.

Parkin, a wonderfully reliable back pocket, grew up barracking for Melbourne and was recruited from Melbourne High School. He won the Hawks' best and fairest

David Parkin.

in 1965, was club captain from 1969-73 and captained the 1971 Hawthorn premiership side. A great football thinker, Parkin coached WA club Subiaco after he left Hawthorn as a player and was always seen as the logical successor to John Kennedy as Hawk coach. He took over from the Hawthorn legend in 1977, the year after the Hawks had won their second premiership. The Hawks were defeated by North Melbourne in the preliminary final, but bounced back in 1978 to defeat the Roos in the Grand Final. Parkin temporarily was king of Glenferrie, only for finishes of seventh and eighth to follow.

Hawthorn announced just after the 1980 Grand Final that it had appointed St Kilda's premiership coach Allan Jeans as its new coach and, just days later, Carlton announced Parkin as its new coach. Parkin immediately launched a new era of success at Princes Park through his team ethic, discipline and shrewd football brain. The Blues finished second on the ladder in 1980, but crashed out of the premiership race in straight sets. It spurred the Blues to even greater efforts in 1981 and, after topping the ladder, defeated Collingwood in the Grand Final. Parkin again had proven his coaching ability and the Blues won back-to-back flags in defeating Richmond in the 1982 Grand Final. Despite his enormously impressive coaching record, Parkin was sacked after the Blues went down to North Melbourne in the 1985 elimination final.

Carlton's decision seemed inexplicable and lowly Fitzroy swooped to sign him as coach for 1986. Ironically, The Age's Ron Carter during the season wrote that Carlton and Fitzroy would switch coaches, with Parkin joining the Lions and Robert Walls moving to the Blues. Both clubs denied the suggestion, but it turned out to be prophetic. Parkin, despite extremely limited resources with Fitzroy, lifted the Lions to the 1986 finals only for them to go down to Hawthorn in a preliminary final. Although Fitzroy slid down the ladder from there,

Parkin's record again was impressive. Parkin was invited back to Carlton in 1991 and, despite the Blues finishing eleventh and then seventh in his first two seasons back, he led them another flag in 1995 and Grand Final losses to Essendon (1993) and North Melbourne (1999). Parkin in 2000 indicated that he would retire at the end of the season and groomed successor Wayne Brittain and was often happy to take a back seat in matches.

PARRATT, Percy

PLAYING CAREER: Fitzroy, 1908-17 and 1920-23, 196 games, 202 goals.

COACHING CAREER: Fitzroy, 1913-15 and 1920-21, 91 games, 62 wins, 26 losses, 3 draws, 6 finals, 1 premiership. Winning percentage – 62. Carlton, 1924, 16 games, 5 wins, 10 losses, 1 draw, 0 finals. Winning percentage – 31. Geelong, 1935, 18 games, 6 wins, 11 losses, 1 draw. Winning percentage – 33.

A champion forward after being recruited from the Rose of Northcote club, Parratt was appointed playing Fitzroy coach in 1913 even though Bill Walker was club captain. Parratt guided the Maroons to a Grand Final victory over St Kilda and was named one of his side's best players. Parratt was named club captain the following year, so therefore was captain-coach over the

Percy Parratt coached three clubs.

1914-15 seasons, taking Fitzroy to third in both seasons. He was replaced by George Holden in 1916, but played in Fitzroy's premiership that season before enlisting in the AIF. Parratt therefore missed the 1918-19 seasons before returning to Fitzroy as captain-coach in 1920 and taking the Maroons to fourth and then fifth before being replaced as coach in 1922 by former South Melbourne star Vic Belcher. Fitzroy won the 1922 flag with Parratt kicking three goals from a half-forward flank against

Collingwood. Parratt retired in 1923, but was non-playing coach of Carlton in 1924. In his only season at Princes Park, the Blues finished seventh. Parratt then coached country clubs Castlemaine and Colac and, while he was living in Colac, was asked to return to the VFL coaching scene with Geelong. He coached the Cats in 1935, for a ninth finish. Parratt died in May, 1971, at 84 years of age.

PATERSON, A.J. 'Jack'

PLAYING CAREER: Did not play at senior VFL/AFL level.

COACHING CAREER: St Kilda, 1938, 1 game, 0 wins, 1 loss, 0 draws, 0 finals. Winning percentage – 0.

Paterson, known as "Banjo", was St Kilda's head trainer for many years and when coach Ansell Clarke was rushed to St Vincent's Hospital with appendicitis before the round nine, 1938, game against Melbourne at the Junction Oval, Paterson was asked to address the players. He told them in what was described as "a vigorous speech" that they had to play with tremendous determination. Melbourne defeated St Kilda by 16 points and, at a meeting the following day, the committee asked reserves coach Dan Minogue to fill in while Clarke recovered. Paterson retired as St Kilda's head trainer in 1942 because of ill-health.

PATTERSON, Mike

PLAYING CAREER: Richmond, 1959-69, 152 games, 73 goals.

COACHING CAREER: St Kilda, 1978-80, 46 games, 14 wins, 31 losses, 1 draw, 0 finals. Winning percentage – 30. Richmond, 1984, 22 games, 10 wins, 12 losses, 0 draws, 0 finals. Winning percentage – 45.

A feared ruckman, Patterson was a great protector at Richmond who played in the Tigers' 1967 premiership side. He moved to North Adelaide as captain-coach in 1970 and guided the Roosters to the 1971-72 SANFL flags. Patterson's resume was so impressive that South Melbourne offered him its coaching position, but he rejected all overtures until he took over from Brownlow Medal winner Ross Smith at St Kilda in 1978. He inherited a poor playing list but lifted the Saints from the bottom of the ladder to sixth position in his first season in charge. The Saints were unlucky to miss the finals as they finished just two match points behind fifth-placed Geelong. However, St Kilda slumped to the bottom again in 1979 and, after defeats by Melbourne and Hawthorn in the opening two rounds of the 1980 season, he was replaced by Alex Jesaulenko, who had joined the Saints as a player after being captain-coach of the 1979 Carlton premiership

Mike Patterson.

side. Patterson returned to Richmond in 1984 as coach but, after the Tigers finished eighth, he was replaced by Paul Sproule. He died in April, 2002, at just 61 years of age.

PEMBERTON, Jack

PLAYING CAREER: Richmond, 1908, 3 games, 0 goals.

COACHING CAREER: North Melbourne, 1931, 8 games, 0 wins, 8 losses, 0 draws, 0 finals. Winning percentage – 0.

After Pemberton played three VFL games with Richmond in 1908, he moved to VFA club North Melbourne and became a club stalwart, retiring as a player in 1914.

He took over as coach with eight games left in the 1931 season following the departure of former Carlton star Norman Clark. Pemberton, born in Colac, also was the Royal Melbourne Show's Master of the Ring for many years and was a well-known dog-racing starter, as well as a stipendiary steward for the Victorian Athletic League.

PIANTO, Peter

PLAYING CAREER: Geelong, 1951-57, 121 games, 144 goals.

COACHING CAREER: Geelong, 1966-70, 105 games, 70 wins, 34 losses, 1 draw, 7 finals. Winning percentage – 67.

Geelong recruited Pianto from Eaglehawk and he proved himself to be one of the best rovers of his era. He played in the Cats' 1951-52 premiership sides and won the club best and fairest the following year. He surprised Geelong at the end of the 1957 season when he accepted the position as captain-coach of country club Coragulac at just 27 years of age. Pianto later coached WA club Claremont for three years and rejoined Geelong as senior coach in 1966, succeeding 1963 premiership coach and former teammate Bob Davis. Pianto was Geelong coach over five seasons and was unlucky not to land a flag with the Cats as they went down by just nine points to Richmond in the

1967 Grand Final. Geelong made the finals in four of Pianto's five seasons, missing out only in his final season of 1970 when it finished fifth. Pianto later ran a sports store in Colac and died in February, 2008.

PLUMMER, Elton

PLAYING CAREER: Essendon, 1934 and 1936-44, 141 games, 1 goal.

COACHING CAREER: Essendon, 1944, 7 games, 3 wins, 3 losses, 1 draw, 0 finals. Winning percentage – 43.

A courageous and reliable back pocket specialist recruited from VFA club Preston, "Duffy" Plummer played in the Dons' 1942 premiership side. He coached Essendon in seven games during the 1944 season when captain-coach Dick Reynolds was unavailable because of appendicitis. Plummer the following season moved to VFA club Brunswick as captain-coach.

PRIMUS, Matthew

PLAYING CAREER: Fitzroy, 1996, 20 games, 5 goals. Port Adelaide, 1997-2005, 137 games, 76 goals.

COACHING CAREER: Port Adelaide, 2010-12, 47 games, 13 wins, 34 losses, 0 draws, 0 finals. Winning percentage – 28.

A big-hearted ruckman in his playing career, Primus was named Port Adelaide captain in 2001, but missed the Power's 2004 flag triumph because of a knee reconstruction. He was born to coach as his grandfather was legendary Geelong mentor Reg Hickey. Primus took over as Power coach following Mark Williams' departure with seven rounds to play in 2010. Port won five of those seven games and Primus was named coach for the following season. However, the Power won just three games that season and avoided the wooden spoon only on percentage. He and the Power parted company with just four rounds to play in 2012 after a disastrous loss to AFL newcomer Greater Western Sydney. Primus after that match was asked about his coaching future and replied: "We'll find out I suppose." He joined Gold Coast as an assistant coach at the end of 2012.

QUADE, Rick

PLAYING CAREER: South Melbourne, 1970-80, 164 games, 111 goals.

COACHING CAREER: Sydney Swans, 1982-84, 57 games, 25 wins, 32 losses, 0 draws, 0 finals. Winning percentage – 44.

A big-hearted ruck-rover recruited from country zone club Ariah Park (NSW), Quade captained the Swans from 1977-79 and was earmarked as successor to coach Ian Stewart for the 1982 season after serving one year as chairman of selectors. However, the 1981 season proved the most divisive in club history because of the club's proposed move to Sydney. When the Keep South at South movement took control of the club it appointed former champion half-back John Rantall as coach. However, with the internal war still rumbling, Rantall graciously agreed to step aside and Quade therefore became the Swans' first coach in Sydney. It was a traumatic era for the Swans, especially as the VFL gave the club little assistance for the big move. Despite poor training facilities and lack of equipment, Quade guided the Swans to the night series premiership in his first season as coach. The Swans finished seventh in 1982 but, as difficulties mounted, they slipped to

Rick Quade, Sydney's first coach.

eleventh the following season. Then, in 1984, Quade succumbed to serious health problems and was replaced mid-season by temporary coach Tony Franklin (one game) and then South Australian Bob Hammond. Quade later returned to the club for a second stint as chairman of selectors and then as a director.

QUINLAN, Bernie

PLAYING CAREER: Footscray, 1969-77, 177 games, 241 goals. Fitzroy, 1978-86, 189 games, 576.

COACHING CAREER: Fitzroy, 1995, 19 games, 2 wins, 17 losses, 0 draws, 0 finals. Winning percentage – 11.

A champion full-forward who shared Brownlow Medal honours with South Melbourne's Barry Round in 1981, Quinlan was on a hiding to nothing when he put his hand up to coach Fitzroy in 1995. The Lions had finished above only the Sydney Swans under Robert Shaw the previous season and were desperately short of playing talent. Quinlan's tenure started disastrously as Fitzroy was scoreless over the first half in an opening round match against Essendon at the Western Oval and the Lions eventually went down by 74 points. The Lions defeated St Kilda by 11 points at Waverley Park in round six and had a shock 33-point victory over

Bernie Quinlan.

Adelaide at Football Park in round eight before slumping to defeat after defeat. Fitzroy hit rock bottom at the Western Oval in round 19 when it went down by 126 points to the Sydney Swans, with Swan full-forward Tony Lockett kicking 16 goals. Fitzroy reacted by dumping Quinlan and replacing him with reserves coach Alan McConnell. Quinlan was bitterly disappointed with the club decision to replace him and said at the time: "At least I had a crack at it."

T. QUINN

QUINN, Tom

PLAYING CAREER: Geelong, 1931-40, 168 games, 169 goals.

COACHING CAREER: Geelong, 1946-48,

57 games, 22 wins, 35 losses, 0 draws, 0 finals. Winning percentage – 39.

Quinn caught Geelong's eye when he starred for South Australia at the 1930 Carnival. A chunky rover, he played in Geelong's 1931 and 1937 premiership sides and twice won the club best and fairest award, in 1936 and 1937. After serving Geelong on the committee, Quinn defeated a field of four other applicants (including former Geelong premiership teammate Les Hardiman) for the position of senior coach. He was appointed just three months before the start of the new season, but vowed to have his side fitter than it had since resuming in the VFL in 1944 after a hiatus of two years because of World War II. Immediately before Geelong's first game of the 1946 season, against Melbourne at the Punt Road Oval, he told his players that they had to have the determination to win. Melbourne defeated Geelong by 46 points and the Cats finished the season in tenth position with just four wins. Geelong retained Quinn's services in 1947 and explained that it wanted "continuity" with its coaches. Geelong finished a creditable seventh, but when the Cats slid to ninth (with seven wins) in 1948, Geelong returned to Red Hickey as coach.

RADEMACHER, Arthur

PLAYING CAREER: South Melbourne, 1913-20, 101 games, 0 goals.

COACHING CAREER: Hawthorn, 1933, 4 games, 1 win, 3 losses, 0 draw, 0 finals. Winning percentage – 25.

Rademacher was a small defender recruited from Leopold. He played in South Melbourne's 1918 premiership side and later was captain-coach of Hawthorn in the VFA. Rademacher then found himself Hawthorn's VFL coach in 1933 under unusual circumstances. Hawthorn had appointed St Kilda's Fred Phillips as coach that season, but he died of blood poisoning before the start of the season. He had had a boil on his arm and the dye from a football jumper infected the wound. Hawthorn was left without a coach and chased former Collingwood star Bill Twomey. Rademacher therefore stepped in until Twomey became available. The former South star coached the Mayblooms to a victory over St Kilda in the opening round, but Hawthorn then went down to Carlton, North Melbourne and Footscray over the next three rounds.

RANKIN, Cliff

PLAYING CAREER: Geelong, 1915 and 1919-28, 153 games, 400 goals.

COACHING CAREER: Geelong, 1925-27, 57 games, 45 wins, 12 losses, 0 draws, 4 finals, 1 premiership. Winning percentage – 79.

Rankin will for ever be known as Geelong's first premiership coach, in 1925. Yet Rankin's football career had barely started in 1915 when he enlisted in the AIF and missed three VFL seasons while serving in France. A champion forward, Rankin was the centre of controversy in 1923 when brother Bert was dumped for a semi-final against Fitzroy even though he was club captain. Cliff Rankin pulled out of the Geelong side, stating that he "would not do himself or the team justice" because he would not be mentally prepared for the big match. Rankin continued with Geelong and was appointed captain-coach in 1925. Geelong finished on top of the ladder with just two defeats, but went down to Melbourne in a semi-final. As minor premier, Geelong had the right to challenge the winner of the Melbourne-Collingwood preliminary final, which the Magpies won by 37 points. Rankin, who usually played at full-forward, named himself on a forward flank for the Grand Final, convinced this unusual move would unsettle the Magpies. He was right as he kicked five goals in Geelong's 10-point triumph. Geelong crashed out of the 1926 premiership race through a semi-final loss to Essendon and, after Collingwood defeated Geelong in a 1927 semi-final, Rankin stepped down and was replaced by Tom Fitzmaurice.

RATTEN, Brett

PLAYING CAREER: Carlton, 1990-2003, 255 games, 117 goals.

COACHING CAREER: Carlton, 2007-12, 120 games, 60 wins, 59 defeats, 1 draw, 4 finals. Winning percentage – 49.

A hard-working centreman, Ratten played with wonderful commitment after working his way through the ranks and won the club best and fairest in the 1995 premiership season. He started his coaching career as an assistant at Melbourne before spending a season with suburban club Norwood. Ratten was appointed an assistant Carlton coach under Denis Pagan in 2007 and was handed the senior position 17 rounds into the season following Pagan's dismissal after a 117-point thumping by the Brisbane Lions. He was appointed coach in his own right in 2008 and immediately set about rebuilding the team. The Blues made the finals each season from 2009-11 and there was talk of a premiership in 2012. Injuries cruelled the Blues but, with just about a full list, they crashed out of finals reckoning when Gold Coast pulled off one of the shocks of the season in defeating them by 12 points at Metricon Stadium, virtually ending Ratten's tenure at Princes Park. Carlton the following week announced that Ratten would not be coach in 2013, even though he had a year to run on his contract. He coached the Blues in their final round defeat by St Kilda and likened his dismissal to the falling of a guillotine. Ratten was gracious in his departure and even wrote to Carlton members to say: "I wish to thank you, as a Carlton member, for lending me your support throughout. I urge you now to get behind the new coach and the team. Because it's all about 'team'."

RATTRAY, Gordon

PLAYING CAREER: Fitzroy, 1917, 1919-24 and 1928, 87 games, 65 goals.

COACHING CAREER: Fitzroy, 1928 and 1937-39, 72 games, 25 wins, 46 losses, 1 draw, 0 finals. Winning percentage – 35. Melbourne, 1924, 16 games, 4 wins, 12 losses, 0 draw, 0 finals. Winning percentage – 25.

Rattray was recruited from Wesley College and made his debut with Fitzroy at 18 years of age in 1917 before serving in World War I. A classy forward, he was a regular Victorian representative who played in Fitzroy's 1922 premiership side. However, he shocked the football world in 1924 when he was appointed non-playing coach of Melbourne, without a clearance. Amazingly, he returned to Fitzroy late in the season to play in a semi-final against Richmond before moving on to VFA club Brighton. Rattray returned to Fitzroy as captain-coach in 1928, but retired as a player after just five games. Fitzroy won only seven games to finish eighth and he was replaced by former Brighton teammate Doug Ringrose as captain-coach. However, he returned to Brunswick Street as non-playing coach in 1937, with the Maroons finishing seventh, tenth and eighth in his three seasons in charge before he was replaced in 1940 by Dan Minogue.

RAWLINGS, Jade

PLAYING CAREER: Hawthorn, 1996-2003, 116 games, 62 goals. Western Bulldogs, 2004-05, 29 games, 32 goals. Kangaroos, 2006, 3 games, 2 goals.

COACHING CAREER: Richmond, 2009, 11 games, 3 wins, 7 loses, 1 draw, 0 finals. Winning percentage – 27.

A talented key position player in his playing days, Rawlings joined Richmond as an assistant coach on retirement and coached VFL affiliate club Coburg Tigers. He took over as Richmond's senior coach when Terry Wallace stepped down halfway through the 2009 season. Rawlings guided the Tigers to a 15-point win over West Coast at the MCG in his first game in charge, only for Richmond to fall away with just two more wins and a draw over the rest of the season to finish above only Melbourne. After Richmond appointed Damien Hardwick as coach from 2010, Rawlings spent two seasons as an assistant coach with the Brisbane Lions before filling a similar role with Melbourne.

REYNOLDS, Dick

PLAYING CAREER: Essendon, 1933-51, 320 games, 442 goals.

COACHING CAREER: Essendon, 1939-60, 415 games, 276 wins, 133 losses, 6 draws, 37 finals, 4 premierships. Winning percentage – 67.

Essendon's greatest identity, Reynolds originally wanted to play with Carlton and when the Blues rejected him, he went to Windy Hill. The boy from local club Woodlands went on to become the greatest rover of his era and won three Brownlow Medals (1934 and 1937-38). He was appointed co-coach, with former player Harry Hunter, when Jack Baggott quit as coach during the 1939 season. Reynolds then took over the role of captain-coach in his own right the following season and held the coaching position until the end of the 1960 season, even though he retired as a player at the end of 1950 and then making a brief comeback during the finals series the following year.

Reynolds was the heart and soul of Essendon for almost 30 years and the man Bomber fans revered as "King Dick" inspired his team over 224 games as captain. He led from the front and, when he was appointed captain-coach in 1940, he was just 25 years of age. Under "King

Dick Reynolds was known as "King Richard".

Dick's" reign as captain-coach, Essendon won four flags, in 1942, 1946 and 1949-50. He was acknowledged as the best player on the ground in the 1942 Grand Final defeat of Richmond and was one of his team's best in the 63-point defeat of Melbourne in the 1946 Grand Final. Reynolds announced his retirement as a player on the morning of the 38-point defeat of North Melbourne in the 1950 Grand Final.

The Essendon champion wrote in The Argus of September 23, 1950: "I've played for Essendon for over half my lifetime, but I've lost that yard – the extra yard I used to have over the other fellow – and I know it's time for me to get out. It was one of the hardest decisions I have ever made ... The game itself has changed during the years. It's more scientific now; it's faster and it's better ... You have to keep learning.

In my own last few years I've copied good players and tried to adapt their best points to my own game ... During my time as captain and coach I've tried never to let anything but football ability influence me in judging players. I think my teammates know that."

Reynolds continued as coach but made a brief playing comeback for the losing (to Geelong) 1951 Grand Final when Essendon had been savaged by injuries. Although he guided Essendon to four flags as captain-coach, Reynolds' record as non-playing coach was less impressive as the Bombers failed to win another flag under his stewardship, even though they were runners-up in 1951, 1957 and 1959. Reynolds' coaching was criticised in his final seasons, with suggestions that he was out of touch with the latest football developments. He therefore retired at the end of the 1960 season and was replaced by former champion goalkicker John Coleman. Reynolds, who was named captain of the Essendon Team of the Century, coached South Australian club West Torrens before returning to Windy Hill as a committeeman. He died in 2002.

RICHARDS, Ron

PLAYING CAREER: Collingwood, 1947-56, 143 games, 114 goals.

COACHING CAREER: Collingwood, 1974, 2 games, 2 wins, 2 losses, 0 draws, 0 finals. Winning percentage – 100.

The brother of Lou Richards, he was a clever small man who played on a wing in the Magpies' 1953 premiership side. On retirement, he coached suburban club East Hawthorn before moving back to Victoria Park as coach of the Under 19s and then the reserves. Richards was in charge of the senior side for two games when regular coach Neil Mann was unavailable and also served the Magpies for many years as a selector.

RICHARDSON, Barry

PLAYING CAREER: Richmond, 1965-74, 125 games, 134 goals.

COACHING CAREER: Richmond,1976 and 1977-78, 47 games, 25 wins, 20 losses, 2 draws, 2 finals. Winning percentage – 53.

Richardson, recruited from St Pat's, Ballarat, was an outstanding full-back who could pinch-hit at full-forward. He once kept champion Hawthorn full-forward goalless and played in the 1967, 1969 and 1974 Tiger premiership sides. After standing in for coach Tom Hafey in one game in 1976, he controversially was handed the senior job at Hafey's expense the following season. Richmond made the finals in 1977 but after defeating South Melbourne in the elimination final crashed to North Melbourne in the first semi-final. When

Barry Richardson.

1913-14, 16 games, 11 goals. St Kilda, 1921, 5 games, 1 goal.

COACHING CAREER: South Melbourne, 1909 and 1912, 41 games, 30 wins, 11 losses, 0 draws, 5 finals, 1 premiership. Winning percentage – 73. Richmond, 1914-16, 47 games, 18 wins, 29 losses, 0 draws, 1 final. Winning percentage – 38. St Kilda, 1920-21, 27 games, 5 wins, 21 losses, 1 draw, 0 finals. Winning percentage – 19.

Ricketts, one of the best rovers of his era, played most of his early football in the VFA with Richmond and joined

Richmond slipped to seventh the following season, Richardson was replaced by Tony Jewell. He later filled support coaching roles with Melbourne, West Coast, Geelong, Carlton and Footscray. It was while he was with Melbourne that he played a big part in the recruitment of Dubliner Jim Stynes. Richardson briefly was Richmond Football Club president and also coached amateur club Old Xaverians.

RICKETTS, Charlie

PLAYING CAREER: South Melbourne, 1906-12, 82 games, 47 goals. Richmond,

South Melbourne in 1906. He went on achieve immortal club fame as South's first premiership leader. South decided in 1909 that it wanted to follow Carlton's example with John Worrall of having a designated coach. Ricketts therefore was named captain-coach and lifted the Southerners from fifth to top of the ladder. South then defeated Collingwood by 21 points in a semi-final and then Carlton by two points in the Grand Final, with Ricketts kicking one of his side's four goals. Football scribe "Markwell" later wrote of Ricketts: "Consummate skill in leadership on the field belongs to few men. It would, perhaps, be an exaggeration to say that captain Ricketts is the possessor of such skill." South then was rocked early the following year when Ricketts informed the club that he was seriously ill and did not know whether he could play at all in 1910. South therefore appointed Bill Thomas as captain-coach. Ricketts managed one game and continued with South to the end of the 1912 season, when he again was captain-coach. South went down to Essendon by 14 points in the Grand Final. It was Ricketts' last game with the Southerners as he returned to Richmond, this time as captain-coach in 1914. He had three seasons in charge, but the Tigers made only one finals appearance under him – and that was in bizarre circumstances as Richmond finished third in a four-team competition and then crashed to Carlton in a semi-final. Ricketts was appointed non-playing coach of St Kilda in 1920 but, after the Saints finished on the bottom with just two wins, he made a brief (five games) comeback in 1921 when the Saints finished above only Essendon. Ricketts then was replaced by Dave McNamara. Ricketts died in September, 1928, at just 43 years of age. In a Sporting Globe feature published in 1936, it was noted: "As a captain, there were few with better leadership qualities."

RIDLEY, Ian

PLAYING CAREER: Melbourne, 1954-61, 130 games, 228 goals.

COACHING CAREER: Melbourne, 1971-73, 66 games, 28 wins, 37 losses, 1 draw, 0 finals. Winning percentage – 42.

Few men have given Melbourne greater service, on and off the field, than Ridley. He joined the Demons from Hamilton Imperials and developed into a classy rover even though he had poor eyesight. He played in five Melbourne premiership sides and coached suburban club Ringwood before coaching the Demon reserves. Ridley succeeded former premiership captain John Beckwith as coach in 1971 and although he did not have the playing talent for success, he got the best out of his men. The Demons finished seventh, eighth and then tenth in his three seasons

Ian Ridley.

in charge and was replaced in 1974 by former South Melbourne champion Bob Skilton. Ridley became a football writer with a Sunday newspaper and then served Melbourne as club president. He sometimes was seen wandering parkland surrounding the MCG whenever his beloved Demons were involved in a tight finish. Unfortunately, his presidency coincided with the push to merge with Hawthorn, yet it often is forgotten that the Melbourne members voted 4679 to 4229 in favour of the merger, only for Hawthorn members to reject the proposal. Ridley died in November, 2008.

RILEY, Mark

PLAYING CAREER: Did not play at senior VFL/AFL level.

COACHING CAREER: Melbourne, 2007, 9 games, 3 wins, 6 losses, 0 draws, 0 finals. Winning percentage – 33.

Riley played in the WAFL with Claremont and was an assistant coach with the club before being appointed senior coach and guiding it to the 1994 Grand Final. He spent three years with Fremantle as a development coach before joining Melbourne as an assistant coach in 2003. Riley took over as the Demons' caretaker coach following the departure of Neale Daniher after 13 rounds in 2007. Melbourne defeated Carlton by 23 points in Riley's first game in charge, but it won only two more games over the rest of the season to finish above only Carlton and Richmond. Dean Bailey took over as coach in 2008 and Riley became an assistant coach with Carlton.

RINGROSE, Doug

PLAYING CAREER: Fitzroy, 1928-29, 35 games, 30 goals.

COACHING CAREER: Fitzroy, 1929, 10 games, 2 wins, 8 losses, 0 draws, 0 finals. Winning percentage - 20.

A Tasmanian, Ringrose was recruited

from VFA club Brighton after he had played in Albury. The classy rover was 28 years of age when he made his VFL debut and was appointed Fitzroy's captain-coach in 1929, in only his second season. He replaced former Brighton and Fitzroy teammate Gordon Rattray, but lasted just 10 games in charge, being relieved of his coaching duties after a defeat by South Melbourne. Ringrose guided the Maroons to just two victories, with Colin Niven taking over for the rest of the 1929 season. Ringrose continued to play with Fitzroy but ended his VFL career at the end of the season after he was appointed captain-coach of Gippsland club Yarram. He died in December, 1953, at 58 years of age.

ROHDE, Peter

PLAYING CAREER: Carlton, 1985-87, 46 games, 6 goals. Melbourne, 1988-95, 117 games, 22 goals.

COACHING CAREER: Western Bulldogs, 2002-04, 45 games, 9 wins, 35 losses, 1 draw. Winning percentage – 20.

A big-hearted defender who had been recruited from Sandhurst to play with Carlton, Rohde coached South Australian Norwood club from 1996-99 and landed a premiership with the Redlegs in 1997. He then joined the Western Bulldogs as an assistant coach under Terry Wallace and was handed the senior job late in 2002 when Wallace severed his connection with the club. Rohde had just one game as coach in 2002, but was handed the reins on a permanent basis in 2003. The Bulldogs won just three games (plus a draw), but Rohde was in charge again in 2004 when the Bulldogs won five games to finish above Hawthorn and Richmond. He was replaced by Rodney Eade in 2005 and he later joined Port Adelaide as General Manager, Football.

ROOS, Paul

PLAYING CAREER: Fitzroy, 1982-94, 269 games, 270 goals. Sydney Swans, 1995-98, 87 games, 19 goals.

COACHING CAREER: Sydney Swans, 2002-10, 202 games, 116 wins, 84 losses, 2 draws, 16 finals, 1 premiership. Winning percentage – 57.

Roos, recruited by Fitzroy from Beverley Hills, started his senior career as a winger but developed into a champion centre half-back who also could play at centre half-forward. He won five Fitzroy best and fairest awards and, after originally being wooed by Collingwood, joined the Sydney Swans in 1995 and played in their losing 1996 Grand Final side. Roos retired at the end of 1998 season but remained with the Swans as an assistant coach. When Rodney Eade stepped down after the Swans lost to Geelong at the

Paul Roos.

SCG in round 12, 2002, Roos was asked to take the coaching reins for the rest of the season. He told the players that he would tolerate mistakes as long as they committed themselves wholeheartedly to the team cause. The Swans in Roos' first game in charge defeated Fremantle by 77 points and wins against Carlton, the Kangaroos, St Kilda and Melbourne followed. By the time the Swans played their last game of the season, against Richmond at Stadium Australia, there were suggestions that former Bulldog coach Terry Wallace would coach the Swans in 2003. Wallace had resigned his position at the Whitten Oval and many

observers believed this was so he could take on the Sydney job. There also were suggestions that 1996 and 1999 Roo premiership coach Denis Pagan would be given the job. Swan fans at the Tiger match expressed their opinion vocally and with banners demanding that Roos be given the job in his own right. They won the day after the Swans defeated the Tigers by 40 points.

Roos represented a new broom and quickly instilled confidence, partly through giving the senior players more autonomy. He also introduced a new match-plan, of smothering the opposition and relying on quick rebounds. The Swans finished third in 2003 and fifth the following year before launching a genuine premiership challenge in 2005. After the Swans went down to West Coast by just four points in a qualifying final at Subiaco, they bounced back to defeat Geelong by three points in a semi-final at the SCG, thanks to a late goal from Nick Davis. The Swans then defeated St Kilda by 33 points in a preliminary final at the MCG before defeating the Eagles by four points in the Grand Final. As Roos held the premiership trophy aloft for the club's first flag in 72 years, he proclaimed: "Here it is." The premiership was a triumph for Roos as AFL boss Andrew Demetriou scoffed mid-season that the Swans could not win a premiership playing their tight,

Bob Rose, coaching Footscray against Collingwood at Victoria Park.

congested football. Yet Roos graciously did not mention this jibe at the club's premiership celebrations. Roos, who also guided the Swans to a heartbreaking one-point loss to West Coast in the 2006 Grand Final, continued with the Swans to the end of the 2010 season when he stepped aside for heir apparent John Longmire. His 202 games as Swan coach is a club record. He said when he retired that he was finished with coaching and reiterated this when Carlton approached him at the end of the 2012 season.

ROSE, Bob

PLAYING CAREER: Collingwood, 1946-55, 152 games, 214 goals.

COACHING CAREER: Collingwood, 1964-71 and 1985-86, 193 games, 121 wins, 70 losses, 2 draws, 13 finals. Winning percentage – 63. Footscray – 1972-75, 89 games, 42 wins, 45 losses, 2 draws, 1 final. Winning percentage - 47.

Arguably Collingwood's favourite son, Rose was recruited from Nyah West and developed into a brilliant and powerful on-baller. He won Collingwood's best and fairest four times and played in the 1953 premiership side before retiring in 1955. Rose coached country club Wangaratta and returned to Victoria Park in 1964 to succeed Phonse Kyne. Although Rose proved himself to be a wonderful coach, he was desperately unlucky in not landing a premiership with the Magpies. St Kilda defeated them by a point in the 1966 Grand Final and Carlton defeated them by 10 points in 1970 after Collingwood led by 44 points at half-time. Rose joined Footscray as coach in 1972 but, in four seasons in charge, he guided them to just one finals series – in 1974 when, ironically, Collingwood defeated them by 69 points in the elimination final. Rose returned to Collingwood in 1985 but, just three games into the 1986 season, relinquished the coaching position in favour of Leigh Matthews. Rose, whose son Robert played with both Collingwood and Footscray, also served the Magpies as a director and vice-president. Enormously popular with all football fans, Rose spent the last 30 years of his life caring for Robert, who was crippled in a motor accident in 1974. Bob Rose died in May, 2003, at 74 years of age.

ROSE, Kevin

PLAYING CAREER: Collingwood, 1958-67, 159 games, 47 goals.

COACHING CAREER: Fitzroy, 1975-77, 66 games, 22 wins, 44 losses, 0 draws, 0 finals. Winning percentage – 33.

One of Collingwood's famous Rose brothers, Kevin Rose was a rough, no-nonsense ruck-rover who played in the Magpies' 1958 premiership side. He later coached VFA club Prahran to two premierships and therefore was perfectly qualified for the vacant Fitzroy coaching position in 1975. However Fitzroy had three poor seasons under Rose, finishing ninth, eleventh and tenth before he was replaced by the man he succeeded – Graham Campbell.

ROWE, Des

PLAYING CAREER: Richmond, 1946-57, 175 games, 24 goals.

COACHING CAREER: Richmond, 1961-63, 54 games, 15 wins, 39 losses, 0 draws, 0 finals. Winning percentage – 28.

The son of champion Collingwood follower Percy Rowe, he played under his father's coaching with VFA club Coburg and was residentially tied to Richmond. Des Rowe developed into a quality defender who captained the Tigers from 1952-57. A natural leader who played in mainly poor Richmond sides, he replaced Alan McDonald as coach in 1961 and, in three seasons in charge, took the Tigers to tenth, eighth and tenth positions. The early '60s were lean years for the Tigers and Rowe had the dubious distinction of coaching Richmond in a game in which it failed to score even one goal. The Tigers scored 0.8 to St Kilda's 12.19 in round 16, 1961. Rowe later spent three years as a Tiger selector.

ROWE, Percy

PLAYING CAREER: Collingwood, 1920-24 and 1927-28, 96 games, 37 goals.

COACHING CAREER: Fitzroy, 1935, 18 games, 8 wins, 9 losses, 1 draw, 0 finals. Winning percentage – 44. Carlton, 1937, 18 games, 11 wins, 7 losses, 0 draws, 0 finals. Winning percentage – 61.

Rowe was one of the toughest players of his era after being recruited from Rutherglen. He was appointed Collingwood captain in 1923, but the burly follower stood down after just three games because he believed the leadership role was affecting his play. Rowe then stunned Victoria Park when he was appointed captain-coach of Albury in 1924, even though he returned to Collingwood to play two games at the end of the season. It was only a brief return as Rowe in 1925 was appointed captain-coach of Wangaratta, which went through that season undefeated. Rowe returned to Collingwood in 1927 and played in the 1927-28 Magpie premiership sides before joining VFA club Northcote as captain-

coach. He guided Northcote to the 1929 flag and his success as a coach saw Fitzroy invite him to coach the Maroons in 1935. Fitzroy finished seventh but Rowe stepped down, only to bob up as coach of Carlton in 1937. Carlton at that time was trying to secure the services of South Melbourne's Brighton Diggins as playing coach, but the Swans refused to clear him. Rowe therefore was seen as an interim coach but, even so, the Blues missed the finals by just half a game from fourth-placed Richmond. Diggins took over the following year and guided the Blues to the 1938 flag. Rowe later coached Coburg.

ROWELL, Ted

PLAYING CAREER: Collingwood, 1901-04 and 1907-15, 189 games, 175 goals.

COACHING CAREER: Collingwood, 1907-08, 30 games, 15 wins, 15 losses, 0 draws, 1 final. Winning percentage – 50.

Rowell was Collingwood's third coach, after Bill Strickland and Dick Condon. A brilliant full-back, Rowell was dogged by controversy early in his playing career as he was accused of "laying down" in a match against Fitzroy and moved to Western Australia. When Rowell, a professional bookmaker, agreed to return to Collingwood, the VFL blocked his clearance and he had to stand out of football. Rowell played in the 1902-03 premiership sides and his natural

COACHING CAREER: Essendon, 1945 and 1946, 2 games, 0 wins, 2 losses, 0 draws, 0 finals. Winning percentage – 0.

Ruddell, recruited from VFA club Northcote after originally playing with Fitzroy reserves, played in Essendon's 1942 and 1946 premiership sides. A brilliant full-back, he was club vice-captain from 1945-48 who twice stood in as Essendon coach when captain-coach Dick Reynolds was unavailable – once in 1946 and once again the following season. Ruddell played one game in 1949 before retiring because of ankle problems and became captain-coach of VFA club Camberwell.

RUSH, Bob

PLAYING CAREER: Collingwood, 1899-1908, 143 games, 1 goal.

COACHING CAREER: Collingwood, 1930, 1 game, 1 win, 0 losses, 0 draws, 2 finals, 1 premiership. Winning percentage – 100.

Rush has the unique distinction of coaching just one senior game for one premiership. This bizarre circumstance arose when coach Jock McHale had influenza and was confined to bed when Collingwood played Geelong in the 1930 Grand Final. Rush, who served the Magpies as player, committeeman, assistant secretary, treasurer and delegate to the VFL,

leadership qualities saw him named captain-coach in 1907. Collingwood finished fourth, but crashed out of the premiership race in a 34-point semi-final defeat by South Melbourne. He was replaced as coach late in 1908 by early Magpie star Bill Strickland and as captain by Bob Nash. Rowell continued to play with Collingwood and, after being a member of the 1910 flag side, retired in 1915 at 39 years of age.

RUDDELL, Cec

PLAYING CAREER: Essendon, 1940-49, 122 games, 0 goals.

stepped in as Collingwood went in chase of a fourth consecutive premiership. When Geelong led by 21 points at half-time, Rush asked his players what McHale would be thinking while listening to the match on radio. The Magpies responded with an eight-goal third quarter and won by 30 points. Rush, recruited from CBC Parade, was a talented defender in his 10 seasons with the Magpies and gave the club its motto of "Floreat Pica" – "May the Magpies Flourish". He died on March 13, 1975, at 94 years of age.

RUTHVEN, Allan

> **PLAYING CAREER:** Fitzroy, 1940-41 and 1943-54, 222 games, 442 goals.
>
> **COACHING CAREER:** Fitzroy, 1952-54, 57 games, 28 wins, 28 losses, 1 draw, 2 finals. Winning percentage – 49.

A brilliant rover, Ruthven was recruited locally and won the 1950 Brownlow Medal. He was one of Fitzroy's most experienced players when coach Norm Smith decided before the 1952 season that he wanted to return to his original club, Melbourne. The Maroons therefore were left with a dilemma as there were six applicants for the vacant coaching position. Fitzroy did not name the applicants, but they included former club champions Haydn Bunton and Frank Curcio. Ruthven and full-back Vic Chanter also applied to be appointed

playing-coach, with Ruthven getting the nod. Ruthven, 28 and captain of Fitzroy in 1947, described his appointment as "very nice". He guided Fitzroy to third position in his first season as captain-coach and kicked the winning behind when the Maroons defeated Carlton by a point in the first semi-final. Fitzroy crashed to Collingwood in the preliminary final and the Maroons slipped to sixth position in 1953 before finishing above only St Kilda the following season. Ruthven retired as a player and coach and Bill Stephen was appointed captain-coach.

RYAN, Joe

> **PLAYING CAREER:** Footscray, 1937-48, 167 games, 261 goals.
>
> **COACHING CAREER:** Footscray, 1959-60, 2 games, 0 wins, 2 losses, 0 draws, 0 finals. Winning percentage – 0.

Recruited from local club Seddon Rovers, Ryan was a brilliant rover who won the club best and fairest in 1946-47 and represented Victoria. A great Bulldog stalwart, he coached the reserves from 1948-60 and stood in as senior coach when Ted Whitten missed a game in each of the 1959-60 seasons. Many believe Ryan should have been appointed Footscray coach in 1957 after 1954 premiership coach Charlie Sutton was sacked. Whitten was handed the job at just 23 years of age.

SANDERSON, Brenton

PLAYING CAREER: Adelaide, 1992-93, 6 games, 4 goals; Collingwood, 1994, 4 games, 1 goal; Geelong, 1995-2005, 199 games, 29 goals.

COACHING CAREER: Adelaide, 2012- , 25 games, 18 wins, 7 losses, 0 draws, 3 finals. Winning percentage – 72.

Although Sanderson was in Adelaide's original AFL squad in 1991 and made his senior debut the following season, he did not make a name for himself until he moved to Geelong in 1995 and became a reliable, hard-running defender. On his retirement in 2005, he spent a season with Port Adelaide as a development coach before being appointed an assistant coach with Geelong in 2007. He applied for the senior Geelong job when Mark Thompson left at the end of 2010, but missed out to Chris Scott. Sanderson remained with the Cats as an assistant and then won the Adelaide coaching position ahead of a large field of candidates, including former Collingwood captain and West Coast assistant coach Scott Burns. In his debut season of 2012, he guided the Crows to the pre-season championship and rejuvenated the squad to climb the ladder. The Crows, after finishing the home and away season in second position, went down to Hawthorn by just five points in a preliminary final.

SAUNDERS, Harry

PLAYING CAREER: Collingwood, 1916-26, 133 games, 10 goals.

COACHING CAREER: Footscray, 1926, 10 games, 3 wins, 7 losses, 0 draws. Winning percentage – 30.

Saunders was one of the VFL's finest defenders after being recruited locally (Collingwood Cadets) and was full-back in the Magpies' 1917 and 1919 flag sides. He took over as Footscray's non-playing coach when Jim Cassidy took ill halfway through the 1926 season. Saunders' coaching debut was the round nine match against Richmond at the Western Oval, which the Tigers won by 11 points. The Bulldogs defeated St Kilda the following week and then North Melbourne the following week. However, their only other win under Saunders was against Richmond (by 44 points at the Punt Road Oval) in the final round. Despite this big win, Footscray the following season appointed South Melbourne's Paddy Scanlan captain-coach. Saunders, who was just 28 years of age when appointed Footscray coach in 1926, died of pancreatitis just four years later.

SCANLAN, Paddy

PLAYING CAREER: South Melbourne, 1920-26, 100 games, 49 goals. Footscray, 1927-28, 33 games, 15 goals.

COACHING CAREER: Footscray, 1927-28, 36 games, 15 wins, 21 losses, 0 draws. Winning percentage – 42. South Melbourne, 1930-31, 26 games, 18 wins, 18 losses, 0 draws. Winning percentage – 50. North Melbourne, 1935-37, 46 games, 8 wins, 38 losses, 0 draws, 0 finals. Winning percentage – 17.

Scanlan's VFL playing career was delayed by his service in World War I. He was touted as a VFL star pre-war while playing with South Melbourne YCW and then the Leopold club. A public servant, he made his debut in 1920 and was appointed South captain in 1923. A brilliant ball-winner, the Sporting Globe that season ran a poll for the best player in each position and the public voted Scanlan the best centreman in the VFL. Scanlan stepped down as club captain when coach Charlie Pannam eventually won his release from Collingwood to play with South as captain-coach in 1926. Scanlan continued as South vice-captain but, before the start of the 1927 season, received an offer from Footscray he could not refuse. The Bulldogs paid him a then unheard of fee of nine pounds a week to be Footscray's captain-coach.

Ironically, Scanlan's brother Joe took over the South captaincy and they were photographed together at the toss of the coin before a Bulldogs-Southerners match at the Western Oval on July 8, 1928. Footscray won by two points. Scanlan took the Bulldogs from tenth in 1927 to seventh the following season but then was replaced by former Geelong player Alec "Bunny" Eason for the 1929 season. Scanlan therefore crossed to Richmond as reserves captain-coach and guided them to the flag before returning to South as coach in 1930. The South Melbourne Record of November 23, 1930, said: "Scanlan is a footballer of wide experience, and has proved a very successful coach and his return to South Melbourne will be hailed with delight by supporters of the local club, many of who considered that the Red and Whites should never have lost his services."

South finished seventh in both 1930 and 1931, but Scanlan then was replaced by West Australian Johnny Leonard. Undeterred, Scanlan was appointed North Melbourne coach as a replacement for Tom Fitzmaurice during the 1935 season. On his appointment he said in an address at a team dinner that he had heard there was disunity at the club, but was pleased that, rather, "the players were a happy family and that a cordial relationship existed between the team and officials". North finished on the bottom in 1935,

but Scanlan was reappointed for the 1936 season and, according to the Argus newspaper was chosen ahead of 20 other applicants. North finished eleventh that season and when North finished on the bottom in 1937, Scanlan was replaced by former Essendon player Keith Forbes. He then helped coach local sides and, in 1951, was assistant coach of amateur club Old Paradians when it won the B Grade flag under the captaincy of his son Patrick. Scanlan died on New Year's Day, 1977.

SCHIMMELBUSCH, Wayne

PLAYING CAREER: North Melbourne, 1973-87, 306 games, 354 goals.

COACHING CAREER: North Melbourne, 1990-92, 66 games, 31 wins, 35 losses, 0 draws, 0 finals. Winning percentage – 47.

Schimmelbusch was one of the greatest players of his era and excelled on a wing or on a half-forward flank. He played in North's 1975 and 1977 premiership sides and captained the Roos from 1979-87. Recruited from VFA club Brunswick, he was a regular Victorian representative and took over as coach from John Kennedy in 1990. North finished sixth in "Schimma's" first season in charge, but slipped to eighth in 1991 and then to twelfth the following season. When Adelaide thrashed the Roos by 147 points in a pre-season match at Football Park in 1993, Schimmelbusch stepped down as coach and he was replaced by Denis Pagan.

SCHMIDT, Billy

PLAYING CAREER: Richmond, 1908-11 and 1921, 75 games, 71 goals. St Kilda, 1912-14 and 1918-20, 90 games, 67 goals.

COACHING CAREER: Richmond, 1933, 21 games, 16 wins, 5 losses, 0 draws, 3 finals. Winning percentage – 65.

Schmidt played with Richmond in its VFA days and therefore was a ready-made star when the Tigers were admitted to the VFL in 1908. A brilliant rover, Schmidt also was a perfectionist whose hectoring annoyed teammates. He captained Richmond in 1910 but, two years later, accepted an offer to join St Kilda. He copped a lengthy suspension in 1914 and, because St Kilda pulled out of the competition for the 1916-17 seasons, he did not resume until 1918. It is believed that Schmidt was unofficial coach of St Kilda for a couple of games when Jim Smith resigned because of business commitments in 1918. Following his retirement in 1920, he spent seven years as coach of Wimmera club Warracknabeal and then Mt Gambier. He bobbed up as official coach of Richmond in 1933 and took the Tigers to a Grand Final defeat by South Melbourne in his only season in charge. Schmidt, who also

coached Murtoa, died in 1975 at 86 years of age.

SCHWAB, Peter

PLAYING CAREER: Hawthorn, 1980-91, 171 games, 38 goals.

COACHING CAREER: Hawthorn, 2000-04, 109 games, 52 wins, 57 losses, 0 draws, 5 finals. Winning percentage – 48.

Schwab, whose father Frank umpired the 1961 Grand Final, was a classy utility recruited from Bennettswood. He played in Hawthorn's 1983, 1986 and 1988 flag sides, but missed the 1989 premiership win because of suspension. On retirement, he joined Richmond as an assistant coach and had a brief stint in charge of the AFL umpiring department before being appointed Hawthorn coach for 2000, taking over from Ken Judge. Schwab lifted Hawthorn from ninth in 1999 to the final eight in his first season in charge and the Hawks then defeated Geelong in an elimination final before going down to North Melbourne in a semi-final. Hawthorn defeated the Sydney Swans and Port Adelaide in finals matches in 2001, but went down to Essendon in a preliminary final. Hawthorn seemed to be on the rise, but tenth placing in 2002 was bitterly disappointing, as was missing the finals in ninth position in 2003. Schwab declared before the start of the 2004 season that Hawthorn had the potential to win the premiership and when the Hawks struggled to win even a handful of games, Schwab's fate was sealed. When North Melbourne defeated Hawthorn by 80 points in round 17, Schwab was informed he would be replaced at the end of the season. He elected to stand down immediately and Donald McDonald was appointed interim coach. Schwab later became chairman of the AFL Match Review Panel, was CEO of AFL Victoria and, late in 2010, was appointed the AFL's Director of Coaching.

SCOTT, Brad

PLAYING CAREER: Hawthorn, 1997, 22 games, 6 goals. Brisbane Lions, 1998-2006, 146 games, 39 goals.

COACHING CAREER: North Melbourne, 2010-12, 67 games, 35 wins, 32 losses, 0 draws, 1 final. Winning percentage – 52.

Scott, recruited from East Doncaster, might have played 22 games with Hawthorn in 1997, but found himself traded to Brisbane, where he joined twin brother Chris. A tough-nut in the Lion midfield, he played in Brisbane's 2001-02 premiership sides. On retirement as a player, he joined Collingwood as an assistant coach and spent three years with the Magpies before winning the senior North Melbourne position from 2010. Scott took North to ninth position in both 2010 and 2011 and into the finals in 2012

only for the youthful Kangaroos to be humiliated by West Cast in an elimination final. He signed a new contract with North in August, 2011, tying him to the Arden Street club until the end of the 2013 season.

SCOTT, Brett

PLAYING CAREER: Sydney, 1981-88, 59 games, 44 goals.

COACHING CAREER: Sydney, 1993, 2 games, 0 wins, 2 losses, 0 draw, 0 finals. Winning percentage - 0.

Scott, a talented centreman whose playing career was hampered by injuries, was on the Swans' match committee when coach Gary Buckenara was sacked just four rounds into the 1993 season. Scott took over as interim coach, but the Swans went down by 93 points to Fitzroy and then by 124 points to North Melbourne in Scott's two games in charge. The legendary Ron Barassi then took over as coach.

SCOTT, Chris

PLAYING CAREER: Brisbane Bears/Lions, 1994-2007, 215 games, 79 goals.

COACHING CAREER: Geelong, 2011-12, 48 games, 37 wins, 11 losses, 0 draws, 4 finals, 1 premiership. Winning percentage – 80.

Brad Scott's twin brother, he already was in Brisbane when Brad joined the club in 1998. Chris played in the Lions' 2001-02 premiership sides and, on retirement, joined Fremantle as an assistant coach. When Geelong coach Mark Thompson shocked the football world in walking away from Kardinia Park late in 2010, Scott beat a highly-rated field to take over as senior coach. It proved to be an almost seamless transition and Scott lifted the Cats to the 2011 flag in his first season as coach. This made him the first coach to achieve this feat since Hawthorn's Alan Joyce in 1988. The Cats won their first 13 games under Scott, breaking the record of wins for a new coach, set by South Melbourne's Johnny Leonard in 1932. The Cats stuttered through the 2012 home and away season and although rated a chance to take out the flag, crashed out to Fremantle in an elimination final at the MCG.

SEWELL, Greg

PLAYING CAREER: Essendon, 1952-61, 171 games, 34 goals.

COACHING CAREER: Esendon, 1965, 1 game, 1 win, 0 losses, 0 draws, 0 finals. Wining percentage – 100.

A great Essendon stalwart, Sewell played mainly on a wing after being recruited locally and was Bomber reserves coach under John Coleman and then Jack Clarke from 1965-68. He took over from Coleman in one match in 1965 when the Bomber coach was on interstate duties. Sewell also served Essendon as a committeeman, was chairman of the match committee over the 1974-75 seasons and was club president.

SHAW, Robert

PLAYING CAREER: Essendon, 1974-81, 51 games, 8 goals.

COACHING CAREER: Fitzroy, 1991-94, 86 games, 28 wins, 58 losses, 0 draws, 0 finals. Winning percentage – 33. Adelaide, 1995-96, 44 games, 17 wins, 27 losses, 0 draws, 0 finals. Winning percentage – 39.

Shaw, recruited from Tasmanian club Sandy Bay, was plagued by injuries during his seven seasons as a defender with Essendon and returned to his home state to coach Clarence from 1984-85. Shaw returned to Windy Hill as an assistant coach from 1986-88 before coaching the Fitzroy reserves to the 1989 flag and being appointed senior coach in 1991. He had mainly poor sides at Fitzroy and did well to drag the Lions up the ladder to finish tenth in 1992 and eleventh in 1993. Although the Lions then slipped to near the bottom, he had won himself a reputation as a fine football thinker and was appointed Adelaide coach to replace South Australian legend Graham Cornes in 1995. Shaw spent two seasons with the Crows, but his tenure was marked by fan abuse and even intimidation. Despite his sharp football brain, he was regarded as an "outsider" in the South Australian community. The Crows finished eleventh and twelfth in Shaw's two seasons in charge and he returned to Essendon as an assistant coach in 1999 and spent the 2005-08 seasons as Fremantle's General Manager, Football, before working in the football media, especially with Inside Football.

SHAW, Tony

PLAYING CAREER: Collingwood, 1977-94, 313 games, 159 goals.

COACHING CAREER: Collingwood, 1996-99, 88 games, 30 wins, 58 losses, 0 draws, 0 finals. Winning percentage – 34.

Tony Shaw.

Shaw, recruited from Reservoir-Lakeside, developed into one of the most courageous midfielders in the competition. He won the club best and fairest in 1984 and 1990 and was Magpie captain from 1987-93. The highlight of his career was leading Collingwood to the 1990 premiership, the club's first since 1958. Shaw took over as Collingwood coach when Leigh Matthews stepped down at the end of the 1995 season but, in four seasons in charge, his highest finish was tenth in 1997. Collingwood under Shaw landed the dreaded wooden spoon in 1999 and he was replaced by Mick Malthouse. He then became a leading media commentator.

SHEA, Keith

PLAYING CAREER: Carlton, 1932-37, 91 games, 101 goals. Hawthorn, 1945, 8 games, 8 goals.

COACHING CAREER: Hawthorn, 1945-46, 39 games, 9 wins, 30 losses, 0 draws, 0 finals. Winning percentage – 23.

A brilliant, flamboyant centreman, Shea joined Carlton from Bacchus Marsh and developed into one of the finest players of his era and was a regular Victorian representative. He moved to Western Australia in 1938, but was lured back to Victoria as captain-coach of Hawthorn in 1945. Shea at that time was almost 31 years of age and past his best. He retired as a player halfway through the season to concentrate on his task of developing talent at Glenferrie Oval. He was regarded as a good football teacher, but Hawthorn finished a modest tenth with just six wins in 1945. Shea retained the coaching position for 1946, but the Mayblooms slipped to the bottom with just three wins and Shea was replaced by Alec Albiston. Shea died in February, 1951, at just 36 years of age.

SHEEDY, Kevin

PLAYING CAREER: Richmond, 1967-79, 251 games, 91 goals.

COACHING CAREER: Essendon, 1981-2007, 635 games, 386 wins, 242 losses, 7 draws, 43 finals, 4 premierships. Winning percentage – 61. Greater Western Sydney, 2012 – , 22 games, 2 wins, 20 losses, 0 draw, 0 finals. Winning percentage – 9.

One of the most endurable coaches in VFL/AFL history, Sheedy has been involved in football at the elite level since he crossed to Richmond from VFA club Prahran

Kevin Sheedy.

without a clearance in 1967. He made a name for himself as one of the toughest players in the VFL over his 13 seasons with the Tigers, either in the centre or in defence, and captained Richmond in 1978. Sheedy played in the Tigers' 1969 and 1973-74 premiership sides and, on retirement, found himself a wanted man after spending just one season in a development role at Punt Road. He was appointed non-playing Essendon coach for 1981 and most observers saw this as a massive gamble by the Bombers as Sheedy was an unknown quantity as a coach. After a slow start in which he threatened to make a playing comeback. Sheedy went on to guide the Bombers to the 1984-85, 1993 and 2000 premierships. He built and rebuilt his sides to meet new challenges and had the happy knack of defying his critics with a combination of cunning and expertise.

For example, his sternest critics suggested Sheedy was trigger happy with tactical moves. However, Sheedy switched his Bomber line-up around when they trailed Hawthorn by 25 points at the final change during the 1984 Grand Final and saw his team triumph by 24 points. Sheedy also revelled in the bizarre, often thumbing his nose at his critics in the process. He often was the centre of controversy and, for example, once referred to umpires as Martians. Sheedy was willing to "stir the pot" whenever he thought it would suit his team. Although Sheedy even had his critics within the confines of Windy Hill, he proved himself to be a master of survival and, in 2006, coached his 600th game. When Essendon finished thirteenth in 2005 and then fifteenth the following season the writing was on the wall. Essendon eventually parted company with Sheedy at the end of 2007. He had coached the Bombers in 635 games, easily a club record, bettering the 415 games by Dick Reynolds from 1939-60. Sheedy's departure from Windy Hill, replaced by another former Richmond player in Matthew Knights, was a seismic change at Windy Hill but Sheedy did not have to wait long to find a new football home. Although he was touted as a chance to take over at Melbourne, he eventually was appointed coach of new

franchise club Greater Western Sydney, which made its debut in 2012. The Giants won only two games in their debut season, but the victory over Port Adelaide in round 19 had massive repercussions as the Power later severed connections with coach Matthew Primus.

SHELDON, Ken

PLAYING CAREER: Carlton, 1977-86, 132 games, 170 goals. St Kilda, 1987-89, 523 games, 24 goals.

COACHING CAREER: St Kilda, 1990-93, 89 games, 48 wins, 40 losses, 1 draw, 3 finals. Winning percentage – 54.

A cheeky rover recruited from Mitiamo, Sheldon played in Carlton's 1979, 1981 and 1982 premiership sides, but crossed to St Kilda in 1987. He retired as a player when he was appointed coach to replace Darrel Baldock in 1987 and, in only his second season in charge, took the Saints to their first finals series since 1973. St Kilda finished the home and away season in fourth position but crashed to Geelong by seven points in an elimination final. The Saints again made the finals in 1992, going down to Footscray in the first semi-final, but when they slipped to twelfth in 1993, the Saints replaced Sheldon with Stan Alves. He then coached South Adelaide, Echuca and VFL club Springvale before rejoining St Kilda as Football Operations

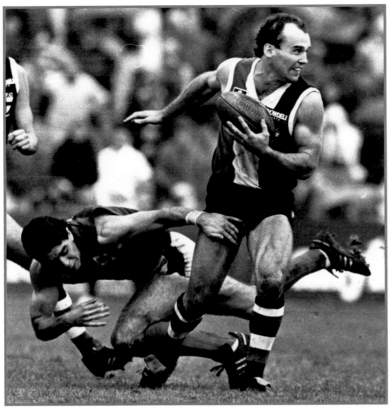

Ken Shelden evades the tackle of Garry Lyon.

Silvagni was recruited from CBC Parade and became one of the most reliable ruck-rovers in the game. He captained the Blues in 1964 and played in the 1968 and 1970 premiership sides. He took over as senior coach when former St Kilda and Richmond champion Ian Stewart had to resign because of ill-health just five rounds into the 1978 season. Silvagni was in charge for three matches – all losses – until the Blues gave the job to club captain Alex Jesaulenko after originally trying to talk St Kilda Brownlow Medal winner Neil Roberts into a coaching career. Silvagni served the Blues for many years as a team selector and son Stephen played 312 games with Carlton from 1985-2001.

Manager. Son Sam played for the Brisbane Lions.

SILVAGNI, Sergio

PLAYING CAREER: Carlton, 1958-71, 239 games, 136 goals.

COACHING CAREER: Carlton, 1978, 3 games, 0 wins, 3 losses, 0 draws, 0 finals. Winning percentage – 0.

One of Carlton's greatest identities,

SIMMONDS, Roy

PLAYING CAREER: 1950-61, 192 games, 78 goals.

COACHING CAREER: Hawthorn, 1973, 1 game, 0 wins, 1 loss, 0 draws, 0 finals. Winning percentage – 0.

A great Hawthorn favourite, Simmonds won enormous sympathy when he missed selection for Hawthorn's 1961 premiership side. A tough back pocket, he had been offered country coaching jobs but wanted to stay with the Hawks to help them land their first premiership. Simmonds coached Hawthorn in one game in 1973 when John Kennedy was unavailable because of state duties. He later served Hawthorn as chairman of selectors and was an assistant coach with Melbourne.

SKILTON, Bob

PLAYING CAREER: South Melbourne, 1956-71, 237 games, 412 goals.

COACHING CAREER: South Melbourne, 1965-66, 35 games, 16 wins, 19 losses, 0 draws, 0 finals. Winning percentage – 46. Melbourne, 1974-77, 88 games, 28 wins, 60 losses, 0 draws, 0 finals. Winning percentage – 32.

Skilton, a champion rover who won three Brownlow Medals and won the Swans' best and fairest nine times, was just 26 years of age when asked to be South captain-coach in 1965. South had won just two games under Noel McMahen in 1964, but Skilton lifted the Swans to respectability in his first season in charge, with South winning nine games to finish eighth. Skilton had inherited a poor quality playing list and despite the Swans

again finishing eighth in 1966, he stepped aside as coach. He cited the difficulties of combining coaching and playing and, despite retaining the captaincy, he was replaced as coach by Allan Miller. Skilton continued playing until the end of the 1971 season and, following a brief stint away from football, was appointed Melbourne coach for 1974. The Demons collected the wooden-spoon that season and, after finishing tenth the following year, challenged for the finals in 1976. Melbourne, which had not made the finals since winning the 1964 flag, had to defeat Collingwood at Victoria Park in the final round AND rely on Carlton defeating Footscray at Princes Park. The Demons did their bit in defeating the Magpies by 15 points but, in an extraordinary result, the Blues and the Bulldogs drew, giving Footscray fourth position half a game ahead of Melbourne. Skilton stepped down as Melbourne coach after the Demons finished above only St Kilda in 1977.

SLOCUM, Ray

PLAYING CAREER: Fitzroy, 1957-65, 121 games, 47 goals.

COACHING CAREER: Fitzroy, 1968, 1 game, 0 wins, 1 loss, 0 draws, 0 finals. Winning percentage – 0.

Recruited from West Preston YCW, Slocum was a talented small man who could rove or play on a wing. He later became playing and then non-playing coach of the Lion reserves and was in charge for one senior match in 1968 when regular coach Bill Stephen was ill. Slocum later coached Diamond Valley Football League club Eltham to a premiership.

SMITH, Dave

PLAYING CAREER: Essendon, 1903-11 and 1913, 142 games, 114 goals. Richmond, 1914, 1 game, 3 goals.

COACHING CAREER: Essendon, 1908-09, 39 games, 26 wins, 13 losses, 0 draws, 2 finals. Winning percentage – 67.

Smith has the distinction of being Essendon's first official coach. A brilliant centre half-forward, he also was an outstanding cricketer and was selected for the Australian tour of England in 1912. He had played in the 1911 Essendon flag side and almost certainly would have been a member of the 1912 premiership side if he had not sailed to England. On return, he played one game with Richmond. Smith, who had been recruited from Richmond district junior club Sherwoods, was appointed Essendon coach in 1908, but with Billy Griffith as captain. Essendon went down to Carlton by just nine points in the Grand Final and went down again (by 36 points) to the Blues in a semi-final the following year. Alan Belcher took over as captain-coach in 1910.

SMITH, Jimmy

PLAYING CAREER: St Kilda, 1899-1906 and 1908-09, 130 games, 22 goals.

COACHING CAREER: St Kilda, 1909, 1915 and 1918, 49 games, 15 wins, 34 losses, 0 draws, 1 final. Winning percentage – 31.

One of the St Kilda's earliest champions after being recruited from West Melbourne, Smith had several stints as club captain and set a fine example in the ruck. He spent the 1907 season as an umpire and was appointed St Kilda

J SMITH ST KILDA

coach in 1909, with Vic Barwick as captain. He played just the one game that season and the Saints finished tenth. Smith returned as coach in 1915, with the Saints finishing seventh. Although St Kilda went into recess over the 1916-17 seasons because of World War I, he was appointed St Kilda coach for the 1918 season and guided the Saints to fourth position before they went down to Collingwood in a semi-final. Smith was replaced by Wels Eike in 1919 and temporarily moved to Queensland. A visionary, Smith in 1914 had planned an Australian football tour to Europe, only for his plans to be scuttled by the Great War.

SMITH, Len

PLAYING CAREER: Melbourne, 1934-35, 19 games, 3 goals. Fitzroy, 1937-43 and 1945, 76 games, 52 goals.

COACHING CAREER: Fitzroy, 1958-62, 92 games, 50 wins, 40 losses, 2 draws, 3 finals. Winning percentage – 54. Richmond, 1964-65, 15 games, 3 wins, 12 losses, 0 draws, 0 finals. Winning percentage – 20.

The brother of legendary coach Norm Smith, Len also was an excellent coach whose career was cut short by heart problems. Smith had just two seasons as a player with Melbourne before spending a season in the VFA with Northcote. He was lured to Fitzroy in 1937 and quietly established himself as a fine defender who also could pinch-hit up forward. Smith coached the Fitzroy under 19s on retirement and was handed the senior job in 1958. Fitzroy had finished eleventh under Bill Stephen in 1957, but Smith immediately lifted the Lions to the 1958 finals, only for them to go down by just four points to North Melbourne in the first semi-final. Smith used pace and slick handball to break open even the tightest of defences and was a particularly shrewd tactician who was able to get the best out of his players. Although Fitzroy finished fifth in 1959, it finished the following season in second position before going down to Melbourne in the second semi-final and then to Collingwood – by just five points – in the preliminary final. Fitzroy did not make the finals in either of Smith's last two years with the Lions and he was replaced in 1963 by Kevin Murray. Smith coached VFA club Coburg before being appointed Richmond coach in 1964. Unfortunately, he was dogged by heart problems and Dick Harris had to take over late in the season. Although Smith was reappointed for the 1965 season, he had to retire because of health problems just three games into the season. Smith, who wrote a meticulous coaching manual during his short but brilliant career, died following a heart attack in 1967; he was just 55 years of age.

SMITH, Norm

PLAYING CAREER: Melbourne, 1935-48, 210 games, 546 goals. Fitzroy, 1949-50, 17 games, 26 goals.

COACHING CAREER: Fitzroy, 1949-51, 55 games, 30 wins, 23 losses, 2 draws, 0 finals. Winning percentage – 55. Melbourne, 1952-67, 307 games, 195 wins, 107 losses, 5 draws, 23 finals, 6 premierships. Winning percentage – 64. South Melbourne, 1969-72, 87 games, 26 wins, 61 losses, 0 draws, 1 final. Winning percentage – 29.

Smith, the younger brother of Len Smith, was one of the finest full-forwards of his era after being recruited from Northcote Juniors. He played in Melbourne's 1939-41 and 1948 premiership sides and topped the VFL goalkicking in 1941. The Demons' captain from 1945-47, he crossed to Fitzroy as captain-coach in 1949 and guided the Maroons to seventh, fifth and fifth again in his three seasons in charge, He retired as a player during the 1950 season and Fitzroy was desperately unlucky to miss the finals as Geelong won fourth position ahead of the Maroons

Norm Smith, football's most revered coach.

only on percentage. However, Melbourne in 1952 wanted Smith to replace Allan La Fontaine as coach and Fitzroy, which had wooed Smith from the Demons in the first place, could hardly stand in his way. The 1951 Fitzroy annual report, released just before the start of the 1952 season, said: "During his three years at Fitzroy he has made many friendships which will continue for all time. His relations with the players were always excellent and the progress of many of the younger players has been solely due to his advice and encouragement."

Smith lifted Melbourne from the bottom to sixth position in his first season in charge and, in 1954, guided his young side to a Grand Final appearance against Footscray. Although the Bulldogs defeated the Demons by 51 points, Melbourne made amends the following season and went on to win further flags in 1956 and 1957. Collingwood in 1958 destroyed Melbourne's dream of four consecutive premierships, but Smith's Demons bounced back to win the 1959-60 flags. Smith was the perfect ring-master, his discipline absolute and his demand for perfection drilled into every Demon. Melbourne was the dominant side of the late '50s and early '60s and when Smith landed a sixth premiership for Melbourne in 1964, no one could have predicted the events of the following season, Melbourne, in bizarre circumstances, sacked the competition's most successful

coach. It was a bitter dispute revolving around Smith's perceived total control of the club and although the matter eventually was settled with Smith's return, the damage had been done and Melbourne slid down the ladder. Finally, Smith was replaced by John Beckwith from 1968.

When South Melbourne was looking for a coach from 1969, club president Brian Bourke suggested Smith would be ideal. South swung into action and signed the former Demon mentor. Amazingly, Smith donated half his modest coaching fee to the Swans. In a demonstration that he would rule the Lake Oval with an iron fist, one of Smith's first gestures as coach was to chide club hero Bob Skilton for being late for the club's annual general meeting. Although the Swans finished ninth in 1969, they climbed into the final four the following season for the first time since 1945. St Kilda defeated South by 53 points in the first semi-final, but the 1970 season was a dream come true for Swan fans. The Swans finished on the bottom in 1971 and after rising just one position the following year, Smith was replaced by Graeme John. The South players held a farewell for their coach and, pointedly, no committeemen were invited. The legendary coach already was struggling with health problems and he died in July, 1973, at just 59 years of age. The best player on the ground in each Grand Final is presented with the Norm Smith

Medal, an award inaugurated in 1979. Ironically, Smith's nephew – Carlton's Wayne Harmes – won the first Norm Smith Medal. Smith's son Peter played 23 games with Melbourne over the 1966-67 seasons and 15 with Carlton from 1968-70.

SMITH Ross

> **PLAYING CAREER:** St Kilda, 1961-72 and 1975, 234 games, 231 goals.
>
> **COACHING CAREER:** St Kilda, 1977, 22 games, 3 wins, 17 losses, 2 draws, 0 finals. Winning percentage – 14.

Smith, a brilliant rover recruited from Hampton Scouts, played in St Kilda's 1966 premiership side and won the Brownlow Medal the following year. After captaining St Kilda from 1970-72, he moved to Western Australia to complete a master's degree and to coach Subiaco. In 1973 he guided the WA club to its first premiership in 49 years and rejoined St Kilda as an assistant coach in 1975. However, injuries to rovers Bruce Duperouzel and Paul Callery saw him make a comeback. Smith continued as an assistant to Allan Jeans in 1976 and when Jeans retired he looked the logical successor. The problem was that St Kilda wanted a full-time coach and Smith was not prepared to end his career in education. The Saints wanted former Richmond ruckman Mike Patterson as coach and, when he pulled out of the running, Smith was given the nod. The Saints had just three wins (plus two draws) under Smith in 1977 and Patterson was appointed coach the following year. Smith continued his career in education and later became a director at the Australian Institute of Sport.

SPARROW, George

> **PLAYING CAREER:** South Melbourne, 1898, 14 games, 2 goals. St Kilda, 1899, 11 games, 0 goals.
>
> **COACHING CAREER:** St Kilda, 1913, 1920 and 1928-29, 45 games, 26 wins, 19 losses, 0 draws, 4 finals. Winning percentage – 58.

Sparrow was a latecomer to the VFL as he played with Richmond in the VFA before joining South Melbourne. He once was charged with affray following an incident in his junior playing days in the Richmond district, but developed into a fine footballer. Sparrow was the first man to coach St Kilda to a Grand Final, but in bizarre circumstances. St Kilda had appointed former star Dave McNamara as captain-coach for the 1913 season but he had been playing with Essendon Town and the VFA club refused to clear him back to St Kilda. McNamara therefore was non-playing coach, but stepped down at the end of the home and away season in the belief that some elements within the club begrudged the team its success. Sparrow took over and the Saints defeated South Melbourne in a semi-final and then Fitzroy in a preliminary final, with the Maroons having right of challenge in a Grand Final. Fitzroy defeated St Kilda by 13 points and Saint fans still wonder whether their team could have won if McNamara had been available. Sparrow moved to Western Australia to coach East Perth from 1914 and coached St Kilda for five games in 1920 when Charlie Ricketts was unavailable because of illness. He had been coaching Tasmanian club Ulverstone when given a third stint as St Kilda coach, this time in his own right, for the start of the 1928 season. Sparrow guided the Saints to a 1929 first semi-final appearance, but they went down by eight points to Carlton. He then was replaced by Bill Cubbins and St Kilda did not reach another finals series for 10 years.

SPROULE, Paul

PLAYING CAREER: Essendon, 1968-71, 60 games, 60 goals. Richmond, 1972-75, 86 games, 93 goals.

COACHING CAREER: Richmond, 1985, 22 games, 9 wins, 13 losses, 0 draws, 0 finals. Winning percentage – 41.

A talented midfielder, Sproule was recruited from Hobart and played in Richmond's 1973-74 premiership sides. He moved back to Tasmania to coach Sandy Bay from 1976 and guided it

Paul Sproule.

to premierships from 1976-78 before coaching Hobart to a flag in 1980. Sproule therefore had tremendous credentials when appointed Richmond coach to succeed Mike Patterson in 1985, with former Tiger rover Peter Hogan as his assistant. Sproule introduced a new reign of discipline at Punt Road and the Tigers finished eighth in 1985. However, this did not save Sproule from the axe after just one season when the Tigers recalled 1980 premiership coach Tony Jewell.

STEPHEN, Bill

PLAYING CAREER: Fitzroy, 1947-57, 162 games, 4 goals.

COACHING CAREER: Fitzroy, 1955-57, 1965-70 and 1979-80, 214 games, 68 wins, 145 losses, 1 draw, 2 finals.

Winning percentage – 27. Essendon, 1976-77, 44 games, 16 wins, 27 losses, 1 draw, 0 finals. Winning percentage – 36.

Stephen grew up barracking for Fitzroy and, after being recruited from Thornbury CYMS, developed into one of the best back pocket specialists of his era and won the club's best and fairest in 1950 and 1954. A regular Victorian representative, he was appointed captain-coach of Fitzroy in 1955 and was replaced as non-playing coach by Len Smith in 1958. Stephen moved to the country to coach Yarrawonga. He returned to Fitzroy as non-playing coach in 1966 but, in five

seasons, the Lions finished no higher than ninth (1970) and he was replaced by former Carlton ruckman Graham Donaldson. The affable Stephen then bobbed up as Essendon coach in 1976 when the Bombers were looking for a stabilising influence. He fulfilled his "father figure" role admirably, even though the Bombers finished tenth and then ninth in his two seasons in charge before being replaced by club favourite Barry Davis. Stephen had a third stint as Fitzroy coach from 1979-80, and this time he took the Lions to a finals series, in 1979 when they finished fourth and defeated Essendon in a preliminary final before bowing out to Collingwood in the first semi-final. Stephen's proudest moment was coaching the Lions to a then VFL record score of 36.22 (238) against Melbourne at Waverley Park in round 17, 1979.

STEWART, Ian

PLAYING CAREER: St Kilda, 1963-70, 127 games, 25 goals. Richmond, 1971-75, 78 games, 55 goals.

COACHING CAREER: South Melbourne, 1976-77 and 1979-81, 111 games, 49 wins, 61 losses, 1 draw, 1 final. Winning percentage – 44. Carlton, 1978, 3 games, 1 win, 2 losses, 0 draws, 0 finals. Winning percentage – 33.

Stewart won three Brownlow Medals

From L-R: Barry Round, Ian Stewart and Ricky Quade.

after moving from Tasmania and was one of the greatest centremen the game has seen. He played in St Kilda's 1966 premiership side but few saw him as a future VFL coach. South Melbourne therefore surprised the football world when it named him coach the year after he retired as a player with Richmond. Stewart immediately made his presence felt, sacking ruckman Brian Roberts and instilling discipline levels not seen at the Lake Oval for years. The Swans improved from being the wooden spooner of 1975 to finish eighth and then climbed into the final five in 1977 before going down to Richmond in an elimination final. Stewart had made such a huge impression that Carlton swooped for his services. But, after just three rounds in 1978, he was forced to step aside for health reasons. Stewart then bobbed up again with South the following year in bizarre circumstances. Des Tuddenham had coached the Swans during Stewart's absence and believed he was contracted for the 1979 season. He and Stewart both turned up for training in the lead-up to the new season, but the Swans eventually settled the matter in Stewart's favour. He remained with the Swans for three seasons, with a best finish of sixth in 1980. Stewart announced his retirement during the highly controversial 1981 season in which the Swans announced they were moving to Sydney and heir apparent Rick Quade took over as coach for the start of the 1982 season.

STRICKLAND, Bill

PLAYING CAREER: Collingwood, 1897, 16 games, 0 goals.

COACHING CAREER: Collingwood, 1904 and 1908, 13 games, 8 wins, 5 losses, 0 draws, 2 finals. Winning percentage – 67.

Strickland had played in the VFA with Carlton for eight years before moving to Collingwood in 1893 and establishing himself as a club leader. He was set to retire after he led Collingwood to the VFA premiership (the club's first flag) in 1896, but was cajoled into another season in the newly-formed VFL. When Collingwood was looking to follow the trend of appointing a coach in 1904, Strickland was the logical choice. He therefore holds pride of place in Collingwood history as the club's first official coach. The Magpies finished third under Strickland in 1904, losing a semi-final to Fitzroy. The great early Collingwood favourite was replaced as coach after just one season by Dick Condon, but Strickland continued to give the Magpies great service as vice-president and a VFL delegate. He died in November, 1959, at 95 years of age.

SUTTON, Charlie

PLAYING CAREER: Footscray, 1942 and 1946-56, 173 games, 65 goals.

COACHING CAREER: Footscray, 1951-57 and 1967-68, 163 games, 82 wins, 79 losses, 2 draws, 7 finals, 1 premiership. Winning percentage – 48.

Sutton was a tough-as-teak back pocket recruited from Spotswood Citizens who embodied the Bulldog spirit. He missed the 1943-45 seasons because of army duties and, on return to the Western Oval, won himself a reputation as one of the most feared small men in the VFL. Sutton in 1951

was appointed captain-coach to replace Arthur Olliver and guided the Bulldogs into the finals in his first season in charge. Footscray went down to Essendon in the first semi-final and, after a disappointing tenth in 1952, the Bulldogs made the preliminary final the following year. Although Geelong defeated Footscray by 26 points in that match, the big-match experience proved invaluable for the Bulldogs as they finished the 1954 home and away season behind only the Cats and then defeated them by 23 points in the second semi-final to march straight into their first Grand Final. Sutton then led Footscray to its first VFL premiership in defeating Melbourne by 51 points in the Grand Final. He had told his players pre-match that if they played "full of grit" they would win the big match. Sutton continued as Bulldog coach to 1957 season after retiring as a player the previous season. The end of his coaching tenure was controversial as he was sacked during 1957 over criticism of his training methods, with a youthful Ted Whitten named captain-coach. However, Sutton had a second stint as coach from 1967-68 after earlier serving as chairman of the match committee. The Bulldogs finished on the bottom in 1967 and tenth the following season. Sutton then relinquished the coaching position to concentrate on running his hotel in Yarraville. Sutton, who gave the Bulldogs almost a lifetime of loyal service, also served the club as president. He died in 2012 at 88 years of age.

SUTTON, Herb

PLAYING CAREER: South Melbourne 1921, 1923-24 and 1926-27, 49 games, 34 goals. Hawthorn, 1928, 15 games, 3 goals.

COACHING CAREER: Hawthorn, 18 games, 0 wins, 18 losses, 0 draws, 0 finals. Winning percentage - 0.

Although Sutton had a modest playing career as a half-forward flanker after joining South Melbourne from VFA club Williamstown, he had carved himself a reputation as a fine coach, landing a premiership with North Launceston in 1925 in between stints with the Southerners. He earlier had been captain-coach of the St Patrick's club, Albury, and took it to a Murray Association premiership. Sutton was South vice-captain in 1927 when the Mayblooms became convinced he not only would be a good coach, but would add to their lean playing stocks. Hawthorn appointed him captain-coach only a month before the start of the 1928 season after Dan Minogue had stood down. It proved to be one of Hawthorn's worst seasons as it did not win a single game. The closest it went to victory was in going down to South Melbourne by five points at the Glenferrie Oval when South rover Terry Brain kicked a goal just seconds before the final bell. Sutton was replaced by Bert Chadwick as captain-coach for the 1929 season.

TAYLOR, Bert

PLAYING CAREER: Fitzroy, 1919-22, 49 games, 7 goals.

COACHING CAREER: Geelong, 1923, 17 games, 9 wins, 8 losses, 0 draw, 0 finals. Winning percentage – 53.

Gilbert Taylor joined Fitzroy from Warragul and played in a back pocket in the Maroons' 1922 flag side. Geelong believed it had hit pay-dirt when it convinced Taylor to join it the following season as captain-coach. However, the Pivotonians had not counted on a Victoria Police ruling which stipulated that police officers could not take outside remuneration and commissioner Sir Thomas Blamey eventually enforced this vigorously. Although Taylor lifted Geelong from second last in 1922 to fourth (and a semi-final defeat by Fitzroy) in 1923, he was replaced by Lloyd Hagger the following season. Taylor moved to Western Australia on leave of absence from Victoria Police and, on return to Victoria, found it difficult to win coaching positions because of the strict police ruling.

TAYLOR, Dick

PLAYING CAREER: Melbourne, 1922-31 and 1935, 164 games, 100 goals. North Melbourne, 1932-34, 40 games, 25 goals.

COACHING CAREER: North Melbourne, 1932-34, 42 games, 14 wins, 27 losses, 1 draw, 0 finals. Winning percentage – 33.

One of the finest centreline players of his era, Taylor played in Melbourne's 1926 premiership side. Taylor, originally from South Yarra, was appointed North Melbourne captain-coach in 1932, but broke a finger in his first match with the Shinboners. He lifted North from the wooden spoon position in 1931 to eighth in his first season in charge. Taylor retired as a player during the 1934 season and although he indicated to the North committee that he was willing to continue with the club as a non-playing coach, North appointed Tom Fitzmaurice as captain-coach. Taylor said on his retirement: "There is no room in the game for the clever player now. All that is wanted is brutal strength." North did not win a game that season and Taylor returned to Melbourne in 1935 for one

R. TAYLOR
NTH.-MELBOURNE

final season and later served on the Redlegs' match committee.

THAW, Alan

PLAYING CAREER: Essendon, 1949-50 and 1952-54, 41 games, 0 goals.

COACHING CAREER: Essendon, 1959, 1 game, 1 win, 0 losses, 0 draws, 0 finals. Winning percentage – 100.

Thaw, recruited locally, played in a back pocket in Essendon's 1949 flag side. He was Essendon's reserves coach from 1955-59 and stood in for Dick Reynolds for one match in 1959 when the senior coach was ill with an infected throat.

THOMAS, Bill

PLAYING CAREER: South Melbourne, 1903-15, 135 games, 2 goals. Richmond, 1914-19, 62 games, 3 goals.

COACHING CAREER: South Melbourne, 1910-11, 39 games, 26 wins, 12 losses, 1 draw, 3 finals. Winning percentage – 67.

Thomas, recruited from Rose of Northcote, was a brilliant defender who played in South Melbourne's 1909 premiership side under captain-coach Charlie Ricketts. When Ricketts fell ill in 1910, Thomas succeeded him as captain-coach and held the position for two seasons. South finished third in 1910 but, after defeating Carlton in a semi-final, went down to Collingwood in the preliminary final. South finished the 1911 home and away season in second position, but crashed out of the premiership race in going down to Collingwood in a semi-final. Ricketts returned as South captain-coach in 1912 but crossed to Richmond as captain-coach in 1914 and Thomas followed him to Punt Road. Thomas was appointed Tiger captain for 1919 but severely broke a leg and never played again.

THOMAS, Grant

PLAYING CAREER: St Kilda, 1978-83, 72 games, 21 goals. North Melbourne, 1984, 7 games, 1 goal. Fitzroy, 1985, 4 games, 0 goals.

COACHING CAREER: St Kilda, 2001-06, 123 games, 63 wins, 59 losses, 1 draw, 6 finals. Winning percentage – 51.

A powerful centre half-back, Thomas joined Warrnambool at the end of his VFL playing career and guided the Hampden Football League club to four premierships. He then coached amateur club Old Xaverians before being appointed North Melbourne chairman of selectors in 1993. Thomas joined St Kilda as an assistant coach in 1993 and, after a stint away from football, was appointed interim senior coach when the Saints dumped Malcolm Blight during the 2001 season. He was handed the job in his own right the following season and although the Saints finished above only Carlton in 2002, they improved considerably from there and Thomas took them to preliminary finals in 2004-05 and a pre-season trophy in 2004. When St Kilda went down to Melbourne in an elimination final in 2006, the Saint hierarchy reacted by releasing a statement indicating that Thomas and the club were parting by mutual agreement. Thomas, however, said he had been asked to resign. He then became a media commentator.

THOMAS, *Hugh*

PLAYING CAREER: Did not play at senior VFL/AFL level.

COACHING CAREER: St Kilda, 1944-45, 38 games, 8 wins, 28 losses, 2 draws, 0 finals. Winning percentage – 21.

The brother of Artie Thomas, who played 53 games with St Kilda from 1910-13, he spent 27 years as Jock McHale's assistant coach at Collingwood in an era in which the reserves trained separately from the seniors. VFA club Sandringham tried to sign him as coach in 1938 and, instead, he joined St Kilda as reserves coach and coached his youngsters to two premierships before being appointed senior coach to replace Reg Garvin in 1944. He lifted St Kilda from the bottom (with just one win) in 1943 to ninth in 1941, with six wins and two draws. But, when the Saints crashed to the bottom again in 1945, with just two wins, he was replaced by Allan Hird. Thomas later coached VFA club Preston.

THOMAS, *Len*

PLAYING CAREER: South Melbourne, 1927-38, 187 games, 56 goals. Hawthorn, 1939, 16 games, 15 goals. North Melbourne, 1940, 6 games, 9 goals.

COACHING CAREER: Hawthorn, 1939, 18 games, 5 wins, 12 losses, 1 draw, 0 finals. Winning percentage – 27. North Melbourne, 1940, 12 games, 4 wins, 8 losses, 0 draws, 0 finals. Winning percentage – 33.

The son of South Melbourne and Richmond's Bill Thomas, he was recruited from Albert Park Stars and developed into a brilliant centreman who won South's best and fairest in 1931 and played in the club's 1933 premiership side. Thomas was appointed captain-coach of Hawthorn for the 1940 season but, after the Mayblooms finished ninth with seven wins, did not apply for the position for 1941. Instead, he accepted an offer to captain-coach North Melbourne. Thomas was almost 33 years of age when he moved to Arden Street and was married with two children. However, this did not prevent him from abandoning his football career and enlisting in the army during the 1941 season. He was posted to the Middle East and then to New Guinea and was killed in action on August 17, 1943. Corporal Len Thomas is buried at the Lae War Cemetery, New guinea.

THOMAS, Stan

PLAYING CAREER: Geelong, 1915 and 1917-25, 137 games, 6 goals.

COACHING CAREER: North Melbourne, 1926, 1 game, 0 wins, 1 loss, 0 draws, 0 finals. Winning percentage – 0.

Thomas was a tough, fearless defender for Geelong after being recruited from Barwon and later became North Melbourne secretary. He took over as North coach for one game when Wels Eicke returned to St Kilda during the 1926 season.

THOMPSON, Mark

PLAYING CAREER: Essendon, 1983-96, 202 games, 50 goals.

COACHING CAREER: Geelong, 2000-10, 260 games, 161 wins, 96 losses, 3 draws, 18 finals, 2 premierships. Winning percentage – 62.

Thompson developed into one of the competition's most reliable defenders after being recruited from Airport West. He won Essendon's best and fairest in 1987 and 1990 and led the Bombers to the 1993 premiership after playing in the 1984-85 flag successes. Thompson became an assistant coach at Windy Hill on his retirement as a player and moved to the Kangaroos to fill a similar role in 1999. He was named Geelong coach in 2000 and, in his first season, guided the Cats to fifth position, only for them to go down to Hawthorn by just nine points in an elimination final. Geelong slipped to twelfth position the following year and, despite narrowly missing the finals in 2002, the Cats retained their faith in Thompson. It seemed Thompson's tenure at Kardinia Park was at stake when the Cats again missed the finals in 2003, but they improved dramatically in 2004 to finish fourth and then go down to the Brisbane Lions by just nine points in a preliminary final. Although the Cats finished sixth in 2005, they missed the finals the following year and Thompson's position was put under the microscope in a sweeping review of all positions at Kardinia Park.

Thompson retained his position for 2007 and rewarded Geelong's faith in him with a premiership, their first since 1963. The Cats thrashed Port Adelaide by 119 points in the Grand Final and although a new era dawned for Geelong, it went down to Hawthorn by 26 points in the 2008 Grand Final. This was seen as a shock result, but Geelong bounced back to defeat St Kilda by 12 points in the following year's Grand Final. Thompson guided Geelong to a preliminary final in 2010 but, after Collingwood defeated the Cats by 41 points, Thompson shocked the football world by announcing his retirement. He said he had "no idea" about his football future and insisted he just did not want to coach any more. "I just got tired of coaching," he said. Geelong therefore was rocked when Thompson just a month later accepted a position at James Hird's assistant at Essendon.

THOROGOOD, Ian

PLAYING CAREER: Melbourne, 1957-62, 93 games, 1 goal.

COACHING CAREER: Carlton, 1976-77, 46 games, 29 wins, 16 losses, 1 draw, 2 finals. Winning percentage – 63.

Thorogood was a hard-hitting half-back flanker who played in three Melbourne premiership sides but left the VFL scene at just 27 years of age to be captain-coach of VFA second division club Waverley. He not only lifted Waverley into division one, but guided the Panthers to the 1965 premiership. When former Melbourne coaching legend Norm Smith joined South Melbourne as coach in 1969, he insisted that Thorogood be appointed his assistant. Thorogood later coached VFA club Prahran and joined Carlton as an assistant coach in 1976. However, John Nicholls sensationally stepped down before the start of the season and Thorogood found himself promoted to the senior position. He guided the Blues to the top of the ladder, only for them to crash by 17 points to Hawthorn in the second semi-final and then get pipped by North Melbourne by one point in the preliminary final. Thorogood was retained for the 1977 season, but the Blues missed the finals by just half a game after going down to Footscray in the final round. He was replaced by Ian Stewart for the following season and returned to Melbourne as an assistant coach before coaching the Demon Under 19s and then becoming a Melbourne committeeman.

TITUS, Jack

PLAYING CAREER: Richmond, 1926-43, 294 games, 970 goals.

COACHING CAREER: Richmond, 1937, 1941 and 1965, 17 games, 12 wins, 5 losses, 0 draws, 0 finals. Winning percentage – 72.

"Skinny" Titus became a Tiger legend after being recruited from Castlemaine. He topped the club's goalkicking from 1929-30 and from 1934-42 and won the Richmond best and fairest in 1929 and 1941. He retired from VFL football in 1943 and, after a season in retirement, made a comeback with VFA club Coburg and kicked 111 goals. Titus stood in for captain-coach Jack Dyer for one game in 1941 and, after serving the Tigers as a committeeman and selector, he took over as senior coach after just three rounds in 1965 when Len Smith took ill. The dapper Titus, famous for his bow ties, guided the Tigers to fifth position, but missed the final four by two games. Titus before one game had a side of beef hanging from a hook and, as he started pummelling it with his fists, blood flew everywhere and he implored his Tigers to do the same to the opposition. Tom Hafey took over as coach the following season. Titus died in 1978, at 70 years of age, following an incident at a North Melbourne hotel.

TODD, John

PLAYING CAREER: Did not play at senior VFL/AFL level.

COACHING CAREER: West Coast, 1988-89, 45 games, 20 wins, 25 losses, 0 draws, 1 final. Winning percentage – 44

Todd was a teenage football sensation who made his senior debut with South Fremantle at just 16 years of age and won the 1955 Sandover Medal at just 17 years and four months. However, he severely injured a knee the following season and had to wear a leg brace. He was captain-coach of South Fremantle in 1959 and non-playing coach from 1966-1968. Todd also coached East Fremantle from 1973-76, taking the Sharks to the 1974 WAFL flag. However, his greatest success as a coach was with Swan Districts from 1977-87 and 1990-94, with four premierships. Then, returning to South Fremantle, he took his original club to the 1997 premiership. Todd also coached Western Australia to a State of Origin victory over Victoria in 1984 and was rewarded with the position of coaching an Australian side in Ireland in the first International Rules Series. He was West Coast coach over the 1988-89 seasons, but almost crossed to South Australian club Woodville. Todd guided the Eagles to fourth position in his first season in charge, only for the Eagles to go down to Melbourne by just two points in the elimination final. When the Eagles slipped to eleventh the following season, he was replaced by Mick Malthouse.

TREZISE, Neil

PLAYING CAREER: Geelong, 1949-59, 185 games, 272 goals.

Neil Trezise.

COACHING CAREER: Geelong, 1963, 1 game, 0 wins, 1 loss, o draws, 0 finals. Winning percentage – 0.

Rover Trezise had a stellar career with Geelong after joining the Cats from Redan and played in the 1951-52 premiership sides. He was playing coach of the reserves over the 1960-61 seasons and non-playing coach from 1962-64. Trezise took charge of the seniors for one match in 1963 when Bob Davis was unavailable and sat on the Geelong board from 1961-83, including a term as club president from 1974-75. Trezise entered the Victorian parliament in 1964 and was Minister for Youth, Sport and Recreation

for more than a decade. He died in August, 2006, at 75 years of age.

TUDDENHAM, Des

PLAYING CAREER: Collingwood, 1962-71 and 1976-77, 182 games, 251 goals. Essendon, 1972-75, 69 games, 66 goals.

COACHING CAREER: Essendon, 1972-75, 90 games, 47 wins, 43 losses, 0 draws, 2 finals. Winning percentage – 52. South Melbourne, 1978, 22 games, 9 wins, 13 losses, 0 draws, 0 finals. Winning percentage – 41.

A ferocious competitor, Tuddenham joined Collingwood from Ballarat YCW and immediately carved himself a reputation as one of football's hard men. The hard-hitting half-forward won Collingwood's best and fairest in 1963 and captained the Magpies from 1966-69 and in 1976. He shocked the football world in 1972 when he accepted the offer to join bitter rival Essendon as captain-coach. The Bombers believed their side needed more steel and that Tuddenham would be just the man to instil it. He immediately launched a severe code of discipline and, at one stage, even had his players crawling around the perimeter of the Windy Hill oval. Tuddenham lifted the Bombers from eleventh in 1971 to fifth in both 1971 and 1972. However, Essendon slumped to eighth in 1976 and when it finished in the same position the following year, it replaced Tuddenham with former

Des Tuddenham revs up the South players.

Fitzroy defender Bill Stephen. Tuddenham, with a point to prove to the Bombers, was appointed South Melbourne coach in place of Ian Stewart in 1978 but, after the Swans finished eighth, they turned to Stewart again after he had resigned at Carlton early in the 1978 season because of ill health. South at one stage had two coaches – Stewart and Tuddenham – turning up to take charge of pre-season training until the matter was settled. Tuddenham later coached VFA club Werribee and several suburban clubs.

TYSON, Charles

PLAYING CAREER: Collingwood, 1920-26, 106 games, 42 goals. North Melbourne, 1927-29, 38 games, 37 goals.

COACHING CAREER: North Melbourne, 1928-29, 23 games, 5 wins, 18 losses, 0 draws, 0 finals. Winning percentage – 22.

Tyson was a tireless follower for Collingwood after being recruited from Kalgoorlie Railways and should have been revered as a Magpie hero. Instead, however, was reviled after he was accused of "playing dead" in the 1926 Grand Final loss to Melbourne. Collingwood refused to list him for the following season and Tyson, who had captained Collingwood in 1926, vigorously defended himself against the accusations. It seemed his only crime was to buy a new car. Tyson moved to North Melbourne in 1927 and was appointed captain-coach the following year in place of Syd Barker. North won just five games to finish above only the winless Hawthorn and, after five winless games to the start of the 1929 season, Tyson was replaced as coach by Paddy Noonan and as captain by Tim Trevaskis. Tyson, who later captained Richmond reserves, died in September, 1985, at 87 years of age.

TWOMEY, Bill

PLAYING CAREER: Collingwood, 1918-22, 54 games, 5 goals. Hawthorn, 1933-34, 10 games, 0 goals.

COACHING CAREER: Hawthorn, 1933-34, 32 games, 5 wins, 27 losses, 0 draws, 0 finals. Winning percentage -16.

The patriarch of the great Twomey family, sons Bill, Mick and Pat all played for Collingwood. Bill Snr won the 1924 Stawell Gift and therefore was regarded as the fastest footballer of his era. He played mainly on a wing, but left Victoria Park at just 22 years of age to coach in the country. His clubs included Stawell, Ararat and South

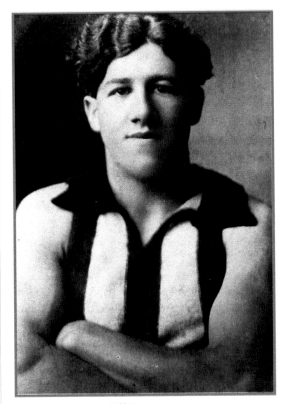

Bill Twomey.

Ballarat. Twomey was appointed Hawthorn coach in unusual circumstances in 1933. The Mayblooms had named St Kilda's Fred "Flop" Phillips as captain-coach, but he died of blood poisoning just before the start of the new season and former South Melbourne and Hawthorn star Arthur Rademacher stepped in as interim coach until Twomey took over. Hawthorn won just three games in each of the 1933 and 1934 seasons and Twomey was replaced by Ivan McAlpine. Twomey later coached the South Melbourne and North Melbourne reserves.

VALENTINE, Viv

PLAYING CAREER: Carlton, 1911-18, 116 games, 90 goals.

COACHING CAREER: Carlton, 1919, 17 games, 10 wins, 7 losses, 0 draws, 1 final. Winning percentage – 59.

Valentine, a champion rover recruited from Tasmanian club Latrobe, played in Carlton's 1915 flag side. He was handed the Carlton coaching job in 1919 after he retired as a player at the end of the previous season. Valentine replaced Norman Clark, who had been in charge for five seasons and had guided the Blues to that 1915 premiership triumph. Carlton finished the 1919 home and away season in third position, but crashed out of the premiership race in going down by 18 points to Collingwood in a semi-final.

VINEY, Todd

PLAYING CAREER: Melbourne, 1987-99, 233 games, 92 goals.

COACHING CAREER: Melbourne, 2011, 5 games, 1 win, 4 defeats, 0 draws, 0 finals. Winning percentage – 20.

A courageous midfielder, Viney joined Melbourne from SA club Sturt and captained the Demons in 1993. He was an assistant coach with Melbourne in 2000 before coaching Victorian country club Murtoa. Viney was an assistant coach with Hawthorn from 2005-08 before filling a similar role with Adelaide from 2009-10. He returned to Melbourne in 2011 and was interim coach after the Demons parted company with Dean Bailey with five rounds to play in 2011 following a humiliating 186-point defeat by Geelong in round 19, 2011. His only win as Demon coach was against Gold Coast in round 23 that season. Melbourne appointed Mark Neeld as coach for 2012 and Viney reverted to his role as manager of player development.

VOSS, Michael

PLAYING CAREER: Brisbane Bears/Lions, 1992-2006, 289 games, 245 goals.

COACHING CAREER: Brisbane Lions, 2009-2012, 90 games, 35 wins, 54 losses, 1 draw, 2 finals. Winning percentage – 39.

Voss was an outstanding junior footballer

who made his AFL debut at just 17 years of age. He went on to win a Brownlow Medal in 1996 and led the Lions to three premierships from 2001-03. The champion midfielder retired in 2006 and then spent two seasons in the media before agreeing to join West Coast as an assistant coach in his plan to win a senior position. However, the Lions surprised the football world when it appointed Voss senior coach to succeed Leigh Matthews. Many observers felt that Voss would be learning on the job, but the Lions made the finals in his first season in charge. Although the Lions then finished thirteenth and fifteenth over the following two seasons and the media questioned Voss' position, his side rallied in 2012 to finish thirteenth, with 10 wins.

Michael Voss celebrates Brisbane's 2001 flag triumph.

WALLACE, Terry

PLAYING CAREER: Hawthorn, 1976-86, 174 games, 96 goals. Richmond, 1987, 11 games, 7 goals. Footscray, 1988-91, 69 games, 20 goals.

COACHING CAREER: Footscray, 1996-2002, 148 games, 79 wins, 67 losses, 2 draws, 7 finals. Winning percentage 53. Richmond, 2005-09, 99 games, 37 wins, 60 losses, 2 draws, 0 finals. Winning percentage – 37.

Wallace, recruited from VFA club Camberwell, was a ball magnet as a centreman with Hawthorn and played in the Hawks' 1978, 1983 and 1986 premiership sides before moving to Richmond and then Footscray. He won the Bulldogs' best and fairest in 1988 and 1989 and, on retirement as a player, was an assistant coach at the Western Oval. Wallace was appointed senior coach when the Bulldogs dumped Alan Joyce during the 1996 season and immediately set about redeveloping the side using innovative placements and tactics. The Bulldogs jumped from fifteenth in 1996 to finish the home and away season in third position in 1997. They crashed out of the premiership race in heart-breaking circumstances as, after looking certain winners against Adelaide, they faltered over the final minutes and went down by two points. Unfortunately for Wallace and the Bulldogs, history repeated itself the following year when Adelaide again defeated them in a preliminary final. When Wallace's Bulldogs finished fourth in 1999 and seventh the following year, their window of opportunity appeared closed. They slid down the ladder and, near the end of a disappointing 2002 season, there were reports that Wallace would replace Rodney Eade as coach of the Sydney Swans. Wallace increased speculation when he resigned his position, only for the Swans to hand Paul Roos the job after impressing as an interim coach. Wallace then spent a period in the football media before being appointed Richmond coach for 2005 on a five-year contract. He failed to lift the Tigers, who finished twelfth in 2005 and ninth in 2006 before collecting the wooden spoon in 2007. Not even a ninth finish in 2008 could save Wallace's skin as there was mounting speculation he would be replaced at the expiration of his contract. After a string of early defeats in 2009, Wallace announced he would not seek an extension to his contract and resigned mid-season. His last game as Tiger coach was, ironically, against the Bulldogs, who won by 68 points.

WALLS, Robert

PLAYING CAREER: Carlton, 1967-78, 218 games, 367 goals. Fitzroy, 1978-80, 41 games, 77 goals.

COACHING CAREER: Fitzroy, 1981-85, 115 games, 60 wins, 54 losses, 1 draw, 5 finals. Winning percentage – 52. Carlton, 1986-89, 84 games, 55 wins, 29 losses, 0 draws, 5 finals, 1 premiership. Winning percentage – 65. Brisbane Bears, 1991-95, 109 games, 30 wins, 78 losses, 1 draw, 1 final. Winning percentage – 28. Richmond, 1996-97, 39 games, 17 wins, 22 losses, 0 draws, 0 finals. Winning percentage – 44.

Robert Walls.

Walls made his VFL playing debut at 16 years of age after being recruited from Coburg Amateurs. He developed into one of the best centre half-forwards of his era and played in Carlton's 1968, 1970 and 1972 premiership sides. He was cleared to Fitzroy in 1978 and made such a big impression as a team leader that he was appointed non-playing coach in 1981. Walls was so impressive in taking the Lions to three finals series that Carlton sought his return to replace coach David Parkin for the 1986 season. Fitzroy and

Carlton therefore swapped coaches, with Walls guiding the Blues to the 1987 premiership. It was the highlight of Walls' coaching career, but Carlton slipped to third the following year and when the lowly Brisbane Bears defeated the Blues at Princes Park in 1989, thanks to a late goal by Warwick Capper, Carlton reacted with typical brutality and dumped its coach.

Walls then had stints with the Bears and Richmond but, in both coaching positions, lacked the playing material for success. He also sparked controversy with his tough training methods, especially with the Bears. However, he introduced a young Michael Voss to senior ranks and predicted his protegy would become one of the game's champions. Walls also guided the Bears to their first finals series, in 1995. The Bears finished eighth and were gallant in going down to top side Carlton by just 13 points in a qualifying final. Walls joined Richmond the following season but, after taking the Tigers to within two match points of a finals series, he was dumped in favour of Jeff Gieschen during the 1997 season. A wonderful tactician, Walls' ability to analyse games saw him become one of football's most incisive television, radio and newspaper commentators.

WARE, Norman

PLAYING CAREER: Footscray, 1932-42 and 1944-46, 200 games, 220 goals.

COACHING CAREER: Footscray, 1941-42, 33 games, 20 wins, 13 losses, 0 draws, 1 final. Winning percentage – 61.

Ware, recruited from Sale, was one of the Bulldogs' greatest players and won the 1941 Brownlow Medal. The powerful ruckman won five club best and fairest awards and was club captain in 1940. Ware was appointed captain-coach in 1941 to succeed Joe Kelly and, after finishing sixth in his first season in charge,

the Bulldogs made the finals in 1942. South Melbourne defeated Footscray by 27 points, but it was a remarkable coaching effort by Ware as he had enlisted in the army and took charge of training on leave from his post at Royal Park. However, he had to relinquish the coaching position as he was posted to New Guinea and missed the entire 1943 season, with Arthur Olliver taking over as captain-coach. Ware returned to VFL action in 1944, but played just five games under Olliver that season. He continued with the Bulldogs to 1946, playing his last game in the first semi-final defeat by Melbourne. Ware died in August, 2003, at 92 years of age.

WARNE-SMITH, Ivor

PLAYING CAREER: Melbourne, 1919 and 1925-32, 146 games, 110 goals.

COACHING CAREER: Melbourne, 1928-32, 92 games, 48 wins, 42 losses, 2 draws, 2 finals. Winning percentage – 52.

One of Melbourne's greatest identities, Warne-Smith played in the club's 1926 premiership side and he won Brownlow Medals in 1926 and 1928. Warne-Smith was named Melbourne captain-coach in 1928 and, through splendid leadership and astute tactics, guided the Fuchsias to third position. They drew with Collingwood in one of the two semi-finals and went down by just four points in the

Ivor Warne-Smith.

replay. It was Melbourne's best season under Warne-Smith as there then were finishes of fifth in both 1929 and 1930, eighth in 1931 and ninth in his final season as captain-coach. He later served Melbourne as chairman of selectors and helped legendary coach Norm Smith build a string of premiership sides. Warne-Smith, a World War I veteran who fought at Gallipoli and on the Western Front, rejoined the army for World War II; he died in 1960 at just 62 years of age.

WATSON, Colin

PLAYING CAREER: St Kilda, 1920, 1922-25 and 1933-35, 93 games, 34 goals.

COACHING CAREER: St Kilda, 1934, 18 games, 9 wins, 9 losses, 0 draws, 0 finals. Winning percentage – 50.

Watson, recruited from South Warrnambool, was a brilliant footballer who joined St Kilda in 1920 after he played a handful of games with VFA club Port Melbourne the previous season. However, he returned to the country after just one season and, after being lured back to the Junction Oval, won the Brownlow Medal in 1925. Amazingly, Watson immediately turned his back on the VFL and was offered the job as coach of Stawell. He then was appointed captain-coach of Maryborough in 1927 and when St Kilda blocked the move, he played without a clearance and earned himself a two-year VFL ban. Maryborough won a premiership under Watson's coaching, but he then spent four years back with South Warrnambool. St Kilda lured him back in 1933 and although he had been out of the top bracket for more than seven years, he looked as fit and as classy as ever. St Kilda appointed Watson captain-coach for the 1934 season and he lifted the Saints to seventh position, only for him to be replaced the following season by non-playing coach Dan Minogue, with Clarrie Hindson appointed captain. Watson

Colin Watson.

Watson made his VFL debut at just 15 years and 305 days after being recruited from Dimboola and developed into one of the game's greatest ruck-rovers. He won the Bombers' best and fairest four times, captained the club from 1989-91 and played in the 1984-85 premiership sides and, after a brief retirement, returned to play in the 1993 flag side. Watson became a high-profile football commentator and made such a big impression with his incisive comments that he was a surprise choice as St Kila coach in place of Stan Alves in 1999. St Kilda finished that season in tenth position and when the Saints continued to struggle the following season, he stood down and returned to the media. Son Jobe, who won the 2012 Brownlow Medal, followed in his father's footsteps when named Essendon captain from 2010.

played just one game (for two goals) with the Saints in 1935 before ending his VFL career once and for all. A fitness fanatic who did not smoke or drink, he died in May, 1970, at 69 years of age.

WATSON, Tim

PLAYING CAREER: Essendon, 1977-91 and 1993-94, 307 games, 337 goals.

COACHING CAREER: St Kilda, 1999-2000, 44 games, 12 wins, 31 losses, 1 draw, 0 finals. Winning percentage – 27.

WATTERS, Scott

PLAYING CAREER: West Coast, 1989-92, 46 games, 13 goals. Sydney Swans, 1993-94, 37 games, 11 goals. Fremantle, 1995-96, 26 games, 6 goals.

COACHING CAREER: St Kilda, 2012 – , 22 games, 12 wins, 10 losses, 0 draws, 0 finals. Winning percentage – 55.

A talented rover in his playing days, Watters was Fremantle vice-captain in its inaugural AFL season of 1995, but injuries forced him into retirement the following year. He coached Subiaco to the WAFL flags of 2007-08 and also coached Western Australia representative sides before becoming an assistant coach at Collingwood. His work with the Magpies was highly valued and it was no surprise that he won the St Kilda coaching position from 2012 following the sudden and unexpected departure of Ross Lyon. Watters immediately set about revamping the St Kilda playing style, allowing his team more freedom and adventure.

WEIDEMAN, Murray

PLAYING CAREER: Collingwood, 1953-63, 180 games, 262 goals.

COACHING CAREER: Collingwood, 1975-76, 45 games, 19 wins, 26 losses, 0 draws. 1 final. Winning percentage – 42.

Weideman was one of the most feared big men of his era and could play in the ruck or at centre half-forward. He was acting Collingwood captain when the Magpies defeated Melbourne in the 1958 Grand Final and was captain in his own right from 1960-63. Weideman, who won Collingwood's best and fairest three times, coached country club Albury and then SANFL club West Adelaide after retiring from the VFL. He was lured back to Victoria Park as non-playing coach to succeed Neil Mann in 1975, but it was an unhappy period for the Magpies. Weideman had a running feud with club president Ern Clarke

and was accused of being "too soft" on the Magpie players. Although Collingwood finished fifth in Weideman's first season in charge, it slumped in 1976 to collect its first VFL wooden spoon and, when Weideman was replaced by Tom Hafey in 1977, he returned to South Australia.

WELLS, Jack

PLAYING CAREER: St Kilda, 1906-09, 39 games, 4 goals. Carlton, 1910-14, 66 games, 51 goals.

COACHING CAREER: Carlton, 1913, 18 games, 9 wins, 8 losses, 1 draw, 0 finals. Winning percentage – 49.

Wells, recruited from WA club Midlands after being born in Victoria, was St Kilda captain in 1907-08, but left the Saints when he became involved in an internal row. A brilliant centreman, he was Carlton captain under the coaching of Norman Clark in 1912, but was appointed captain-coach the following season. The Blues finished sixth and Clark returned as coach the following year, with Bill Dick as club captain. Wells played just five games with the Blues that year and moved on to play in the VFA with North Melbourne.

WHEELER, Terry

PLAYING CAREER: Footscray, 1974-83, 157 games, 18 goals.

COACHING CAREER: Footscray, 1990-94, 91 games, 50 wins, 40 losses, 1 draw, 3 finals. Winning percentage – 55.

Recruited from Warburton, Wheeler was a tough and niggardly back pocket who joined VFA club Williamstown as captain-coach at the completion of his VFL playing career and guided the Seagulls to the 1986 premiership. He returned to the Western Oval as assistant coach in 1989 and replaced Mick Malthouse as senior coach in 1990. They were tough times for the Bulldogs as there were moves to merge the club with Fitzroy. Although the merger never eventuated, Wheeler had to take pre-season training in difficult circumstances. Despite all this, the Bulldogs in 1990 won 12 games to finish seventh. Wheeler in 1992 guided the Bulldogs to second position by the completion of the home and away season, only for his young team to crash out of the premiership race in going down by 64 points to Geelong in the preliminary final. Wheeler was named coach of the All-Australian side but, less than two years later, was sacked as Bulldog coach following an 88-point loss to Geelong and was replaced by Alan Joyce.

WHITTEN, Ted

PLAYING CAREER: Footscray, 1951-70, 321 games, 360 goals.

COACHING CAREER: Footscray, 1957-66 and 1969-71, 228 games, 91 wins, 137 losses, 0 draws, 3 finals. Winning percentage – 40.

One of football's greatest identities, Whitten joined the Bulldogs from local club Braybrook after originally trying to win a release to Collingwood. A champion key position player, he became synonymous with the Footscray club and is revered as the club's greatest product. Whitten played in Footscray's 1954 premiership side and won the club best and fairest five times. He took over as Footscray captain-coach following the sacking of premiership coach Charlie Sutton during the 1957 season and held

Ted Whitten.

the coaching position until the end of 1966 when, ironically, he was replaced by Sutton. Whitten, had guided the Bulldogs to the 1961 Grand Final against Hawthorn, partly through the use of the now banned flick-pass, only for his side to go down by 43 points. It was the only season in which the Bulldogs made the finals under Whitten's coaching.

Whitten returned as captain-coach in 1969, again replacing Sutton, but retired as a player in 1970. His three-quarter time address to his players in his final match as a player, against Hawthorn, now is part of football folklore. He told them: "It's got to be a do-or-die effort. You've got to show all the guts and determination you've got in your bodies. You've got to inspire me." The Bulldogs won by three points. Whitten was non-playing coach in 1971 and his second stint as Bulldog coach lasted just three seasons, for finishes of eleventh, seventh and eighth. He was replaced by former Collingwood coach Bob Rose and Whitten later become synonymous with Victorian State of Origin sides as chairman of selectors. The greatly-loved Whitten, known as Mr Football, developed prostate cancer in 1995 and was given tremendous applause as he and son Ted Jnr, who played 144 games with the Bulldogs from 1974-82, were driven around the MCG before a State of Origin match. Football's most loved identity died a few weeks later and was given a state funeral at St Patrick's Cathedral.

WIGRAFT, Len

PLAYING CAREER: Fitzroy, 1917-27, 135 games, 41 goals.

COACHING CAREER: Fitzroy, 1934, 16 games, 6 wins, 10 losses, 0 draws, 0 finals. Winning percentage – 38.

Recruited from VFA club Preston, the big-hearted Wigraft played as a follower in Fitzroy's 1922 premiership side and was a regular Victorian representative. A three-time best and fairest winner, he left the Maroons to be captain-coach of Echuca over the 1928-29 seasons and later was coach of the Richmond reserves and then Abbotsford Brewery. Wigraft took over as Fitzroy coach after two rounds into the 1934 season when Jack Cashman resigned because he felt he did not have the confidence of the committee and was cleared to Carlton. Fitzroy finished eighth in Wigraft's only season as coach and he was replaced by former Collingwood star Percy Rowe. Wigraft continued to serve the Maroons in a number of areas and was an advisor when captain-coach Fred Hughson guided Fitzroy to the 1944 premiership. He died in January, 1982, at 85 years of age.

WILLIAMS, Jack

PLAYING CAREER: Geelong, 1925-34, 175 games, 9 goals.

COACHING CAREER: Geelong, 1945, 20 games, 2 wins, 18 losses, 0 draws, 0 finals. Winning percentage – 10.

The powerfully-built Williams played in Geelong's 1925 and 1931 premiership sides. A great club stalwart who served the Cats in many capacities, he continued playing with the Geelong reserves at the end of his senior career. Williams, who played mainly on a half-back flank or wing, then coached North Geelong. Williams was appointed senior Geelong coach for the 1945 season, but Geelong won only two games – against Hawthorn and St Kilda – to finish above only the Saints. He was replaced by Tommy Quinn in 1946 and later coached Geelong West.

WILLIAMS, Mark

PLAYING CAREER: Collingwood, 1981-86, 135 games, 178 goals. Brisbane Bears, 1987-90, 66 games, 58 goals.

COACHING CAREER: Port Adelaide, 1999-2010, 274 games, 151 wins, 121 losses, 2 draws, 17 finals, 1 premiership. Winning percentage – 55.

Mark Williams.

The son of South Australian football legend Fos Williams, he played with the Port Adelaide Magpies before joining Collingwood in 1981. Williams, a tireless and gritty no-frills midfielder captained Collingwood from 1983-86 before a contract dispute saw him cross to the Brisbane Bears. The dual Collingwood best and fairest winner returned to the Port Magpies as a player and then coached SANFL club Glenelg before joining Essendon as an assistant coach. Williams joined Port Power as an assistant coach in 1997 and was elevated to the senior position in 1999. Although the Power won consecutive minor premierships over the 2002-03 seasons, they were seen as finals "chokers" as they failed to reach the Grand Final in either season. All that changed in 2004 when the Power defeated the Brisbane Lions in the 2004 Grand Final. Williams controversially grabbed his tie and pretended to choke himself and also suggested that a club sponsor was wrong in suggesting the Power boss could not coach. Port finished a modest eighth the following season and although it defeated North Melbourne in an elimination final, it bowed to cross-town rival Adelaide in the first semi-final. Port bounced back to finish second in 2007, but went down to Geelong by a record 119 points in the Grand Final. It was the last finals game for Williams as Port coach and he resigned in July 9, 2010. Ironically, his last game as coach was against Collingwood. Williams in 2010 joined new franchise club Greater Western Sydney as senior assistant to veteran coach Kevin Sheedy but, at the completion of the 2012 season, announced he would join Richmond as a development coach.

WILLIAMS, Paul

PLAYING CAREER: Collingwood, 1991-2000, 189 games, 223 goals. Sydney Swans, 2001-06, 117 games, 84 goals.

COACHING CAREER: Western Bulldogs, 2011, 3 games, 2 wins, 1 loss, 0 draws, 0 finals. Winning percentage – 67.

Williams, a brilliant midfielder with great pace, surprisingly was allowed to cross to the Sydney Swans in 2001 and won their best and fairest award in 2001-02. He went on to play in the Swans' 2005 premiership side. Williams spent two years as an assistant coach with Melbourne and was an assistant coach with the Western Bulldogs in 2011 when senior coach Rodney Eade stepped down with three rounds to play. Williams had three games in charge and guided the Bulldogs to victories against Port Adelaide and Fremantle. He joined Carlton as an assistant coach in 2012 but was dumped in a coaching reshuffle at the completion of that season.

WILLIAMS, Tommy

PLAYING CAREER: Fitzroy, 1928-37, 136 games, 41 goals.

COACHING CAREER: Fitzroy, 1964, 1 game, 0 wins, 1 loss, 0 draw, 0 finals.

A great Fitzroy stalwart after being recruited from East Brunswick, Williams was a fine half-back flanker who represented Victoria three times. He coached the Fitzroy Under 19s and was in charge of the senior for one match in

1964 when captain-coach Kevin Murray was unavailable.

WILLIAMSON, Colin

PLAYING CAREER: St Kilda, 1937-46, 165 games, 44 goals.
COACHING CAREER: St Kilda, 1952-53, 37 games, 7 wins, 30 losses, 0 draws, 0 finals. Winning percentage – 19.

Williamson, who joined St Kilda from VFA club Northcote, was a safe and reliable defender who had the unique distinction of captaining the Saints to its first flag – a lightning premiership in 1940. Williamson in 1948 coached Brighton to its only VFA premiership and then coached local club Bentleigh. He was invited to take over from Fred Green as St Kilda coach in 1952 and had two seasons in charge at the Junction Oval. The St Kilda playing cupboard at that time was bare but, after collecting the wooden spoon in 1952, St Kilda improved to finish ninth in 1953. However, Williamson heard whispers that the Saints had approached North Melbourne's Les Foote to take over as coach in 1954 and his tenure as St Kilda coach was over.

WILSON, Percy

PLAYING CAREER: Collungwood, 1909-20, 183 games, 71 goals. Melbourne, 1921-24, 51 games, 20 goals.
COACHING CAREER: Melbourne, 1921-23, 48 games, 16 wins, 30 losses, 2 draws, 0 finals. Winning percentage. St Kilda, 1924, 13 games, 4 wins, 9 losses, 0 draws, 0 finals. Winning percentage – 31.

Wilson was a favourite Collingwood son after being recruited locally. A courageous rover, Wilson won Collingwood hearts with his never-day-spirit and when Melbourne invited him to be captain-coach in 1921, the Magpies reluctantly cleared him "with willingness but a lot of regret". Wilson guided Melbourne to sixth position in the 1921 and 1922 seasons and when the Fuchsias finished ninth in 1923, he was replaced by recently retired Fitzroy star Gordon Rattray. Wilson crossed to St Kilda as non-playing coach in 1924, but walked out during the season when he heard rumours that he was only coaching the Saints for monetary reasons. He moved back to Melbourne and made a brief comeback. He later coached Murtoa and VFA club Port Melbourne. Wilson died in March, 1941, just three days short of his 52nd birthday.

WOOD, Artie

PLAYING CAREER: South Melbourne, 1917-23, 97 games, 14 goals.
COACHING CAREER: South Melbourne, 1921, 16 games, 5 wins, 10 losses, 1 draw, 0 finals. Winning percentage – 31.

A wonderfully-talented small man who excelled on a wing, Wood started his football career with Middle Park and was rated one of the best players on the ground in South's 1918 Grand Final defeat of Collingwood. He was appointed playing coach in 1921, at just 25 years of age, with Carl Willis as club captain. However, South finished seventh that season and Wood was replaced by the legendary Roy Cazaly. Wood left South at the end of the 1923 season and spent three seasons as captain-coach of country club Maryborough. When he moved on to Wimmera League club Horsham, Maryborough officials said "Maryborough's loss in Horsham's gain". Wood, also a talented cricketer, spent 14 seasons playing with Horsham and was enormously popular.

WORRALL, John

PLAYING CAREER: Did not play at senior VFL/AFL level.

COACHING CAREER: Carlton, 1902-09, 144 games, 100 wins, 43 losses, 1 draw, 14 finals, 3 premierships. Winning record – 69. Essendon, 1911-15 and 1918-20, 135 games, 65 wins, 67 losses, 3 draws, 5 finals. 2 premierships. Winning percentage – 48.

It is one of football great misapprehensions that Worrall was the VFL's first official coach. In reality, that honour belongs to Collingwood's Bill Strickland, who was named Magpie coach in 1904. Worrall started coaching Carlton two years earlier, but it was not an official position. Rather, he was appointed club secretary and assumed coaching duties as part of this role, implicit in his demand that he be in charge of training and, to use a modern term, list management. Worrall was a brilliant all-round sportsman who played 11 Test cricket matches for Australia. He also was a champion footballer who started with South Ballarat and then played approximately 115 games in the VFA with Fitzroy. Following his retirement, he kept a close eye on his Maroons from the other side of the fence, offering advice on tactics and training. Carlton recognised his potential as a mentor and, as the Blues' secretary, he insisted on complete control. Worrall, who was single-minded in his quest for success, built a formidable team which won consecutive premierships from 1906-8. However, his very success led to his downfall at Princes Park as several senior players during the 1909 season complained about his rigid discipline and tough training regime. The Blues sacked him and named club captain Fred Elliott as coach. This decision probably cost Carlton a fourth consecutive premiership as South Melbourne defeated the Blues in the 1909 Grand Final.

Several VFL and VFA clubs sought Worrall's services over the next few years and he elected to join Essendon in 1911, again with tremendous success. He guided his second VFL club to the 1911-12 flags. Essendon pulled out of the competition from 1916-17 because of World War I and, because of lack of playing personnel, the Dons struggled on resumption in 1918 and finished last. They improved to sixth the following year, only for the Essendon players in 1920 to emulate their Carlton counterparts in complaining about Worrall's tough tactics. He was replaced by club captain Percy Ogden. Worrall never coached again but, being a trained journalist who had worked on The Age in his years with Fitzroy, covered football and cricket for The Australasian. He died on November 17, 1937, and the Sporting Globe's Hec de Lacy wrote a few years later: "He (Worrall) was a born leader of men. He had the drive; he set the example."

WORSFOLD, John

PLAYING CAREER: West Coast, 1987-98, 209 games, 37 goals.

COACHING CAREER: West Coast, 2002-12, 259 games, 140 wins, 117 losses, 2 draws, 17 finals, 1 premiership. Winning percentage – 54.

Worsfold was a tough and feared small defender after being recruited from South Fremantle. After winning the Eagles' best and fairest in 1988, he was appointed club captain in 1991 at just 22 years of age. Worsfold therefore was captain of the Eagles' first two premiership sides, in 1992 and 1994. He joined Carlton as an assistant coach on retirement as a player and was regarded as a senior coach in waiting. Several clubs, including Richmond, Hawthorn and Fremantle made overtures and, at the end of the 2001 season, Worsfold could have signed with either West Coast or Fremantle as coach. He was appointed West Coast coach from the 2002 season and, after the Eagles made the finals in each of Worsfold's first three seasons, they made a breakthrough in reaching the 2005 Grand Final, only for the Sydney Swans to defeat them by four points. Worsfold's Eagles had their revenge the following season when they defeated the Swans by a point in the Grand Final. The Eagles slumped from there and even collected the wooden spoon in 2010 before Worsfold was able to take them to the finals again in both 2011 and 2012. Worsfold therefore tasted the highs and lows of coaching with his no-nonsense approach and insistence on tight defence. Worsfold's 259 games as Eagle coach is a club record, bettering the 235 games by Mick Malthouse from 1990-99.

INDEX